THE
Church

THE
Church

THE BODY OF CHRIST IN THE WORLD OF TODAY

ED HAYES

CHARLES R. SWINDOLL, GENERAL EDITOR
ROY B. ZUCK, MANAGING EDITOR

WORD PUBLISHING
NASHVILLE
A Thomas Nelson Company

THE CHURCH
Swindoll Leadership Library

Copyright © 1999 by Word Publishing. All rights reserved.

Published by Word Publishing, a unit of Thomas Nelson, Inc.,
P. O. Box 141000, Nashville, Tennessee 37214. All rights reserved. No portion
of this book may be reproduced, stored in a retrieval system, or transmitted in
any form or by any means—electronic, mechanical, photocopy, recording, or
any other—except for brief quotations in printed reviews, without
the prior permission of the publisher.

Unless otherwise indicated, Scripture quotations used in this book are from
the *Holy Bible, New International Version* (NIV),
copyright © 1973, 1978, 1984, International Bible Society.
Used by permission of Zondervan Bible Publishers.

Scripture quotations marked KJV are from the
King James Version of the Bible.

Scripture quotations marked NASB are taken from
the NEW AMERICAN STANDARD BIBLE, copyright © 1960, 1962, 1963, 1971,
1972, 1973, 1975, 1977, 1995 by the Lockman Foundation.
Used by permission.

Published in association with Dallas Theological Seminary (DTS):

General Editor: Charles Swindoll
Managing Editor: Roy B. Zuck

The theological opinions expressed by the author are not necessarily the
official position of Dallas Theological Seminary.

Library of Congress Cataloging-in-Publication Data

Hayes, Edward L.
The church : the body of christ in the world of today / Edward L. Hayes
p.   cm.
Includes bibliographical references and index.

ISBN 0-8499-1376-4

1. Church.   I. Title.

BV600.2.H38   1999   98-39065
262–dc21   CIP

Printed in the United States of America
99 00 01 02 03 04 05 06 BVG 9 8 7 6 5 4 3 2 1

To Marilyn
whose love, patience,
and practical wisdom
helped shape
our marriage,
our home, and
this book

Contents

Foreword ix

Preface xi

Introduction xv

1. The Church as a Community of the Redeemed 1

2. The Church in History: The Spread of Global Wildfire 25

3. The Church and the Headship of Christ 53

4. The Church and the Bible 71

5. The Church and Holy Spirit Power 95

6. The Church and Commitment 113

7. The Church and Its Ministry and Organization 131

8. The Church and Worship 153

9. The Church and the Gospel 173

10. The Church and the World 191

11. The Church and Suffering 213

12. The Church and Its Hope 231

13. The Church and Renewal 251

Endnotes 271

Bibliography 291

Scripture Index 295

Subject Index 301

Foreword

I LOVE THE CHURCH. When it's functioning correctly *nothing* beats the church for effectiveness. Babies are cradled, children are loved, teenagers are challenged, parents are instructed, seniors find fellowship, singles are strengthened, and families are nurtured. When a church is running smoothly on all cylinders, its impact on a community is nothing short of remarkable.

Recent books on the church have swung from one extreme to the other. Someone fires a salvo which proclaims all is wrong in today's churches. Another answers with a missive aimed at pointing out all that God is doing in His church today. The pendulum swings back and forth between the extremes. One work dismisses current trends in evangelism as "entertainment," while the next answers that today's "seeker" needs new forms of communication. What has long been needed is a healthy look at the family of believers called "the church." How pleased I am to add *The Church,* by my longtime friend, Dr. Ed Hayes, to this series.

Ed goes way back to the founding of the church to show how she was started. However, he doesn't stay there. Moving us through church history like a skilled tour guide, he leads us on a journey showing the church's high points and low points. He stops us long enough on the journey to show us what the church has done right and where it has faltered. At times we move with breathtaking speed gliding from one century to the next. At other stops we slow our pace and listen to church fathers, church opponents, and church observers, all the while keeping our goal of learning more about this eternal institution in clear sight.

One of the fascinating aspects of football is observing how the coaches use their players. I've observed that seasoned coaches know their players intimately. They know each player's strengths and weaknesses. They know when to put a specific player into the game and when to pull another out. Many of you reading this work labor in the church. You may serve as a pastor, teacher, nursery worker, or elder. Whatever your role, the church in which you serve would not run as effectively without your being there week in and week out. Because—and this is the bottom line—the church is about people! People like you and me who long to use our gifts in "a spiritual service of worship" (Rom. 12:1).

The church is not a business, a school, or a hospital (though it is often compared to these institutions). Above all, the church is a family; in fact, it's a family of families. Some families are big, others small. Some families are healthy, others dysfunctional. Families come in all shapes, sizes, flavors, and stripes. And so do churches.

So come along on this reading tour of the church. You will love the scenery, and you can trust the tour with Dr. Hayes, an experienced and wise guide.

—CHARLES R. SWINDOLL
General Editor

Preface

WRITING A BOOK ON THE CHURCH is like trying to explore the Louvre of Paris in one afternoon. There are just too many rooms, corridors, and galleries inviting attention. To stay in only one section invites narrowness, while any attempt to see it all is frustrating. You can hardly take in that museum in one afternoon.

The church, however, is far from being a museum. It is a living, vibrant, and expanding institution of God's design and making.

I come to the writing of this book after more than sixty years of life in the church. They have been good years. Nurtured by caring and godly parents, pastors, and teachers, I have never found myself at odds with the church. A critic at times, but not at odds. Quite the contrary. Over the span of many years, and much travel, ministry, and fellowship with believers in various quarters of our globe, God has tutored me in His truth, and my love for the saints has grown and ripened.

A great deal of credit for this love goes to my parents, whose faith was as rich as the soil they farmed in the central valley of California. At an early age, I came to faith in Christ, never seriously wavering or straying from the sound doctrine preached, taught, and lived at the little Baptist church in Ceres, California. Time has taught me that no church is perfect, nor was this one. But there was a lot of love in that place, which overcame a multitude of sins.

Following four transforming years at Dallas Theological Seminary, I was ordained to the gospel ministry. Now, looking back on forty years of ministry, a few central motifs mark what I have learned on my pilgrimage. These I hope to develop in this book. Years in the classroom, church, and conference-center leadership have brought people into my life whose faith struggles and servant styles have left an aroma of life. That is a heritage I shall always treasure as I am led along in what Paul described as a triumphal procession, designed to spread the fragrance of the knowledge of Christ (2 Cor. 2:14–17).

The church, God's great community of hope, is something like the four unfinished marble statues of slaves that sculptor Michelangelo began in sixteenth-century Florence. The characters cry to be released from their prison of roughhewn stone, but the vision of what they were to become died with the artist. Those crude and ghostly shapes will never know the perfection of Michelangelo's greatest work, *David*. In the Galleria dell' Accàdemia, not far from the great Duomo of Florence, Italy, the perfect and imperfect stand in stark contrast.

The church, while imperfect and incomplete, is still being shaped by its living Master, Jesus Christ. This same Lord has promised that one day He will present His church "as a radiant church, without stain or wrinkle or any other blemish, but holy and blameless" (Eph. 5:27). En route to the final consummation of the age, the church lives as a prisoner of hope, expecting the return of Jesus Christ.

Mentioning the word "church" to any audience prompts a wide range of responses. Two millennia have not brought Christian consensus, yet believers hold tenaciously to the biblical truth of one body, one Spirit, one hope, one Lord, one faith, one baptism, and one God and Father of all (Eph. 4:4–6). Our privilege is to watch the Master Sculptor perfect His own work, not merely as passive observers, but as fellow workers in His kingdom.

This book has been put together by many helpers along the way. I am indebted to the fine library staff of the Denver Seminary Carey S. Thomas Library, under the able direction of Professor Sarah Miller, and to the reference librarians of the Voskuyl Library of Westmont College, under the leadership of Librarian John Murray. Diana Phillips, Claudia Scott, and Diane Ziliotto, in particular, aided me in tracing down hard-to-find sources. Manuscript preparation was in the capable hands of Melissa Michaels, assistant to the Department of English and Modern Languages at the beautiful Montecito campus of Westmont College.

No amount of disclaimers will serve to cover for human error, failure to give proper credit, and faulty viewpoints. However, to the best of my knowledge and ability, every attempt has been made to treat this important subject with fairness. Were I a Bach or an angel, I would pen the words *Gloria in excelsis* to this work. I pray that the book will help its readers—and that all glory will go to God alone.

Introduction

You have taken the right line, my dear Pliny, in examining the cases of those denounced to you as Christians, for no hard and fast rule can be laid down. . . . They constitute a very bad precedent, and are also out of keeping with the age.

—Emperor Trajan

The world was not worthy of them.

—Hebrews 11:38

IN OUR LIFETIME we have witnessed both the "death of God" and the "death of theology." The first played itself out in a media frenzy, but the second is a lingering death. Long held to be the queen of the sciences, theology suffers from bad press. Evangelical theology in particular, with its claim that salvation is through Christ alone, is seen as dogmatic, narrow, and bigoted.

As a result, many people feel that the church is not relevant. So, they argue, give people what they want to hear. Steer clear of doctrine and theology. Stroke their psyche and avoid any hints of negatives.

This sounds appealing—or appalling, depending on your perspective. It is appealing to those who strategize to reach people who have tuned God out of their lives. On the other hand, it offends many who honestly believe that the church's primary call is to be faithful to the gospel. Giving people what they want to hear, they are convinced, is a dead-end street. It means a sellout to the prevailing culture and to doctrines that are irreconcilable with biblical revelation.

This was exactly the point the apostle Paul made to Timothy when he warned about slippage in sound doctrine. "To suit their own desires," he wrote, "they will gather around them a great number of teachers to say what their itching ears want to hear" (2 Tim. 4:3).

Much preaching rides the wave of culture and fails to address its maladies. Loss of a heavenly look and disposition is a casualty resulting from attempts to whittle God down to our size. A utilitarian god appealed to by whim and wish is not an adequate god.

Religious commercialism threatens the integrity of Christian proclamation and the church. In *U.S. News and World Report,* Jeffrey L. Sheler asked, "Is God lost as sales rise?"[1] A sizable portion of the Protestant evangelical community has made its peace with commercial culture by deciding to become a bigger roadside attraction.

Sound doctrine, especially the doctrine of the church, offers substantive answers to counterfeit faiths. Just as gold once served our United States economy by setting the standard for monetary value, so truth sets a high standard. Doctrine, adorned by godly living, is needed now more than ever in our churches. This goes for the teachings that define and shape what the church is all about. We should resist the rush to a thin relevancy or an experience-centered faith, despite the appeals of populist religion.

There can be no restoration of Christian values or a revived church apart from a sound theology. Christianity is a radical condemnation of the world. "My kingdom," Jesus affirmed, "is not of this world" (John 18:36). Any renewal of the church must of necessity build on biblical principles. This is no plea for a dull, mindless traditionalism, nor is it to suggest that we not relate truth to life. Rather, it is a call for a powerful declaration of the Word of God, which forms the foundation of all renewal and reformation.

One of the abiding realities is the indestructibility of the church. It may suffer from friend and foe alike—yet it remains. As Jesus promised, "The gates of Hades will not overcome it" (Matt. 16:18). In the end, God's people will not be overpowered. Despite persecution and lethargy, neglect and even apostasy, the true church remains. This is not to say that individual denominations and congregations will not decline or even fail. History reveals that many of them will. The body of Christ, however, refuses to be stamped out. What Christ purchased with His own blood may exist underground or in total freedom, yet it overcomes attacks by Satan himself.

This is a great mystery and can only be attributed to God's power and presence in His true church. This indestructibility can only be the work of the One whose resolve to build His church overcomes both opposition and obstacles. In light of this grand truth, we must heed Paul's exhortation given first to Timothy: "I am writing you these instructions so that, if I am delayed, you will know how people ought to conduct themselves in God's household, which is the church of the living God, the pillar and foundation of truth" (1 Tim. 3:14–15).

Any appeal to proper behavior in the church must go well beyond manners and civility. It encompasses the full range of understanding the nature, composition, leadership, and mission of Christ's church. The doctrine of the church serves as a corrective to abuses of all kinds and, if solidly grounded in biblical truth, will shape its earthly destiny.

Christianity entered a world that was by no means empty of religion. Its entrance came like a shining light in a world filled with a confusing landscape of religions. As Willistin Walker has noted, "Christianity could not build on virgin soil."[2] This new community began as one among several Jewish parties. The Nazarenes, as they were called, took on themselves the name of their founder, Jesus of Nazareth. Christians became known simply as followers of "the Way." The community—and, early on, communal—aspect of this unique fellowship became known as the church or the body of Christ.

At first, the rise of Christianity was insignificant, even despised. Within the first two decades of the church's beginning, a pattern of despised servanthood became evident. Paul, whose intellectual competence was unquestioned, recognized the spiritual power of weakness. He, along with others, had thrown his reputation on the side of those whom the first-century world branded foolish. At one point, he took some satisfaction in being branded a fool for Christ's sake. "Up to this moment," he wrote to the fledgling Corinthian church in A.D. 55, "we have become the scum of the earth, the refuse of the world" (1 Cor. 4:13).

Throughout history, pride has ruined the church. When privilege and power tempt the church to throw its weight around, we do well to remember the humble beginnings of the despised group who were first called "Christians" at Antioch (Acts 11:26). Claiming to be a Christian was then and still is no claim to fame. To be a Christian spelled trouble. Any successes it has known in history and any favor it has gained in the eyes of the world tend not to be normative. In a real sense, to be a member of Christ's church means that one carries the stigma of the Cross. From the world's perspective it means to be on the side of losers.

Resurrection power, however, has to be reckoned with. What is branded "weak" is in reality strength, and what is labeled "foolish" is actually wise. By choosing the poor, the foolish, and the ignoble, John Calvin believed, God has preferred them over the great, the wise, and the noble. "What modesty is called for on our part," Calvin wrote in his commentary on 1 and 2 Corinthians. It is with this perspective that I will address the subject of the church.

Central to the theology of the Christian faith is an understanding of the unique work in calling out a people for Himself. Part of the good news the apostles preached was the direct revelation from Jesus Christ that His redemptive work of grace would bear fruit in the formation of the church.

In his lengthy treatise on the rise of Christianity, Augustus Neander stated a foundational principle:

> The church is not of human origin; it is from God. Now Christianity we regard not as a power that has sprung up out of the hidden depths of man's nature, but as one which descended from above, because heaven opened itself for the rescue of revolted humanity; a power which, as it is exalted above all that human nature can create out of its own resources, must impart to that nature a new life, and change it from its inmost centre. The great source of this power is the person whose life its appearance exhibits to us—Jesus of Nazareth—the Redeemer of mankind when alienated from God by sin. In the submission of faith to him, and the appropriation of the truth which he revealed, consists the essence of Christianity, and of that fellowship of the divine life resulting from it, which we designate under the name of the church.[3]

The earliest writings by the church fathers gave little evidence of a need for a developed doctrine of the church.[4] However, as controversies arose and creedal formulations became necessary to define the true church, a more full-blown theology emerged. As Christianity spread like a flame throughout all the known world of the first century, it left in its path pockets of believers who fulfilled the command of Christ to be salt and light in the world. Such incendiary fellowships, to use Elton Trueblood's description of churches,[5] encountered hostilities and persecutions from the enemies of faith. Living and ministering in pagan contexts did not come without great risk. Threats to the purity of faith came from both without and within. What was rooted and grounded in the truth of the Scriptures in many cases took on more the shape of the prevailing culture than the pure life of Christ. The same criticism is being leveled against evangelical Christianity today. French sociologist and theologian Jacques Ellul warned that Christians need to beware of making the gospel fit every fad of society. "Each generation," he wrote, "thinks it has finally discovered the truth, the key, the essential nub of Christianity by veneering itself with the dominant influences or modeling itself in it."[6] While no perfect church ever existed, the constant quest for purity and holiness has kept Christians searching for a city on a hill.

Throughout the two millennia since Christ uttered his immortal words to Peter, "On this rock I will build my church" (Matt. 16:18), Christians have attempted to flesh out the meaning of the word *church*. This book is one more attempt to do just that. But it also represents something else: Evangelicalism needs to take a serious and fresh look at the church. Never before, it seems, have church leaders been so unsure as to how to carry out their ministries. A time of change and experimentation calls for a recovery of the basics. In our zeal for effectiveness and societal acceptance, the very future of the church is threatened. Evangelicalism may end up corrupting and compromising the very gospel it seeks to proclaim. Substantive faith is in danger of eroding out from under us at a time when people in our culture are engaged in a new spiritual quest. While ours is a spiritual age, it readily seeks the cultic, occult, mystical, or revived paganism of a new age.

In 1996 the framers of the Cambridge Declaration made a plea for a clearly defined doctrine of the church. While the declaration, like all humanly devised creeds, contains mere human words, it nevertheless states a warning in clear terms about the erosion of God-centered worship in our churches:

> Wherever in the church biblical authority has been lost, Christ has been displaced, the gospel has been distorted, or faith has been perverted, it has always been for one reason: Our interests have displaced God's and we are doing His work in our way. The loss of God's centrality in the life of today's church is common and lamentable. It is this loss that allows us to transform worship into entertainment, gospel preaching into marketing, believing into technique, being good into feeling good about ourselves, and faithfulness into being successful. As a result, God, Christ and the Bible have come to mean too little to us and to rest too inconsequentially upon us.[7]

My own plea echoes the concern of the authors of the Cambridge Declaration. Our concern must be for Christ's kingdom and not our own empires, successes, or popularity. History has repeatedly shown that spiritual effectiveness does not depend on winning at the polls.

One of the criticisms of evangelicalism is that it does not have much of a doctrine regarding the church. Ecclesiology, as this doctrine is properly called, is important if for no other reason than that it serves as a corrective to the excesses and abuses of Christians and church bodies that stray from the teaching of the Bible.

Within evangelicalism today the theology of the church reflects considerable diversity, as it should. Much of this is due to the fact that evangelicalism exists as a transdenominational expression of commitment to personal faith in Jesus Christ. With a high commitment to the doctrine of salvation, evangelicalism has been able to accommodate itself to a variety of forms of church order and discipline. As long as it is assured that there is adherence to the biblical doctrine of eternal salvation, other doctrinal and denominational issues seem less important. Lacking a commonly accepted ecclesiology, however, evangelicalism is marked by individualism in church polity, discipline, and worship. While a central focus on the gospel is commendable, lack of theological orientation weakens the church. The present deemphasis on nearly all major doctrines of the Scriptures has produced an alarming biblical illiteracy. Without a cohesive understanding and acceptance of a biblical ecclesiology, evangelicalism in our postmodern world is generally viewed as one more expression of a fragmented religious scene in an already fragmented culture.

From the meaning of the word *church* to its doctrine, duties, and discipline, this book approaches the subject from a biblical perspective. The book may serve as a helpful guide for laypersons and Christian workers who desire to understand the nature and mission of the church. Emphasizing areas I feel have often been treated too lightly, I focus on the marks of the true church: the centrality of Christ as Head of His church, the authority of Scripture, and the power of the Holy Spirit in the life and witness of the church. The traditional and necessary doctrines relating to church polity, leadership, ordinances, ministry, and worship are included. As a basis of understanding, the book also offers a single-chapter overview of church history.

In addition, the book addresses legitimate efforts of evangelism and missions. Identifying with the church in its global expressions, chapters are included on the nature of the gospel, suffering, and hope. A revisitation of the subject of Christian separatism is aimed at helping believers chart a course of relevant cultural engagement without losing biblical distinctives. Emphasis is placed on the Lord's return, the central focus of Christian hope, which purifies the church and prods it into active witness in the world.

The book concludes with an appeal for renewal. The church must never lose its moral authority to address present-day ills. Hopefully readers will gain a greater love for the Savior, bring greater glory to God, and value the significance of a biblically based ecclesiology. The church is one body, yet diverse. Learning to love one another ought to be the prevailing agenda of our evangelical calling.

What our Lord loved and gave His life for, we too must love and offer the sacrifices of praise, time, talent, and stewardship. As pilgrims and strangers on earth, believers are an assembly of the elect, sanctified by the will of God, and called to witness to the salvation offered in the name of our Lord Jesus Christ.

The vision of a coming kingdom does not diminish the church's earthly task of living in unity. The Bible teaches that "none of us lives to himself alone and none of us dies to himself alone" (Rom. 14:7). Yet the apparent individualism and competitiveness of many evangelical churches speak openly to our failure to achieve oneness in Christ.

Every institution on earth is imperfect, but that does not lead us to adopt the "pro-God but anti-church" motto of the dissidents of the 1960s. Nor does it lead us to abandon our search for purity, holiness, and renewal of spirit.

There can be no churchless Christianity. The church is a divine institution called into existence by Jesus Christ and built on the firm witness of the apostles. "No one can lay any foundation," Paul wrote, "other than the one already laid, which is Jesus Christ" (1 Cor. 3:11). Our taproots must run deep, our devotion must never dim, and our zeal to maintain the integrity of the gospel must remain warm and evangelistic.

When we make small what Christ intended to make large, we are disloyal to Christ and His eternal Word. In the Bible the church looms large. We are dealing with the church of the living God. In the words of Origen, one of Christianity's early definers and defenders, who lived from around 185 to 254, "I want to be a man of the church; I do not want to be called by the name of some founder of a heresy."[8]

This book does not intend to say everything about the church. That task would be too vast, its scope endless. One feels a bit like John the Evangelist, who concluded his Gospel with words that revealed the overwhelming task of explaining Jesus to his readers: "Jesus did many other things as well. If every one of them were written down, I suppose that even the whole world would not have room for the books that would be written" (John 21:25). In similar language Cyril of Jerusalem (around 315–386) in his *Catechetical Lectures* expressed the immensity of the task of describing the church: "I should need to lecture for many more hours if I were to say everything about the church that I would like to say."[9]

1
The Church as a Community of the Redeemed

The church is a so deeply hidden thing that no one can see or know it but can only grasp and believe it in baptism, the Lord's Supper, and the word.
                                                                    —Martin Luther

How did the church begin? Where did it come from? And how did it expand into every part of the world? As described in the New Testament, a group of people fired with zeal for the resurrected Christ were followers of "the Way," later called Christians. The church emerged from the barren soil of first-century Judaism and was considered by its enemies to be nothing more than a Jewish sect. Yet its scope and significance transcended the limited soil of an insignificant country in the Roman Empire. Founded by Jesus Christ, built on apostolic preaching and teaching, and spread abroad by persecution and missionary zeal, Christianity has reached into almost every part of the inhabited globe.

The early message of the apostles was not an apology or argument for God's existence. It was simply good news, reciting the great events in the ministry of Jesus Christ. It became a profoundly simple and yet powerful confession of Christ's lordship and of what had happened to the community of disciples. At its heart, the message is summed up in the text of 1 Corinthians 15:1–11. This gospel was "received," not concocted, to fit the times. The fact is that Christ died for our sins in accord with the Scriptures, that He was buried, was raised on the third day according to the Scriptures, and later was seen by the apostles and a host of others who verified His resurrection.

Jesus was not just another human being. He was God in the flesh, a Galilean by family ties, son of Mary, and the Messiah of Israel. He is the supreme expression of God's love for humanity. Proper response to Jesus meant a break with the past, repentance of sins, and personal faith in His saving grace. Proper response to Him meant commitment to a community of faith, the humanity made new in Christ, transformed in mind and spirit. In reality it meant becoming part of the family of God.

As revealed in the New Testament the church is unique and distinct from anything known before. Early Christians understood that God was in Christ reconciling the world to Himself (2 Cor. 5:19) and that they were ambassadors of Jesus. Luke's account of the first days of the church makes it clear that they were fired with zeal because of the resurrection of Jesus Christ from the dead.[1] This assertion of the uniqueness of the church in New Testament revelation does not deny the existence of an assembly of God's covenant people in Israel. From this side of the Cross, however, we must look for the clear statement of Christ and the apostles as to the meaning and mission of the church. "What counts is a new creation," Paul declared to the Galatians (Gal. 6:15). This declaration meant a corporate beginning as well as personal newness of life in Christ.

The relationship of the church to the kingdom will be discussed later, but the important thing is that the church stands unique in the purposes of God.[2] As Roman Catholic theologian Hans Küng has written, the church began with people placing their faith in Christ. "As soon as men gathered together in faith in the resurrection of the crucified Jesus of Nazareth and in expectation of the coming consummation of the reign of God and the return of the risen Christ in glory, the church came into existence."[3]

Exactly what is the church? What is its nature, meaning, and mission? Do we have a clear picture from the New Testament as to its order of governance and its scope of authority as an institution called into existence by the Lord Himself? What is its continuing relationship to its Founder?

We begin to answer these and other questions by searching for a biblical definition of the church. It becomes a task not unlike the unfolding of a flower, one petal at a time.

THE MEANING OF THE WORD *CHURCH*

The English word *church* comes from the Greek word *kyriakos*, which occurs only twice in the New Testament (1 Cor. 11:20; Rev. 1:10). In the first instance the word is used in relationship to the gathering of believers for the Lord's Supper. In the second the word is synonymous with the Lord's Day. The Scottish word *kirk* comes from this Greek term. A biblical doctrine of the church, however, cannot be built on a single word that occurs only twice in the New Testament. The more expansive and active Greek term *ekklēsia*, meaning an assembly, must be understood.

Ekklēsia is derived from two words that together mean "to call out." First used in antiquity to refer to the assembly of citizens of a city, the word is used in the New Testament to refer to the church. In the Septuagint, the Greek translation of the Old Testament, *ekklēsia* occurs about one hundred times. The word was used to translate the Hebrew term *qāhāl*. More often, however, the term *synagōgē* was used to translate *qāhāl*. In the Old Testament *ekklēsia* indicates an assembly (Deut. 9:10; 23:3; Mic. 2:5) or a political body (Ezra 10:8, 12; Neh. 8:2, 17). In 2 Chronicles 6:3 it refers to the gathering of Israelites for the consecration of the temple. From the word itself no claim may be made for the existence of the church in the Old Testament.

L. Coenen makes the claim that *ekklēsia* almost exclusively described the church after the period of the Gospel accounts of the life of Jesus. The notable exceptions, of course, are Matthew 16:18 and 18:17. "One can say with certainty," Coenen writes, "that all the early Christian writers use *ekklēsia* only for those fellowships which come into being after the crucifixion and resurrection of Jesus."[4]

If the church did not come into existence until after Christ's first advent, why did Jesus Himself use the word *ekklēsia* twice? The answer is that in Matthew 16:18 He spoke of the church as yet future ("I will build my church"), and in Matthew 18:17 He used *ekklēsia* of a local body of Christians,[5] who in the future would need to exercise church discipline.

While Acts 7:38 makes reference to the assembly or congregation (*ekklēsia*) of Israelites in the wilderness, Matthew's usage designates a new society independent of Old Testament roots. This new gathering may represent continuity in the sense of a "calling together," as Ryrie contends, [6]just as Israel was an assembly, but there the similarity ends. Jesus intended to engage in a new venture, one that united believers who would believe in response to the apostles' teachings regarding the gospel of salvation found in Christ alone. The church was to become the true congregation or community of the redeemed.

The term *ekklēsia* extends to those believers visible only to God (2 Tim. 2:19), that is, the so-called universal church, and to believers in specific locations (Rom. 16:1; 1 Cor. 1:2; 2 Cor. 1:1; 1 Thess. 1:1). Using the metaphor of a building, Paul said the *ekklēsia* is a local Christian community being built up in Christ (1 Cor. 3:9–10). Timothy was to teach believers how to behave in the church , the household of God (1 Tim. 3:15). The *ekklēsia* can be understood only in relationship to the Lord. It is the church of God (1 Cor. 1:2; 11:16, 22), and is "in Christ" (Gal. 1:22) and "of Christ" (Rom. 16:16).

The church is found in a particular segment of salvation history, the period between the Day of Pentecost and the Rapture. At the Rapture the church will be presented without spot or wrinkle, a reference to the future purity of the church in heaven (Eph. 5:27; see also 1 Thess. 3:13; 2 Pet. 3:14; Jude 24).

THE NEW TESTAMENT CONCEPT OF THE CHURCH

The church consists of believers in Jesus Christ, baptized in the name of the Father, Son, and Holy Spirit, committed to one another in love and called out of this world into a worshiping, caring, and witnessing fellowship. The word *church* may refer to the church universal, that is, all believers in the present era. And it also refers to a specific local body or group of believers meeting in one place: Also there is evidence from the Scriptures of a third category, which I prefer to call *translocal.* Early believers were consciously aware of other congregations, even to the extent of compassionate and sacrificial sharing of money and goods with churches in other locations.

Each of these concepts needs to be explored if we are to grasp the meaning of "church."

The Church Universal

The term *universal* may be inferred from Hebrews 12:23–24. In this verse the faithful are seen as coming to Mount Zion, to the heavenly Jerusalem, the city of the living God. This is an obvious reference to heaven. "The church of the firstborn" is said to be accompanied by thousands and thousands of angels. The members, so to speak, of this church have their names written in heaven. There they will have been made perfect in Christ, the Mediator of the New Covenant. The distinguishing feature of this unique group is that it was made perfect by the sprinkling of blood. This is a reference to Christ's death on the cross in contrast to the sacrifice of Abel (Gen. 4:10). Jesus' blood speaks a "better word" and opens up a way for people into the very presence of God (Heb. 10:19).

Scholars differ as to the exact meaning of this "joyful assembly." Perhaps it is best to view this unusual gathering as a reference to the whole communion of saints, that is, the church on earth and in heaven.[7] John Calvin understood the work of the church as that of establishing a heavenly Jerusalem "to be built throughout the whole world."[8]

The idea of an invisible church is often linked to this concept of a universal body of believers. This idea is found in Augustine's *City of God* and was also taught by some of the Reformers. The Bible, however, does not seem to refer to an invisible body. Perhaps it is best to speak of His body as invisible from only a human standpoint in that we are incapable of knowing about all gatherings of believers in the past twenty centuries. Furthermore, we cannot know who these believers are. Only God knows that. Certainly the church triumphant, consisting of saints in glory, is unknown to us by our limited experience, which is bound to space and time.

I recall once hearing of a Christian who boasted that he was a member of the invisible church. His pastor kindly corrected him, "Yes, but it hasn't met yet!"

The fact of the universal church is implied in passages that speak of the church as a whole, such as "I will build my church" (Matt. 16:18), "the church throughout Judea, Galilee and Samaria" (Acts 9:31), "the church of God" (20:28), "I persecuted the church of God" (1 Cor. 15:9; Gal. 1:13), "Christ is the head of the church" (Eph. 5:22), and "his body which is the church" (Col. 1:24).

The Local Church

While Jesus gathered disciples around Him in His lifetime on earth, this group was never called the church. Even with the institution of the Lord's Supper, the disciples did not carry this noble title. Consciousness of the church arose gradually in the primitive Christian community. Expecting the Lord's imminent return, believers set about to live and work in light of that expectation.

What is clear is that congregations emerged out of the fire of Pentecost. From the biblical record we know of specific local churches: the churches in Jerusalem, Antioch, Rome, Corinth, Philippi, Thessalonica, Ephesus, Colossae, the seven churches of the Revelation, and others. Several local churches met in homes: in Philemon's house (Philem. 2), Chloe's house (1 Cor. 1:11), the house of Aquila and Priscilla (16:19), and Nympha's house (Col. 4:15).

We know nothing of separate church buildings until the third century. Early believers gathered wherever they could. In a real sense Christianity was family business long before it became "church" business. Early saints were content to meet on the first day of the week in synagogues on the Sabbath and perhaps in homes. They did so until the expansion of the gospel into the pagan or Gentile world led to a cleavage between those called Christians and Jews.

The Translocal Church

Visible local churches meeting in various locales developed a certain cohesiveness. It is sometimes difficult to differentiate between one local church in a city and others that may have also been formed in the same area. The apostle Paul was acutely aware of this as a church planter of the first century. For instance, when he wrote to the Corinthians, he addressed his letter to "the church of God in Corinth, to those sanctified in Christ Jesus and called to be holy, together with all those everywhere who call on the name of our Lord Jesus Christ—their Lord and ours" (1 Cor. 1:2). There was unity in the geographic distribution of churches.

Paul understood the existence of a universal witness to the gospel and the fruit of that witness. Much of this fruit was the result of his own tireless labor. There was a corporateness to his ecclesiology that is often lacking today among churches and their leaders.

The idea of a church that transcends race, gender, national boundaries, and ethnic backgrounds is present in the New Testament. What we need today is a recovery of the spirit evident in Paul's words, "together with all those everywhere who call on the name of the Lord Jesus Christ." The basis of our unity is always Jesus—"their Lord and ours."

I would prefer not to call this "church" the invisible church, nor to equate it with the universal body of believers, because the translocal church refers to believers in various locales at any given time, not to all followers of Christ throughout the present church age.

NEW TESTAMENT IMAGES OF THE CHURCH

What's in a name, we may ask? In the richness of divine revelation the multifaceted nature of the church of the living God is revealed. Just as God may be described by His nature and by His attributes, the church may be described by various words or terms.

The Church Militant and Triumphant

While there are many local churches, in another sense there is only one true church of Jesus Christ. Any discussion of the church and its various manifestations need not detract us from affirming "one holy catholic [universal] church." The distinction between the church militant and the church triumphant is a common one.[9] One refers to the present church on earth, the other to the church in heaven. The first describes the worldwide church facing its daily, spiritual battle and advancing gospel witness. The second designates all believers in heaven. Those who have fallen asleep in the Lord (1 Thess. 4:15) comprise the church triumphant.

Paul concluded that Christ "died for us, so that, whether we are awake or asleep, we may live together with him" (5:10). This overarching statement of confidence transcends all petty bickering, schism, and conflicts between local churches. Our oneness in Christ unites us in life or in death. One might say that there will always be a church to attend somewhere on earth or in heaven.

Membership in the church triumphant is not yet complete. It will never be complete until the last believer enters glory. Then, and only then, will its perfection be realized. The gathering of the elect will prompt praise in heaven. On the island of Patmos, John had a vision of the overcomers, the ones who will inherit heaven (Rev. 21:7). The invitation is out: "Come, I will show you the bride, the wife of the Lamb" (21:9). The message of the church militant is also "to come." "The Spirit and the bride say, 'Come!'" (22:17). Just as Christ's incarnation was a coming, and just as His future return is called a coming, believers are to be active in inviting people everywhere to come to Christ.

The final two stanzas of Samuel J. Stone's hymn "The Church's One Foundation" reflect the church militant and the church triumphant.

> 'Mid toil and tribulation,
> And tumult of her war,
> She waits the consummation
> Of peace forevermore;
> Till with the vision glorious
> Her longing eyes are blest,
> And the great Church victorious
> Shall be the Church at rest.
>
> Yet she on earth hath union
> With God the three in One,
> And mystic sweet communion
> With those whose rest is won;
> O happy ones and holy!

Lord, give us grace that we,
Like them, the meek and lowly,
On high will dwell with Thee.

A Fellowship

The earliest of the Greek words used to explain the nature and function of believers who gathered together was *koinōnia*. The church was like a fledgling bird just out of the nest, its wings not yet strong enough to fly. But fly it did, and quite magnificently. Luke described its earliest days: "They devoted themselves to the apostles' teaching and to the fellowship [koinōnia], to the breaking of bread and to prayer" (Acts 2:42).

Here we have a succinct description of the form and function of the primitive church. Within the context of devotion to apostolic teaching, the church is described as a fellowship. The sign over the door of this first church of Jerusalem was simply "the fellowship." The word *koinōnia* means a fraternal group of participants in a common cause. The word itself comes from *koinōs*, meaning common. In secular Greek it referred to a legal relationship of common ownership. It also meant "profane," something being accessible and permissible to all. To make something common removes it from the exclusive-club category of human gatherings. For instance, the word *commons* in English is used to describe a park-like area open to all. Such was the nature of the early church—a *community* of the redeemed.

Acts 2 continues with a description of the life and witness of the *koinōnia*: "Everyone was filled with awe, and many wonders and miraculous signs were done by the apostles. All the believers were together and had everything in common. Selling their possessions and goods, they gave to anyone as he had need. Every day they continued to meet together in the temple courts. They broke bread in their homes and ate together with glad and sincere hearts, praising God and enjoying the favor of all the people. And the Lord added to their number daily those who were being saved" (2:43–47).

This early communal effort is further described in the example of a man the apostles called Barnabas (meaning "son of encouragement").

His example of selfless giving described in Acts 4:36–37 stands in contrast to the human tragedy of Ananias and Sapphira (5:1–11).

The *koinōnia* represented a tight-knit circle of caring, sharing saints, whose example and witness gave ample evidence of the transforming power of the grace of God.

The epistles give further examples of this powerful commonality, although we find little evidence that the practice of selling all and laying it at the apostles' feet continued beyond Acts 5.

Paul made reference to "the right hand of fellowship" extended him by Christians in Jerusalem (Gal. 2:9). When his mission to the Gentiles was confirmed, all the church simply asked was that he remember the poor (2:10). Later Paul was to become active in collecting relief money for the church in Jerusalem, which was experiencing famine and hardship. *Koinōnia* is thus more than an abstract term. It was fleshed out in the early church through acts of generous giving. This is seen in the example of generous Corinthian believers and the exhortations Paul gave the church on the subject of "the collection" (1 Cor. 16:1; 2 Cor. 9:1–15).

The word *koinōnia* is full of significance for the church today. It means much more than a comfortable club for saints. By its very nature it is a compelling community of generous believers doing good things for everyone, especially the family of believers (Gal. 6:10). The acid test of a true fellowship is more than a confession of faith. It is borne out in doing good and sharing with others. As Hebrews 13:16 says, "With such sacrifices God is pleased." Justice, mercy, kindness, and compassion, all virtues of our Lord, are to be fleshed out in the fellowship of believers.

The Body of Christ

No metaphor of the church links Christians to Jesus Christ more clearly than the term "the body of Christ." In this new community of the redeemed, one's Jewish or Gentile identity does not count. The unifying principle is union with Christ, who is Head of the church. The metaphor of a body has led expositors of the Scriptures and theologians to refer to the church as an organism—not merely an organization.

In 1 Corinthians 12 Paul stressed the fact that the body is a unit despite its many parts. The unifying factor is Jesus Christ, whom Paul described elsewhere as the One who made two one (Eph. 2:14). The Prince of Peace is Peacemaker between Jew and Gentile, providing access to the Father by one Spirit (2:18).

We note five key ingredients in the picture of the church as Christ's body. First, we are initiated into the body by the baptism of the Spirit—whether Jews or Greeks, slave or free (1 Cor. 12:13). Second, we are interdependent in the same way parts of our human body depend on each other (12:14–20). Third, while some believers may seem less "honorable" than others, God has bestowed great honor on them (12:21–25). Fourth, we are to celebrate our differences and our dependency (12:26–27). Fifth, Paul made it clear that God has arranged the parts of the body just as He wanted them to be (12:18), and He has combined the members of the body so that there should be no division (12:25). If this is true, then who are we to tamper with God's sovereignty and trash His name by schism and disunity? Sabine Baring-Gould's hymn "Onward Christian Soldiers" expresses the ideal "body language" of the church:

> Like a mighty army
> Moves the church of God;
> Brothers, we are treading
> Where the saints have trod
> We are not divided,
> All one body we—
> One in hope and doctrine,
> One in charity.

The body metaphor described in Ephesians 1:22–23 and 4:15–16 views Christ as the Head. We are to grow in Him, the One who makes the body function properly, and we are to do so in a context of love.[10]

God's Household

The church is also likened to a household of faith. "This metaphor elevated the community of believers as the 'location' of God's presence on earth," Mark Bailey points out.[11] Though believers are also called "God's temple" (1 Cor. 3:16), the term *household* is used in the domestic sense. The case for this is built on numerous references to familial relationships and to homes where early believers met to worship God.

Paul's instructions to young Timothy lifted the metaphor to lofty heights. He wrote, "Although I hope to come to you soon, I am writing you these instructions so that, if I am delayed, you will know how people ought to conduct themselves in God's household" (1 Tim. 3:14–15). Citing the need for purity and holiness, Paul referred to items in a large house as useful or useless, noble or ignoble (2 Tim. 2:20–21). The apostle's exhortation to do good to all people, especially to those who belong to the family of believers, attests to this household imagery (Gal. 6:10). Paul also spoke of believers as members of God's household (Eph. 2:19).

The notion of the church as a household is further strengthened by the New Testament emphasis on our relationship to God the Father. The fatherhood of God is expressed generally in Paul's citation of pagan literature to make a spiritual point. "We are his offspring," Paul told his Athenian listeners at the Areopagus in Athens (Acts 17:28). Believers, however, are called sons or children of God (John 1:12–13; Rom 8:14, 16, 21; 1 John 3:1–2). This imagery is further strengthened by reference in Hebrews 2:10 to God's work through Christ to bring "many sons to glory."

The biblical focus on the household of faith is less on its participants than on its Head. Paul wrote of God's household as "the church of the living God, the pillar and foundation of the truth" (1 Tim. 3:15). This truth is summed up in the next verse with its Christocentric formula: "He appeared in a body, was vindicated in the Spirit, was seen by angels, was preached among the nations, was believed on in the world, was taken up in glory" (3:16). To be a member of the family or household of God, one must believe in Christ.

The Building of God

Paul wrote that believers are "God's building" (1 Cor. 3:9). In a mix of metaphors the great apostle also referred in the same verse to "fellow workers" as "God's field." By the grace of God, Paul was allowed to lay foundations for new churches as an expert builder would carefully construct a foundation. The Greek term for fellow workers, *synergoi*, links common believers to this apostolic task of building something that will last. The image of a field pictures a place where farmers are at work. Thus Paul skillfully interwove three images that would highlight the importance of building and serving well in the church. There is little room in God's building for sloppy work. Service in the church requires our best efforts for the glory of God.

In this spiritual building Jesus Christ Himself is "the living Stone" (1 Pet. 2:4), that is, the "cornerstone" (2:6), and believers, as inhabitants and participants in God's building, are called "living stones" who "are being built into a spiritual house" (2:5).

In Ephesians 2:20–22 Paul moved easily from the household imagery of verse 19 to the metaphor of a building with a foundation built on apostolic and prophetic activity (2:20). This building is seen as a temple of the Lord (2:21) in which the Spirit lives (2:22). Here the Holy Spirit in His ongoing work is seen uniting people together in one dwelling. Heaven is also likened to a building with many rooms (John 14:2). Similarly the church here on earth is seen as a dwelling place or building of God's habitation.

The Bride of Christ

The New Testament also portrays the church as the bride of Christ. Just as a groom loves his bride, so Christ loves us; and just as a bride loves her husband, so the church is to love Christ. In Ephesians 5:32 Paul spoke of the great mystery of the believers' marriage to Christ. Written in the context of instructions to husbands in a marriage (5:25–33), Paul's words in this passage reveal several key ideas about the church. First, Christ's love for His church is held up as the model for every marriage union (5:25). Second, for the church to be presented to Christ holy and blameless, without spot or wrinkle or any other blemish, it must experience cleansing by "the word" (5:26). Third, Christ feeds and cares for His church, just as a responsible husband and wife build each other up in a sound marriage

(5:29). Fourth, the church is Christ's body, just as the marriage of a man and woman unites them as "one flesh" (5:30–31). Fifth, the union of husband and wife symbolizes the love between Christ and the church (5:32).

In Paul's letter to the Corinthian believers, he expressed his godly jealousy over their lack of fidelity. He wrote, "I promised you to one husband, to Christ, so that I might present you as a pure virgin to him" (2 Cor. 11:2). Paul feared that Satan's agents, false teachers of his day, would achieve what the serpent had successfully achieved with Eve in the garden. He pictured himself as the father of the bride, whose purpose is to offer to the bridegroom a virgin daughter who would become his wife. This Near Eastern custom is obscure to us in our culture, but in New Testament times virginity was sacrosanct. Human jealousy is a vice, but Paul labeled his concern as "godly jealousy." Here the purity of the church is held high. The bride of Christ, Christ's church, will be presented to our Lord at His coming.

The use of this metaphor of the bride also occurs in the praise section of Revelation 19:6–8: "The wedding of the Lamb has come, and his bride has made herself ready" (19:7). John here portrayed the church as a bride prepared for this final union with Christ in heaven. Immediately following this outburst of enthusiastic praise John exclaimed in delight, "Blessed are those who are invited to the wedding supper of the Lamb!" (19:9).

The Flock of God

In China today a thriving Christian movement of churches is called "The Little Flock." Their title comes from the rich imagery of sheep in the Bible used to describe the followers of God. In both Old and New Testaments, pastoral imagery is used to express the care of God for Israel and of Jesus for the church. Several times the Old Testament speaks of the Lord as the Shepherd of Israel (Pss. 23:1–6; 80:1; Isa. 40:11; Jer. 31:10; Ezek. 34:11–22; Zech. 10:3, 8).

In the New Testament the church is likened to a flock of sheep (though nowhere in the New Testament is God the Father called "shepherd"). In Paul's farewell message at Miletus he instructed the church, "Keep watch over yourselves and all the flock of which the Holy Spirit has made you overseers. Be shepherds of the church of God" (Acts 20:28–29). Peter, who was personally instructed by our Lord to feed the flock (John 21:15–19), returned to this imagery later in life when he exhorted elders to be "shepherds of God's flock" (1 Pet. 5:2). He further instructed them not to lord it over followers but to be examples to the flock. Good pastoral duty would lead to a reward, he wrote, when the "Chief Shepherd" appears (5:4). Earlier in his epistle Peter compared his readers to sheep who had gone astray but now had returned to the "Shepherd and Overseer" of their souls (2:25).

It seems paradoxical that the Lamb of God (John 1:29) is also the Good Shepherd (10:11, 14). In the metaphor of the church as the flock of God, we have a rich image of the Savior as shepherd and of the responsibility of human overseers to be exemplary leaders or undershepherds of congregations. Leading and feeding are to be the main duties of pastors.

Today we are in danger of seeing this metaphor obscured by a secular overlay of managerial and organizational behavior. Too many ministers see themselves as chief executive officers of a corporation rather than shepherds, or pastors, in the biblical sense of the term.

Other Metaphors

Other metaphors or descriptions of the church describe unique facets of Christ's church, the jewel of God's creation. These include the temple of the Holy Spirit, the pillar and ground of truth, the city of God or the heavenly Jerusalem, a royal priesthood, a holy nation, a mystery, and a vineyard. Many of these are echoes of Old Testament imagery. This poses a question as to whether the early church merely appropriated the older covenant terminology to describe New Covenant reality. Does a continuity or a discontinuity exist between the old and the new?

From an examination of Scriptures, we can conclude that indeed something new took place in the formation of the church on the Day of Pentecost. It was more than a continuation of the assembly in the Old Testament. The Book of Acts views the church as an entirely new structure. "That is why in Acts 11:15," Darrell Bock wrote, "Peter could refer to the events of Acts 2:1–4 as 'the beginning.'"[12]

We will return to this discussion of the church from a different vantage point in chapter 12. There we will explore the church and its hope, as well as similarities and distinctions between it and Israel. Those who embrace the church's message, regardless of national, ethnic, religious, racial, or gender differences and backgrounds, find a oneness in Jesus Christ, who alone is the Savior of the world.

REVISITING THE FOUNDING OF THE CHURCH

John Calvin pointed to the humble beginning of the church: "And this was eminently fitted to excite his disciples to perseverance, that though their faith was little known and little esteemed, yet they had been chosen by the Lord as the first-fruits, that out of this mean commencement there might arise a new Church, which would prove victorious against all the machinations of hell."[13]

This new church, as Calvin and others described it, burst in on the world. Its trajectory eventually exploded in Rome and from there spread like a prairie fire over all the known Roman world (Col. 1:23). The obvious success of the new church, however, does not mean that the fact of its founding is without controversy. How was the church formed? And how can we see through the debate over origin to the reality and power of its existence in the world?

Peter's Confession

Peter's confession, "You are the Christ, the Son of the living God" (Matt. 16:16), is included in all three Synoptic Gospels. Mark simply recorded Peter's words in response to Jesus' question in Mark 8:29: "You are the Christ." Luke also recorded a brief answer by Peter, "The Christ of God" (Luke 9:20).

This confession forms the heart of evangelical ecclesiology. Jesus Christ, the Chief Cornerstone of the church, is indeed the central focus of the doctrine. Peter's pivotal confession formed the setting in Galilee for Jesus' declaration, "I will build my church" (Matt. 16:18).

In Jesus' day people held a variety of opinions about the Man from Galilee (16:14). Some were of the opinion that He was the martyred John the Baptist resurrected to life. Herod held this view (14:1–2). Others thought He was Elijah the prophet (16:14) assigned as a forerunner of the Messiah (see Mal. 3:1; 4:5–6). Matthew added Jeremiah to the list, as well as the general designation, "one of the prophets." But Jesus surprised them all by affirming that He is Christ, the Messiah of Israel.

Jesus placed emphasis on the word *you* in Matthew 16:15: "Who do *you* [the disciples] say I am?" (italics added). Ultimately a confession, if it means anything at all, must be personalized. General answers or options are invalid. Peter memorialized himself with his quickness to respond personally, although he was often a spokesman for the others (15:15; 19:27). Donald Hagner, commenting on Peter's subsequent confession, observed that "Peter is never regarded as isolated from the twelve."[14]

Peter's confession brings together two titles, "the Christ" and "the Son of the living God" (16:16). "The living God" contrasts with the pantheon of gods in the ancient world, even those deities of the region of Caesarea Philippi, where the confession was uttered. Elsewhere in the Bible the words "the living God" are associated with the church (1 Tim. 3:15; 4:10).

Peter's confession, as well as that of all Christendom, forms the essential core of our faith. "No one can lay any foundation other than the one already laid, which is Jesus Christ," wrote Paul to believers at Corinth (1 Cor. 3:11). Peter's words pointed unmistakably to Christ as the Author of salvation, the Founder of our faith, and the Lord of His church. Any other confession will not do. Our own confession of faith must be Christ-centered: "Jesus is Lord" (John 13:13; Rom. 10:9–10).

Peter the Rock

Few Bible verses have sparked as much controversy as Matthew 16:18: "And I tell you that you are Peter, and on this rock I will build my church, and the gates of Hades will not overcome it." The historic division between Protestants and Roman Catholics arose, in part at least, over the meaning of this text.

What did Jesus mean by the use of the word *rock*? In this passage He gave a new and expanded meaning to "Peter," Simon's nickname (Matt. 4:18; Luke 6:14; John 1:42).

In John 1:42 both the Aramaic "Cephas" and the Greek "Peter" (rock) are used. Simon Peter, as the disciples knew him, is always listed first among the disciples, but from this we cannot claim Peter was the first pope. While he may have gone to Rome in his lifetime, there is no historic evidence of his being the first bishop of the church. This tradition came later.

Peter is here in view as the rock with authority and custody of the gospel, as were all the apostles (see Eph. 2:20). In the future Jesus would build a new community through the labor of the apostles, with Peter being the leading apostle to the Jews and Paul to the Gentiles.

Calvin's commentary on Matthew 16:18 speaks of Peter as representative of all believers. "From this it appears how the name Peter belongs both to Peter and to other believers; that is, founded on the faith of Christ they are fitted by a bold concord into the spiritual building, so that God may dwell in their midst. For since Christ here declares that this is the common foundation for the whole Church, He wishes to join with Peter all the believers who are going to exist in the world."[15] The church is built not on the man Peter, but on his God.

The keys to the kingdom mentioned in 16:19 may symbolize the teaching office. By preaching the gospel, Peter made it clear that Jesus is the only door to salvation (Acts 2:38–39; 3:16–20; 4:12; 10:34–43). By proclaiming Jesus as the only Savior and by warning that unbelief has serious consequences, Peter, along with all the apostles, used "the keys to the kingdom." "Binding" and "loosening" may refer to the apostles' announcing one's judgment or salvation, based on his or her rejection or acceptance of Christ.[16]

Doors to the kingdom can be opened or closed solely on the authority of Christ, whose gospel invites everyone to repent of their sins and be saved. Likewise, any authority exercised within the church must be consistent with the teaching of the Word of God.

The Invincibility of the Church

When Jesus spoke of the church, He said, "The gates of Hades will not overcome it" (Matt. 16:18). While *Hades* sometimes refers to the dead, or their "abode" in the grave, other times, as here, it refers to hell itself. While death is the great enemy of us all, overcome only by the resurrected Christ, Satan from hell opposes Christ's church. However, victory is certain for the church—both through our future resurrection from the dead and the present spiritual battle against all evil.

Victory over death and Satan is sure. Not even the death of the Messiah on the cross could prevent the community of faith from arriving victoriously at heaven's gate. The church can never be destroyed. In fact, in persecution it seems to be the strongest. Since its life comes from the Vine, which is Christ (John 15:1–4), the church's growth and ultimate victory is assured.

Martin Luther's immortal hymn "A Mighty Fortress Is Our God" comprehensively gives credit to our mighty, overcoming God:

And tho this world, with devils filled,
Should threaten to undo us,
We will not fear, for God hath willed
His truth to triumph through us
The prince of darkness grim, we tremble not for him—
His rage we can endure,
For lo, his doom is sure: one little word shall fell him.

Pentecost

The early Christians clearly believed that Jesus formed His church. As branches of the Vine, they lived by every word He said. Following Jesus' ascension to the Father, the disciples gathered on the Day of Pentecost. The cataclysmic events that followed altered forever the landscape of the world. What was embryonic in the calling of the disciples, and what was yet future in the Matthew 16:18 account, became reality at Pentecost. New Testament evidence points to the origin of the church at this event in Jerusalem.

Could the church have been formed before? By its nature, as the body and bride of Christ, the prerequisite for the church was the death, burial, and resurrection of Jesus Christ. Furthermore, it was dependent on the coming of the Holy Spirit. Peter's citation of the prophecy of Joel in his sermon at Pentecost makes clear reference to a fresh work of the Holy Spirit.

At Pentecost there was an outpouring of the Holy Spirit. Predicted by our Lord Himself (Acts 1:5), this outpouring was called "the baptism of the Holy Spirit," essential for initiation into the body of Christ. While the phrase "the baptism of the Spirit" is not used in Acts 2, it can be shown, as Saucy has observed, that it had its fulfillment or full expression at Pentecost.[17] The "beginning" (11:15) refers not merely to the early evidence of the Holy Spirit's power on the Day of Pentecost, but also to the beginning of the church, the baptism of the Holy Spirit.

The church is the holy habitation of God built up in Christ the Head. Only when the Holy Spirit came to dwell in the hearts of men and women was the church formed as the temple of God. Thus the church is "a Spirit-indwelt community."[18]

What began as a group within the larger framework of religious Judaism became a full-blown movement in its own right. Its enemies spoke with disdain about the new movement, calling its adherents "Christians" (11:26), that is, followers of Christ. Eventually the chasm grew (seen, for example, in the Jews' opposition to Paul: 17:5, 13; 21:27–36; 23:12, 27–29), and the church moved militantly into enemy territory.

MARKS OF THE CHURCH

How can one tell if a church is really a church? Obviously the sign at the front entrance of a church building does not qualify a local church to be called one of Christ's churches. Even if we were to use the words of Jesus in Matthew 18:20, can we be sure the gathering of two or three constitutes a church? Jesus' words, "For where two or three come together in my name, there am I with them," refers only to the promise of His presence among believers, not to a church gathering. If they meant the latter, then every Christian family consisting of two or more individuals would qualify as a church.

The term *church* has been distorted by formalism on the one hand and individualism on the other. Formalism, with its emphasis on a sacramental approach to worship, suffers from a de-emphasis on personal faith, while individualism opens itself to highly subjective experientialism. In the former the presence of God is defined by form and structure. In the latter the absence of form and structure is heralded as a virtue by the entrepreneurs of a "do-it-yourself" fellowship. Churches ought to have certain commonalities, certain criteria for judging their validity, and certain attributes that unite rather than divide.

Christians in the past have attempted to identify the "marks" of a true church. With some eighty-five major denominations in America alone, it is sometimes difficult to find commonalities. Furthermore, there are at least 225 different independent groups that call themselves "Christian."

The marks of a true church include the preaching of the Word of God, the ordinances of baptism and the Lord's Supper, and the proper exercise of discipline based on obedience to God's Word. (Calvin and other Reformers believed that preaching and the right administration of the sacraments are the irreducible marks of the church. Luther held that the Word is the only infallible mark of the church. Later Reformers and Baptists added discipline as an essential mark.) A brief review of these essentials may help us avoid the two extremes of lifeless formalism and rudderless individualism.[19]

The Preaching of the Word of God

Central to the life of an evangelical church is the preaching and teaching of the Word of God. Jesus taught that the mark of a true disciple is holding to His teachings (John 8:31). Hearing and believing the liberating gospel is the litmus test identifying a believer from an unbeliever. Furthermore obedience to Jesus' teachings marks those who say they love Jesus. Early Christians were warned not to believe every messenger, but to test the spirits (preachers). If they preached that God was come in the flesh (in other words, the incarnation of God in Christ), they were from God. If they did not preach this message, they were not from God (1 John 4:1–3).

Holding high the Word of God, in both belief and proclamation, the apostles set the pattern for all preaching of the Scriptures. The content of the earliest preaching, according to C. H. Dodd, was marked by six elements: (1) the age of fulfillment has dawned; (2) this has taken place through the death and resurrection of Jesus; (3) by virtue of the Resurrection, Jesus has been exalted to the right hand of God; (4) the Holy Spirit in the church is the sign of Christ's present power and glory; (5) the messianic age will reach its consummation in the return of Christ; and (6) preaching included an appeal for repentance, the offer of forgiveness and the promise of salvation to all who believe.[20] Robert Mounce and others have disagreed with Dodd, typifying his categorizations as "a sort of six-headed sermon which the apostles delivered on any and every occasion."[21] Mounce understands preaching as far more dynamic, emphasizing the Cross of Christ. God's saving action in Christ is for him the ultimate test of genuine preaching. Thus the mark of preaching can never be merely a rehearsal of biblical truths. This mark emphasizes the centrality both of the preaching function in the church and of Christ who is preached.

The Ordinances or Sacraments

The second mark of a church is the proper administration of the sacraments (or ordinances, as Baptists and other non-state church groups prefer to call them). Even the way the ordinances are administered is to be rightly governed by the Word (Matt. 28:19; Acts 2:42; 1 Cor. 11:23–30). These ordinances and their meaning are discussed in more depth in chapter 6.

Discipline

The word *discipline* carries with it a breadth of meaning ranging from commitment to excommunication. Reformers and other church leaders believe that while a church consists of believers voluntarily joined together, the exercise of discipline is essential to maintaining purity of witness.

We find our examples for this in the Scriptures, beginning with Matthew 18:18. It is a minister's high privilege to announce forgiveness in Christ's name to repentant persons who have been confronted in a biblical manner. The early church faced the need for discipline, as evidenced in the example of Ananias and Sapphira's deceit (Acts 5:1–11) and the example of incest in 1 Corinthians 5:1–5. The principle of 1 Corinthians 14:40 sets the pattern for discipline in the church: "Everything should be done in a fitting and orderly way." Revelation 2:14–15, 12 may also be cited as evidence of discipline. "I have a few things against you," are the words of "him who has the sharp, double-edged sword." No church is exempt from the discipline of our Lord. Discipline, clearly then, is a mark of the church.

Exactly what constitutes church membership is debated by some. Discipline as a mark of the church carries little meaning apart from the concept of commitment and church membership. True churches also possess certain other attributes, which some may call "marks." These include unity, catholicity, and holiness. (Each of these is discussed in detail later.) For evangelicals, unity is found only in Christ—not in adherence to the church's hierarchy. "Catholicity" refers to the breadth and scope of the existence of a global church—not to a particular church with its headship in Rome. Holiness, for which all Christians should aspire, refers to emulating Christ's righteousness and being consecrated to God. The use of the term *holy* excludes all unbelievers from Christ's church. The apostle Paul referred to churches of the saints (1 Cor. 1:2; 2 Cor. 1:1; Phil. 1:1). These and other major attributes and marks of the church help us understand what constitutes what we call a church. The marrow of a mature theology of the church, according to Roland Bainton, Luther's biographer, consists of a Christ-centeredness that affirms the called-out nature of the redeemed, forgiven sinners, saved through the utterly unmerited grace of God made possible by the cross of Christ.[22]

2

The Church in History: The Spread of Global Wildfire

There exists not a people, whether Greek or barbarian, or any other race of men, by whatsoever appellation or manners they may be distinguished, however ignorant of arts or agriculture, whether they dwell under tents, or wander about in covered wagons, among whom prayers are not offered up in the name of the crucified Jesus to the Father and Creator of all things.

—Justin Martyr
(around A.D. 100–165)

THE STORY OF THE CHRISTIAN CHURCH encompasses far more than a single chapter's worth of observations. Church historian and Oxford University scholar Henry Bettenson spent his life writing and researching on the church. In the preface to his 1943 edition of *Documents of the Christian Church*, he struggled with the limitations of space and time to treat such a vast subject. In typical English understatement Bettenson wrote of a frustration all of us face when tackling a topic larger than life. "It is unlikely," he wrote, "that any two persons could be found who should agree on what should be included in such a book and what omitted."[1]

The process of examining the living faith of fellow Christians over two millennia is a little like an archaeologist trying to make sense out of some fragments of bones, tools, and a few teeth. Here the similarity ends, for the history of Christendom evidences a thriving movement, a vibrant, pulsating faith that left in its trail all kinds of documentary evidence. For most of its history the church has been one of the most chronicled institutions of society. Narrowing the focus on such a diverse phenomenon is no small task.

Yet why should we be bothered with noting how the church developed over the ages? How can happenings centuries past be relevant for the present? Several benefits accrue from a quick overview of church history. It can help us in these ways:

- to appreciate our past heritage

- to acknowledge with gratitude the sacrifices our forefathers have made in standing true to the Lord and His Word

- to be alert to ways the church has gone astray in doctrine and practice

- to be sensitive to how the church can be influenced for good or bad

- to be motivated to build on the church's strengths

- to be challenged to continue to carry out the responsibilities the Lord has given the church

F. F. Bruce, writing on the rise and progress of Christianity from its first beginnings to the conversion of the English, chose the analogy of a spreading flame.[2] The church moved out from Jerusalem, and in a relatively brief period engulfed the known world like global wildfire.

What was it about Christianity, its beliefs, practices, and early adherents that caused it to spread rapidly into all parts of the world? As a popular movement, the church had several things going for it. For one thing it emerged out of the barren soils of fragmented Judaism. Furthermore it sprang up in a remarkable period of history, ripe for its expansion. The Bible used the words "the fullness of the time" to describe the circumstances at the time of the birth of our Lord and the birth of the church (Gal. 4:4, NASB). There was an established, somewhat orderly empire, and by government edict Roman citizens were assured of rule by law. An extensive international road system, the existence of a common trade language, and the expansionist policies of the Caesars all contributed to the rapid spread of the gospel.

But the rise of the church came about not simply because of human developments and aspirations. What ignited the early believers' enthusiastic faith was the conviction that Jesus Christ had been raised from the dead. News had spread throughout much of the world of an unusual Jewish feast called Pentecost, when the Holy Spirit was poured out and the imminent return of this risen Lord was anticipated. The message of Jesus was confirmed by mighty acts of God.

This explosive "sect" claimed as its followers the poor and the rich, men and women, and Jew and Gentile. Its initiatory rites included baptism by water, but not circumcision. The movement itself was marked by characteristics similar to any social revolution—a new allegiance that placed its members in conflict with prevailing societal norms. The counter reaction of Roman authorities, ignited by suspicion of the Jewish leaders, thrust these followers of the Way outward in every direction. The Christian church represented a separatist movement on the one hand and, on the other, a corps of people bent on transforming their world.[3] However, were it not for the power and presence of God in its midst, the church could have risen and fallen as other movements in history have done. This one was different. The God of heaven, not merely one of several among the pantheon of gods, was at work.

THE CHURCH IN THE NEW TESTAMENT

No great movement begins in a vacuum. Christianity emerged at a time of Roman rule in Palestine. In 37 B.C. Roman armies in alliance with Herod, the son of Antipater, who was in charge of the army, had taken full control of Jerusalem. Under Herod, Jerusalem was rebuilt, wealth and power were amassed, the temple was renovated in magnificent style, and a succession of high priests was established. After Herod's death in 4 B.C., Herod Antipas was awarded his tetrarchy in Galilee. What followed was a chamber of horrors, temple intrigue, a national census under Caesar Augustus, a rising nationalism, and eventually the ruin of the Israelite state in A.D. 70.

After Herod's reign, the country was divided into four parts and leaders were assigned—hence the title *tetrarch*, a Greek word meaning ruler of a fourth of a kingdom. Jerusalem rule fell to high-priest kings, although they were subject to Roman authority. We would call them puppet kings. Two major factions—the Sanhedrin, composed of seventy priests, and the Pharisees, who comprised a majority—kept tensions alive. During this unhappy time, John the Baptist emerged and led a great religious revival that touched the common people, who belonged to no particular sect or party. John came in the succession of Elijah and the older prophets, denouncing state and religious corruption, and calling for repentance of personal sin. His appeal was tremendously popular and powerful.

When John baptized Jesus of Nazareth in the Jordan River, an unusual thing occurred. The Holy Spirit descended from heaven like a dove, and God the Father said, "This is my Son, whom I love; with him I am well pleased" (Matt. 3:17). Eventually John the Baptist was arrested and beheaded, and Jesus' popularity attracted a widening circle of disciples of His own.

From this point on, a series of dramatic events took place in a relatively brief period, events that would alter the course of history. The advent of Jesus split time in half between B.C. and A.D. Eventually His death and resurrection, followed by the events at Pentecost, would propel the church from the launching pad called Palestine, or Israel.

The Jerusalem church, which figured so prominently in the early days of the church, was composed of the original apostles, Jesus' human relatives, and a host of others converted at Pentecost. James, the brother of our Lord, was probably the head of the Jerusalem church. The number of the disciples soon rose from three thousand to five thousand. They met in the temple and in houses. Among its members was Barnabas, whose splendid gift may have done much to help the church through its early financial difficulties (Acts 4:36–37). This tightly knit group held all things in common and engaged in compassionate service, looking after the fatherless, widows, and the sick.

Early persecution came to the Jerusalem church at the hands of the Sanhedrin. As one of the first deacons, Stephen, like our Lord, was charged with sedition and blasphemy, although the specific details of the charges were unclear (6:5–6, 8–15). Following a stirring message to the crowd, he was stoned to death (7:2–60). One called Saul of Tarsus stood by, consenting to Stephen's death (8:1), the church's first martyr. This Saul was the one man who later took the gospel across the known world.

THE PILGRIM COMMUNITY—
GATHERED AND SCATTERED

We gain some understanding of the early expansion of Christianity from a few passages in Paul's letters and the Gospels (Mark 3:7–8; Acts 1:8; 8:1;

2 Thess. 2:8, 14). Peter later referred to believers as "aliens and strangers" (1 Pet. 2:11). The most significant church outside of Jerusalem was located at Caesarea, the residence of the Roman governor. Bearers of the mission, in obedience to the Great Commission of our Lord, carried the gospel to Samaria and beyond. Philip, another of the early deacons (Acts 6:5), was associated with the Samaritan mission (8:4–8).

The expansion of the church moved rapidly northward through Phoenicia (Tyre, Ptolemais, and Sidon, 21:3–4, 7; 27:3) to Cyprus and Antioch (11:19). At Antioch the derisive designation "Christian" was first given to the followers of Christ (11:26). In Acts 10 a centurion named Cornelius came to faith in Christ. Communities arose in Syria and Cilicia (Gal. 1:21). Beyond these efforts the compressed history of Acts 13–14 describes outward expansion, and later we have record of further expansion into Europe.

Tradition tells of the expansion of the gospel as far away as India. Witness in Egypt and Ethiopia could have come from Philip's Ethiopian convert on the road to Gaza (8:26–39). Even the Ukraine has its legends of the gospel reaching Kiev. Missionaries sent by Augustine, the first archbishop of Canterbury (died 604), to Glastonbury, England, reported finding a church already established there.

Until the missionary journeys of Paul, expressions of Christianity, for the most part, carried a dominant Hellenistic influence. The church at Caesarea was an exception. From Peter's experience in Caesarea and from Paul's experiences through evangelism, the gospel was falling on good soil among Gentiles, many of whom came to faith in Christ. While the gentile initiative is attributed to Peter, it was Paul who eventually became the apostle to the Gentiles (Rom. 15:15–16; Gal. 1:16).

The conversion of Gentiles and their membership in the emerging church posed a problem. Some men taught that all aspects of the Jewish Law must be followed. Paul and Barnabas took issue with their dogmatism, which the false teachers summed up in a few words: "The Gentiles must be circumcised and required to obey the law of Moses" (Acts 15:5). A council of apostles and elders met to resolve the dispute, which pitted those favoring an open gospel against those excluding uncircumcised Gentiles from salvation. Peter delivered their conclusion: "We believe it is through the grace of our Lord Jesus that we are saved, just as they are"

(15:11). Later the council sent a letter sanctioning the existence of the gentile church, and affirming that both Jews and Gentiles are recipients of God's unifying grace. "With this agreement," wrote Hans Conzelmann, "the foundation for all the future mission is laid."[4]

The New Testament period ends with a diverse church scattered over the Roman world, because of both missionary design and persecution. The fire of faith was ablaze. Light was entering the dark recesses of the world for which Christ died.

The close of the apostolic age ended in persecution. A great fire in Rome in July, A.D. 64 was blamed on Christians, probably by Nero, to divert popular rumor from himself. If Peter was indeed in Rome at the time, he probably died under Neronian persecution. As stated earlier, no definitive linkage can be made for Peter ever being the first bishop or pope of Rome. That designation came later by tradition.

The continuation of church history after the Jerusalem Council (A.D. 49) and the fall of Jerusalem (A.D. 70) is in reality the continuation of the Acts of the Apostles. W. R. Inge wrote of the powerful flow of church history: "Clement of Alexandria [around 150–215] compared the Church to a great river, receiving affluents from all sides. The great river sometimes flows impetuously through a narrow channel; sometimes it spreads like a flood; sometimes it divides into several streams; sometimes, for a time, it seems to have been driven underground. But the Holy Spirit has never left himself without witness."[5]

The years from A.D. 70 to 110 remain one of the most obscure in church history. Only God knows the unnamed missionaries of this period who spread the gospel everywhere they went. Williston Walker noted that when this period of rapid changes ended, the characteristics of the church showed surprisingly little of the distinctive stamp of Paul. There was, in Walker's words, "an inrush of ideas from other than Christian sources, brought undoubtedly by converts of heathen antecedents, modified Christian beliefs and practices, especially regarding the sacraments, fastings, and the rise of liturgical forms. The old conviction of the immediacy of the guidance of the Spirit, faded without being wholly extinguished. The constitution of the church itself underwent, in this period, a far-reaching development."[6]

THE SPREADING FLAME OF WITNESS

After the destruction of Jerusalem in A.D. 70 by the Romans, Christians continued to engage in vigorous debate and open witness to others. Christianity by its very nature was not yet captive to inwardness. To be sure, there was the example of asceticism followed by Jews of the Qumran sect, but for Christians, the issue of separation from the world had not yet taken on a monastic quality. That would come later from the desert fathers, as the early ascetics were called.

As the gospel reached ever farther outward in the mid to late first century, it became necessary to include a defense or apology of the faith. In this period the Gospels were recorded, giving credible witness to Jesus' life and ministry. Jesus' life and sayings were at the heart of New Testament preaching, but as oral tradition about Jesus became separated in time from the experience of the church, the need for a written record of what Jesus said and did became essential. Some of the epistles were written before the Gospels were written. This is not to say that the Synoptic Gospels (Matthew, Mark, and Luke) did not exist earlier in some form, but they did not appear until after A.D. 50. Twenty years later, they were part of the literature of the church and the emerging canon of Scripture. John's Gospel, however, came late in the first century.

By the time of Justin Martyr, about the middle of the second century, the Gospels were read in the services of worship together with the Old Testament prophets. The process of accrediting the canon was not complete until shortly before A.D. 400.

The center of ecclesiastical power shifted from east to west during this postapostolic period. By the end of the first century, Asia Minor had been extensively evangelized, as had adjoining Syria. A quarrel between Rome and the East arose over the time to observe Easter. Rome won out. By A.D. 200 Rome had assumed a place of prominence and had begun to assert authority over other church bodies. Even the rise of the influential Christian centers in Alexandria and Carthage did not dim Rome's rising star.

The term "apostolic fathers" seems to have been first used by Severus of Antioch. It was applied to those leaders outside the New Testament, including Clement of Rome, Ignatius, Polycarp, Barnabas, and Hermas.[7]

These second- and third-century writers produced a significant body of literature. Some of these writers and later fathers, such as Tertullian (died around 222) and Cyprian (died 258), codified a distinct Roman Catholic influence on the church, in that their homilies served to further establish the power of the Western church.

The early apologists, such as Justin Martyr in his *Apology*, defended the moral character of Christianity. During this period intense persecution of the church was the norm rather than the exception. This violent opposition took place under Emperor Decius (249–251). Commanding all citizens of the empire to give allegiance to the traditional Roman gods, Decius forced Christians to make a choice. Some complied; others resisted to death. Those killed were called "martyrs" (the word in Greek means simply "witness"). Those who endured persecution were called "confessors." The question of admission to the church then became crucial. Should "lapsed" Christians or defectors be allowed into the church?

In this context Cyprian, bishop of Carthage, uttered his famous dictum, "Outside the church there is no salvation." The rise of sacramentalism, veneration of saints, and other symbols of power were centered more around the hierarchy than the congregation. Bruce Shelley aptly summarizes this development: "Grace had come to terms with time. The bishop controlled the Spirit."[8] The immediacy of Spirit guidance in the church now passed to the mediation of the church.

THE WEDDING OF STATE AND CHURCH

Chaos and anarchy ruled the empire prior to the rise of one pivotal leader, Diocletian, who ruled Rome for more than twenty years (284–305). His skill as a statesman overshadowed his weaknesses, but toward the end of his rule he turned full imperial power against Christians. Bishops and ordinary believers were martyred, and church buildings burned.

Popular opinion turned against this cruel policy of Diocletian and his henchmen in A.D. 312, soon after Constantine assumed imperial power. Calling on the God of the Christians, Constantine was converted to Christianity, although he was not baptized until on his deathbed. Constantine permitted certain freedoms and generously allowed institutional Christianity to flourish.

Constantine changed the nature of official Christendom forever. Declaring the empire Christian, Constantine placed a veneer over secular society which became Christian at least in name. The same was true of Theodosius, who ruled the empire from 378 to 395. Society, half-rooted in paganism, used the church as a haven for the politically ambitious. Furthermore, with the populace supposedly becoming Christian by edict, any sense of a disciplined church membership was obliterated.

Architecturally, church buildings began to display domes, a design borrowed from the ancient Persians. This style would later become the symbol of Eastern Orthodox churches.

Christianity, in Constantine's mind, was a unifying factor for a declining empire. It offered one emperor, one law, and one citizenship to all free people. Christianity became the single fully sanctioned religion of both court and country.

Following the death of Constantine the empire was divided, and its rule fell to his three sons. When one son died shortly after the division, the empire was speedily sectioned in two—East and West. The stage was set for a major schism that came centuries later.

THE RISE OF MONASTICISM

Ascetic ideals had long been growing in the church. Monasticism, the belief that purity of soul is achieved by withdrawal from the world, began to flourish. In its beginning, monasticism reflected an attempt to break with the formalism of the church. In time it would create its own formalism.

Anthony, the founder of monasticism, was born in Koma in central Egypt around A.D. 250. He is said to have lived more than one hundred years, most of them as a hermit. He fasted, viewed himself as tormented by demons, practiced self-denial, and prayed. His example attracted disciples whose individualistic styles set early patterns of monasticism. The work of Athanasius (around 293–373) introduced these practices to the West.

From these inauspicious beginnings arose a full-blown movement that eventually engulfed Roman Catholic Christianity and, to a lesser extent,

Eastern Orthodoxy. Essentially a lay movement at first, monasticism gained favor from important church leaders like Ambrose (339–397), Augustine (354–430), and Jerome (around 374–420).

The Benedictine rule, founded by Benedict of Nursia, best expressed the ideals of monasticism. Tradition has it that in 525 he founded a monastery of the Benedictine Order on a hill between Rome and Naples. The ideals of this orderly rule and its center on Monte Cassino spread.

Celibacy, which many have seen as a mark of a holier Christian life, eventually became a requirement for the ministry.

Monasticism has flourished both in the Roman Catholic Church and in Eastern Orthodox churches. While Protestantism rejected it in the sixteenth century, nineteenth-century Anglicanism established a few orders. Monasticism, which spread quickly throughout the Byzantine Empire in the seventh century, was later established in Kiev in 1050 and Moscow in 1354.

Two religious groups, the Dominicans and the Franciscans, emerged as renewal efforts within monasticism and exist to this day. Monasteries declined by the sixteenth century, but they have continued in some form to the present.

Monasticism sought to answer the question, What is the perfect Christian life? In the third century, this and similar questions about purity and holiness were being seriously asked in the church. In the next two centuries monasticism flourished like a vine, engulfing nearly all of Christendom.

Monasticism represented an early revolt against the abusive power of bishops and the clergy. Yet in time monasticism adopted ideas the church had earlier branded as heretical. These included the belief that salvation could be earned, as the Ebionites taught. Flesh and matter were seen as evil, a belief held by the Gnostics. Monasticism, furthermore, tended to develop two classes of Christians—those aspiring to perfection and those captive to a secular world. This was contrary to New Testament teaching that all believers are called saints and are part of a holy priesthood before God.

The good of monasticism may be seen in its missionary movement and in its praiseworthy efforts with the poor. From the sixth century onward, most Christian missionary efforts came from those who had taken monastic vows. Kenneth Latourette saw in monasticism a distinct

Christian ideal of people renouncing their possessions and distributing goods to the poor.[9]

Here and there, both inside and outside of Roman Catholicism, bursts of monastic influence exist. Dreams of Christian centers that radiate both conviction and care are alive even today. Visions of monasticism refuse to die.

THE RISE OF CENTRAL AUTHORITY

The popularity of certain heresies served to develop the need for tighter organizational structure. A wide variety of sects claimed to be Christian in name—the Gnostics and Marcionites, to mention only two. The term *catholic* was first used by Ignatius. Ignatius, who died around 110, held that "wherever Jesus Christ is, there is the catholic church."[10] Latourette believed that several motives prompted the development of the use of that term: "Christians", "to unite all; to preserve, transmit, and spread the Christian gospel; and to bring all Christians together in a visible body of Christ.'"[11]

Three things were essential to achieving these purposes: a comon authority (bishops), a common canon of Scripture, and a proper creed. In time each of these fell into place, but not without struggle—even struggle that threatened the very unity they sought.

The concept that there is an unbroken line of authority between the first apostles and bishops was forcefully promoted by Irenaeus in the second century. The appointment of bishops became the "catholic" church's way of assuring purity of doctrine. They were certain that the apostles faithfully and accurately taught what had been transmitted to them by Christ, and later appointed elders and bishops in unbroken succession.

Despite these mechanisms—originally designed to insure fidelity—controversies continued. In time the great councils of the church unscrambled the arguments and affirmed truths that, over the centuries, have proven unifying to the church.

Constantine's example of calling the Council at Nicaea to reconcile the differences between Arius and Athanasius provided a precedent for ecumenical councils. At Nicaea (325) and Constantinople (381), the doctrine of the Trinity was affirmed, chiefly the relationship of Jesus Christ to God the Father.

As the church expanded, it moved further away from what F. F. Bruce described as doctrines of Christianity that later became theological abstractions.[12] However, the councils were useful in establishing certain definitive answers to key questions.

The Council at Carthage (398), for instance, settled questions regarding the canon of Scripture. The Council of Chalcedon (451) gave final form to the orthodox conviction about the two natures of Christ. Later councils were called to solidify as well as clarify the centralization of papal authority in matters of doctrine and faith: the Fourth Lateran Council, (1215–1216), the Council of Constance (1415), and the Council of Trent (1545–1563).

THE SPLIT BETWEEN EAST AND WEST

The Eastern and Western churches continued to drift apart. One looked to Constantinople and the other to Rome. This took place in stages, not unlike the continental drift that geologists speculate separated South America from Africa in antiquity.

A critical stage in this separation occurred at Constantinople in 692. A council called by the emperor decided that Constantinople should enjoy equal privilege with Rome. The Eastern Church defied Rome by allowing deacons and presbyters to marry, prohibiting fasting during Lent season, and ordering that Christ be depicted in human form. Together, these developments formed a wedge between these two great segments of the church.

In the eighth century the powerful Pope Leo III banned the use of religious images and pictures in worship. The use of pictures or icons to depict the humanity of Jesus had long been in practice in the East. The "iconoclastic controversy," as it was called, also served to drive Eastern Christianity further from Western Christianity. The controversy represented a demand for a "spiritual" realm of power, rejecting images. Under subsequent popes, veneration of icons was banned with religious fervor. Finally, at a general council called in Nicaea in 787, Constantine VI, Byzantine emperor in Constantinople, sanctioned pictures. The West and the East agreed that honor paid to images passes on to that which the image represents. The Greek Orthodox Church, in particular, elevated this form of veneration, while in the West, dimensional imagery—not merely flat paintings—became the norm. In attempts to reach heathen with tangible expressions of the spiritual world, the church slid closer to heathenism itself.

This controversy, which along with other theological points ultimately divided East and West, serves as a warning to modern evangelicals who seek to win unbelievers by secular means. It is still the preaching of the Cross that wins converts, not visual imagery (icons, images, or religious relics).

Official separation between East and West occurred in 1054 under Leo IX, who sought to excommunicate the Church of Holy Wisdom at Constantinople.

In the West, Catholics elevate the pope as the supreme spiritual ruler of the world. Those in Eastern Orthodoxy, on the other hand, teach that the incarnate God came to earth to restore the icon of man. They have no allegiance to the Vatican. Thus East and West, originally separated geographically under Roman emperor Theodosius in 395, came to represent two separate ways of viewing truth. Perhaps it is too simple to say that the East emphasized rule by a mystical presence of God, while in the West, a legal monarchy symbolized by the pope, exercised final authority.

A Holy Roman Empire, it was felt, would assure the legacy of divine truth. Crowned Roman emperor on Christmas Day, 800, Charlemagne, or Charles the Great, as he was known, vigorously sought to restore the glory that once was Rome. He defined the boundaries of power in Western Europe, and the power of the papacy flourished, even more so after his death in 814. From Charlemagne onward, the papacy rose in importance, and under Pope Innocent III (1198–1216), it was brought to its apex of influence and political power. Before him, Leo I, Gregory I, and Gregory VII had enlarged papal power, but Innocent III proclaimed himself "the vicar of him of whom it had been affirmed that he was king of kings and lord of lords."[13]

Under his pontificate, Constantinople was captured by the Crusaders and a significant council met to affirm Roman Church authority (Fourth

Lateran Council, 1215–1216). Confessions to priests, the doctrine of transubstantiation, elevation of the tithe as a tax, and obligatory penance were only a few of its dictates.

A period of papal decline followed, pilgrimages became popular to reinforce faith, and relics of saints were venerated. In the eleventh century, religious music and poetry flourished. After 1050, the "Hail Mary" (*Ave Maria*) was heard in churches, with its prayers to the Virgin.

A host of developments, including the rise of Neoplatonism and scholasticism, the influence of Pierre Abelard (1079–around 1144), Thomas Aquinas (1225?–1274), the Black Plague, the rise of universities, and the rise of the diocesan or parish structure, distinguished this period. Also selling indulgences—payment for purgatory—was a common practice.

THE GREAT SCHISM—RIVALRY OF POPES

In the fourteenth century seven popes, one pope after the other, resided in Avignon, France. This period has been called the Babylonian Captivity of the church, a metaphor Martin Luther later used to expose church abuse. Ideologically Rome remained the proper papal capital successor to Saint Peter in the apostolic church. Then in what came to be known as "the Great Schism" of forty years (1377–1417) popes were elected in both France and Rome. The Council of Constance ended the split in 1417, restoring the papacy to Rome. In grand language the decree *Sacrosancta* stated, "This holy Council of Constance . . . declares first, that it is lawfully assembled in the Holy Spirit, that it constitutes a General Council, representing the Catholic Church, and then therefore it has authority immediately from Christ; and that all men, of every rank and condition, including the Pope himself, are bound to obey it in matters concerning the faith, the abolition of the Schism, and the reformation of the Church of God in its head and members."[14]

Having two papacies—one in Avignon and one in Rome—proved to be expensive. Facing depleted treasuries, the Roman popes set about in earnest to increase revenues. Such efforts and accompanying abuses eventually led to revolt. Papal power could silence a John Wycliffe or a John Hus by martyrdom, but Martin Luther and other Reformers would refuse to be silenced by centralized power in Rome.

DISSENT AND REFORMATION

Early Efforts to Reform Rome

In all these developments there was an undertone of dissent and frus-
trated renewal—all preparation for the Reformation. Mass conversions
to Christianity, first under Constantine and later under Charlemagne and
others, served only to build a superficial faith. As a result of abuses—both
clerical and lay, papal and political—a foment was rising for renewal. More
and more, the vast ecclesiastical machinery necessary to oversee the populace was beginning to show signs of danger.

The existence of mystics served as a prod to Rome to remain "spiritual." Who can minimize the work and writings of the monk from Kempen,
Thomas á Kempis (1379–1471), Catherine of Siena (1347–1380), French
heroine Joan of Arc (around 1412–1431), Julian of Norwich (around 1342–
1416), German mystic theologian Johannes Eckhart (around 1260–1327),
each in their own countries calling for a pure faith?

The moral decline of the papacy prompted calls for reform, and pressure was building throughout Christendom. Churchmen ambitious for
power and prestige, and a succession of popes bent on self-aggrandizement,
corrupted the church. Spiritual leadership, as envisioned by Hildebrand
(an eleventh-century French monk, who later was Pope Gregory VII from
1073 to 1085), and Middle Age Reformers, was thwarted by blatant instances of immorality, bribery, and political intrigue. "The papacy was a
liability rather than an asset," wrote Latourette.[15]

Two Reformers stood out in the midst of the moral mess, John
Wycliffe and John Hus. Wycliffe (1329–1384), an Oxford University
scholar, became increasingly radical and called for the removal of the
worldly popes. To him, salvation depends solely on election by God,
not on any connection with the church. He repudiated indulgences,
masses for the dead, and all formalism. Furthermore, Wycliffe translated the Bible from Latin into English to make it accessible to the
common people. Almost a thousand years earlier Jerome in the fourth
century had done essentially the same thing in producing the Scriptures in common (*vulgare*) Latin, known as the Vulgate. Now this same
activity, ironically, was considered heretical. To spread the gospel, Wycliffe

sent out preachers, "poor priests," who were given the nickname Lollards. They preached in village greens, barnyards, and churchyards. Wycliffe is chiefly known for the final seven or eight years of his life and his writings, more than for his work at Oxford. Both the Wycliffe translation of the Bible and the work of the Lollards contributed to the English Reformation.

John Hus from Bohemia (1373–1415) represented a whole band of scholars and preachers who denounced corruption in the church. Elevated to the position of dean and rector at the University of Prague, he denounced the pope, claimed that Christ rather than Peter is the foundation of the church, and desired moral reform rather than ecclesiastical revolution. Eventually he was excommunicated by the archbishop. Following an unsuccessful appeal to Pope John, Hus was burned at the stake on July 6, 1415. His final words were the same as those of Jesus from the cross: "Lord, into Thy hands I commend my spirit."[16]

Other efforts at reform are too numerous to mention in this brief overview of the history of the church. The grave menace of a corrupt church provoked Reformers. Rising nationalism, the rise of humanism, the Renaissance, and related factors produced ample fodder for revolt. Most pre-Reformation reformers stayed within the church; a few like Hus were cast out of it. But a groundswell was rising. A protest movement— the Protestant Reformation—was not far away.

Looking back on history, we can barely imagine the intensity of emotion that fired the Reformers. As they appeared on their own thresholds of history, they followed a long line of sincerely zealous Christians who desired purity of truth and life within the church.

The Protestant Reformation

Before the Protestant Reformation no religious movement had been more successful in accomplishing reform than the one led by Hus. The influence of Wycliffe, called the "morning star" of the Reformation, led Hus to engage in a nationalistic effort in Bohemia. Czech reform was intellectually fueled by Hus, who wrote a very important book entitled *On the Church* in 1413. This was a full century before Luther. The wheels of reform ground slowly but inexorably, but the Roman Church viewed any attack on established ecclesiastical and civil laws as anarchy.

We have to remember that the existence of the Black Plague had a profoundly disruptive effect on Western Europe during this period, as did the rise of Islam. Constantinople fell to the Turks in 1453, sending shock waves throughout Christendom, and cemeteries were filling fast from the awful plague.

"The Middle Ages were anything but a period of conformist religion and church domination," wrote Steven Ozment.[17] Popular movements like the Lollards and Hussites kept Rome on the defensive. Even the devotionalists and mystics left their mark on Rome's seemingly invincible power. Governmental centralization, apart from Rome's ecclesiastical power, grew in influence. The growth of the monarchy undermined the universal claims of councils and popes. The Hundred Years War (1337–1453) between England and France left royalty in England in a much stronger position to control its people and their religious practices. Autonomous political dynasties, the Palatinate, Saxony, Brandenburg, and Bohemia, and three ecclesiastic powers—archbishoprics at Mainz, Trier, and Cologne—helped shape the direction of the German Reformation.

The stage was set for militant reform and popular dissent by consolidation of secular political domination. In England the king claimed the right to choose the archbishop of Canterbury. Payment to Rome was discontinued, and King Henry VIII became head of the national church. In France a movement called "Gallicanism" restored local clerical authority in the church. Spain, more Catholic than Italy, won its own concessions under Ferdinand and Isabella. Spanish bishops began to be appointed by kings.

Only in Germany did Rome retain a measure of clout, but bit by bit civil magistrates and city councils extracted their pound of flesh. Primarily in sixteenth-century Germany, however, a magnitude of corruption sparked revolt.

Albrecht von Brandenburg, archbishop of Mainz, Germany, promoted indulgences against which Martin Luther protested. German people saw this as another form of taxation by a foreign power. Luther himself viewed the selling of indulgences as a form of foreign taxation, as well as a religious evil.

Several key elements in Western civilization combined to create a mighty launching pad for the Reformation. The rise of humanism was important, as it established a new literacy and an insatiable desire to study the classics. Erasmus's work in recovering the original languages of the Bible by publishing a Greek New Testament, Gutenberg's invention of the printing press, the translation of the Bible into local languages, and a rising new economy—each of these formed planks in the platform of reform.

Martin Luther

On the eve of All Saints' Day in the year 1517, Martin Luther, a highly educated monk of the Augustinian Order, posted on the door of the Castle Church at Wittenberg the famous Ninety-Five Theses, directed against Albrecht, the bishop of Mainz. His theses essentially voiced three concerns: papal exploitation of national dissent, the jurisdiction of the pope over purgatory, and the error of indulgences. On this third point, salvation by faith in Christ alone was declared.

In the ensuing controversy Luther came toe to toe with papal power. A doctor of theology, he was able to confront Romanism at the highest academic levels by affirming several important biblical doctrines. His assertion of justification by faith alone ran counter to papal power to remit penalty for sins by monetary payment. "Luther," wrote Roland Bainton, "had the temerity, when the pope did not endorse his view, to deny the infallibility of the pope, and for good measure of a general council also."[18]

The debate was intense and eventually led in 1521 to a meeting called the Diet of Worms, where Luther was asked to recant. This, of course, he would not do. Luther opposed the view that the Roman pontiff is infallible in matters of faith. No issue could be more crucial. The lines of dissent and of excommunication were enunciated by both sides of the debate. Luther's words, "Here I stand, so help me God," led to an inevitable cleavage between Rome and Luther's followers.

The bishop of Mainz, intent on building his own edifice, had struck a deal with Rome. One-half of indulgence money was to go to build Saint Peter's Basilica in Rome, the other half to stay in Mainz. The sordid details of this sad transaction were probably known to Luther. Through this form of taxation, Rome, he said, was building on the blood of God's sheep. John Tetzel, the local indulgence vendor, had gone too far. His sales pitch offered freedoms too great for fearful parishioners to ignore: "As soon as the coin in the coffer rings, the soul from purgatory springs."[19]

In three major tracts, Luther set forth his views on Christ as the way to salvation, the church's rites, governance, and relationship to society. "The breach was irreparable," cried his contemporaries.

Luther's views still form the basis of twentieth-century evangelical witness:

1. There are only two sacraments (ordinances), baptism and the Lord's Supper.

2. All Christians are priests before God.

3. Transubstantiation, the view that the Mass reenacts the Incarnation and Crucifixion, is unbiblical.

4. Personal faith in Jesus Christ is the prerequisite for the sacraments (although Luther regarded infant baptism as essential to snatch children at birth from Satan).

5. Faith alone, not human merit, is the basis of salvation. Faith itself is a gift from God.

6. The Scriptures alone—not the pope or a church council—are infallible.

7. Popes and bishops have no jurisdiction over God's people.

8. The church is a remnant because the elect are few.

From our vantage point, the Reformation Luther started may seem incomplete. For example, he never relinquished a corporate view of the baptismal font. His congregationalism, furthermore, was never fully developed.

The implications, however, of a conscience captive to the Word of God could only effect revolution. Following the Diet of Worms, Luther went into seclusion under the protection of Frederick the Wise at the castle fortress of Wartburg. Taking advantage of the leisure afforded at Wartburg, Luther translated the entire New Testament in three months' time. The

Old Testament came later. The German vernacular Bible is Luther's greatest accomplishment. It appeared in final form in 1534.

A man of immense energy, talent, and intellect, Luther also developed educational institutions and may be rightly called the father of modern compulsory education. His musical skills were obvious. His fidelity to Katharina von Bora, a former nun whom he married in 1525, suggests that the home was a major institution affected by the Reformation. Every father, Luther believed, was to be a priest to his own family. Katharina and Martin had six children and also raised four orphaned children. This former monk and his wife forged a union that influenced views of marriage for generations. Katharina, Luther said, was his nearest neighbor and therefore should be his dearest friend.

Within a decade, most of northern Germany was won over to Protestant beliefs. A territorial church emerged, sparking its own critique by the Anabaptists and fellow Reformers. Scandinavia also turned to the Lutheran faith.

Ulrich Zwingli

Ulrich Zwingli grew up as a farm boy in eastern Switzerland. As early as 1516 he became an evangelical preacher. Educated at Basil and influenced by Erasmus, Zwingli insisted on independence from Luther's reform in Germany. He found Luther's views closer to the old faith, although the two reforms were similar. He described his reliance on the Bible as a special insight, much like Luther's discovery of the meaning of the righteousness of God.

Eventually Zwingli and his reform party in Zurich affected the removal of the mass and religious images, but they continued the practice of infant baptism. Those more radical than they focused their opposition on infant baptism.

Zwingli differed with Luther on the meaning of the Lord's Supper. He held that neither bread, wine, water, nor the preacher's words contained or conveyed divine grace. This "memorial" view of the Lord's Table is held today by most Baptists and other independent Christian groups.

A series of Protestant–Catholic wars broke out after 1529. The ensuing Peace of Kappel (1531) established the principle of local sovereignty in religion. A militant man of uncompromising conviction, Zwingli died on the battlefield defending his views of the Reformation.

John Calvin

In 1523, at the age of fourteen, John Calvin entered the College de la Marche in Paris, where he began his career in the field of divinity. Here he was introduced to the French Reformers. By the age of twenty-two, he had achieved a master's degree, studied law, and received a doctorate. In 1532, at the age of twenty-three, he converted to Protestantism. Calvin described his conversion this way: "God subdued and made teachable a heart which for my age, was far too hardened in such matters."[20] Because of religious war in France, he ended up in Geneva. While there, he presented an ecclesiastical document, *Articles on the Organization of Church and Worship* (1537). He also wrote a new catechism, *An Instruction in the Faith.* His views of Christian governance of cities emerged, as well as his dissent with official church authorities. Exiled from Geneva in 1538, Calvin met Martin Bucer, a convert of Luther, whose practical skills in effecting reforms he admired and adopted. Bucer became Calvin's mentor. While in Strasbourg, Calvin wrote the first edition of his *Institutes of the Christian Religion* and his first biblical commentary. Invited back to Geneva, Calvin did what few ministers dare do when taking a pastorate. He warned the church council, "If you desire to have me as your pastor, correct the disorder of your lives."[21]

In Geneva, Calvin instituted his own authoritarianism. We may lament his dogmatism and strict rules of conduct, but he did leave a legacy. His *Institutes* gives us the clearest understanding of Reformed thought.

Sociologist Max Weber argued that the root of Calvinist activism was worry over predestination. This is only partly true. Calvin left a major footprint on the expansion of Christianity. Although he was anxious over the human condition of fallenness, he was also confident in the righteousness of God's cause in providing salvation.

The Radical Reformers

Radical Reformers who followed Luther and Zwingli helped to establish other important planks in the platform of modern evangelicalism—the voluntary church, the separation of church and state, and religious liberty. Officially the Swiss Anabaptist ("rebaptizer") movement began in Zurich in January 1525. Conrad Grebel, Feliz Manz, and Georg Blaurock believed that the Bible teaches believers' baptism. Only consenting adults who freely choose to follow Christ are to be baptized, and only these baptized believers constitute the true church. This was indeed a radical departure from the prevailing centuries-old view that every infant, by being sprinkled, becomes a member of the state church.

Modern-day Mennonites and Amish trace their roots to Anabaptist practices and teachings, as do Baptists, the Brethren, and the Hutterites. Later, Pietism and Methodism would partake of the hidden fruit of these champions of a radical brand of Christian faith. Disavowal of mainstream Protestantism marked their ways, as the Reformation itself continued to be reformed.

THE RISE OF EVANGELICALISM

In the years following the Protestant Reformation major revolt from Rome extended to the far reaches of western civilization. Calvinism, in particular, engulfed Scotland. Reformation in England took place under Henry VIII. The archbishop of Canterbury, much earlier freed from papal authority, now was head of the church in England. John Knox (around 1514–1572), whose fiery preaching and strict Calvinism shaped a form of governance unfriendly to rule by kings and queens, forged a reform of his own kind. Scotland today is quite separate from England in its Reformed tradition.

Within Anglicanism a nonconformist dissent arose. Establishment religion, viewed by many as oppressive, created dissent, with several expressions. Nonconformists, as they were called, included Puritans, Baptists, Quakers, and others.

Puritanism was at first opposed to separatism in England but was later driven to it by the Convocation of Canterbury (1604), which said anyone who challenged the apostolic character of the Church of England would be imprisoned, banished, or sentenced to death.

Under King James I (the king under whose reign the Authorized Version or King James Version of the Bible was commissioned), large numbers of separatists and nonconformists fled the country. Around 1606, John Smyth gathered a small group of separatists at Gainsborough, England. This congregation and others from Scrooby Manor were imprisoned near Ely, England. They later fled to the Netherlands and from there to America. Separatism, begun under Elizabeth's reign, suffered persecution under James's tyranny.

The Pilgrim fathers found a haven for their Calvinism in America in the colony of Massachusetts.

Colonists settled America for a variety of reasons. Secular and religious interests were not always distinct. Howard Mumford Jones wrote that the idea of America is difficult to trace to any one single idea.[22] Visions of a kingdom of God on earth drove some to the New World. Others fled persecution, yearning for freedom. With civil war raging in England, one colonial preacher told his congregation, "There hath been both a Church-quake and a State-quake in that Land."[23]

Religion in the New World carried with it a mix of powerful ideas: manifest destiny, divine providence, gospel expansion, mercantilism, millennialism, and utopianism. New Englanders were seen as forerunners of God's army, light-givers in a dark world. They saw the beneficence of God as only one more indicator of the wisdom of westward expansionism.

The doctrine of the church is often obscured by the developments of religion mixed with secularist goals of prosperity. While faith was transplanted from European shores to America, it took its own shape in time. New forms in a new land shaped the faith of the nation.

In Central and South America a more singular form of church life took root—Roman Catholicism. Jesuits, Franciscans, and Dominicans each had a hand in extending the Catholic faith in the Americas, chiefly under the patronage of the Spanish crown (or the Portuguese crown for Brazil).

The growth of Christianity in Canada, or New France as it was first called, was largely the result of immigration. Under the aggressive French bishop of Quebec, François Laval (1623–1708), French Canadian Roman Catholicism became firmly established.

The scene in the American colonies was different. Puritans dominated the northern colonies, where the plain law of the Bible shaped congregationalism. Dissent by Baptists led Roger Williams to form Rhode Island as a free colony. Quakers arrived and, despite persecution, they formed a church in Boston in 1665, only later moving westward.

The Church of England established its presence and influence in Virginia and the Carolinas. The mixed character of these colonies was influenced by Huguenots, Scotch-Irish Presbyterians, and English Baptists, to name a few. Maryland, a proprietary colony, was chartered to Roman Catholics. The middle colonies in particular were shaped by the diversity of immigrant people and their churches. Religion in America reflected a growing pluralism calling for a binding element. Such was found in federalism (power shared by a central government and its colonies) and in the formation of a new nation "under God."

EVANGELICAL REVIVAL

The spread of the spirit of the Enlightenment brought pressure on church doctrine and life. Seventeenth-century Enlightenment was a conscious effort to apply the rule of reason to individual and corporate life. Autonomy, reason, and preestablished harmony influenced Europe, and in the early part of the eighteenth century the New World stood on the doorstep of the Industrial Revolution.

Religion in eighteenth-century England was only a thin veneer over a coarse society. Social conditions cried out for reform. Deism, with its impersonal God, had weakened the theological toughness of an older orthodoxy. The time was ripe for reform. It came by way of the evangelical revival, first in England, then in America, in the form of the Great Awakening.

In England, a groundswell of evangelicalism was fired by the writings of German pietists. German Lutheranism had become rigid and unbending, and was now little more than a lifeless state religion. Philipp Jakob Spener (1635–1705) brought a refreshing love of the Bible to a listless church. He had been influenced by Puritan writers and by the translated works of Richard Baxter (1615–1691), including *The Reformed Preacher*. In *Pia desideria* (1675) Spener spelled out the evils of government influence on religion and of immorality and drunkenness. He proposed gatherings of all believers as priests for purposes of reading the Scriptures and reforming the laity. He succeeded in warming up popular Christian life; he made piety popular.

One of the practical outgrowths of this emerging evangelicalism was missionary expansion. German Pietism penetrated churches in Denmark, Sweden, and Norway, as well as the lower Rhine valley and the Netherlands. It sparked the revival of the Moravian Brethren under the leadership of Count Nikolaus Ludwig von Zinzendorf (1700–1760). The older Hussite church had declined. The consequences of the Thirty Years War (1618 to 1648) had been destructive to Bohemian Protestantism. Out of the refugee camps of Herrnhut, Bohemia came a mighty missionary movement. Moravians envisioned a "church within a church," decrying separatism, seeking only to experience a "heart religion."

These developments led to the establishment of religious societies in England for the cultivation of prayer, Bible reading, and aid to the poor. Samuel Wesley, the father of John Wesley, formed one of these societies patterned after those of Philipp Spener. In time, these enthusiastic societies led to the formation of Methodism.

John Wesley (1703–1791) and Charles Wesley (1707–1788) were educated at Christ Church College, Oxford, and probably did more than any others to shape eighteenth-century evangelicalism. In 1729 Charles Wesley formed a little club, later known as the "Holy Club." Influenced by William Law's book *A Serious Call to a Devout and Holy Life* (1728), the Wesleys and George Whitefield (1714–1770) found opportunities for preaching in America. The Wesleys were converted through experiences of serious illness and as a result of trying to serve God without possessing vital faith. For John Wesley this took place through the reading of Martin Luther's *Commentary on Romans* at a society meeting on Aldersgate Street, London. "I felt my heart strangely warmed," he wrote. "I felt I did trust in Christ, Christ alone, for salvation."[24]

In his lifetime John Wesley performed a work for God that

revolutionized conditions in the English lower and middle classes. He traveled, someone has estimated, nearly a quarter of a million miles for the gospel. After his death in 1791, Methodism separated from the Church of England.

The Great Awakening led to evangelical expansion in America. George Whitefield and Jonathan Edwards (1703–1758) influenced a religious revival in America that affected Anglicanism and Presbyterianism alike. The Awakening led to the rise of dissenting bodies and revival among the Baptists. Methodism mushroomed. The New Light movement was marked by evangelical preaching and the development of small societies to reach American Indians and the poor. The legacy of Edwards's preaching and writing remains with us today. His defense of Calvinism was classically shaped. He defended revivalism as the true work of God and rejected the exploitation of emotionalism. A champion of high academic standards for pastors and high standards for church membership, Edwards later became the president of Princeton University.

One of the most significant results of the evangelical revival was the rise of modern missions and social reform. In the southern colonies the Society for the Propagation of the Gospel was active in spreading the gospel westward. Tract societies were formed, prisons were reformed, the evils of slavery were exposed, and the Sunday school was born. Both in Britain and in America, missionary groups blossomed.

William Carey (1761–1834) became the first missionary of the Baptist Society for Propagating the Gospel among the heathen. In 1795 the London Missionary Society was formed, sending its first missionaries to Tahiti. Other efforts, aimed at Christianizing the world, would follow. Christianity, in large measure, followed the expansionism of western civilization and political rule worldwide.

THE PRESENT STATE OF EVANGELICALISM

The term *evangelical* suffers from some abuse and has been used to describe fairly diverse expressions of faith. I have already used the term to describe the eighteenth-century revival of earlier Reformed ideals and institutions. The post-Enlightenment period of history produced within western Christianity a reaction against rationalism and deism that can rightly be called "evangelical." New focus on the Scriptures, always a purifying element in reform, and fresh witness to the gospel, mark evangelicalism.

The term *evangelical* conjures up orthodox theological connotations: grace alone, faith alone, Scripture alone, and Christ alone. These truths form the heart of evangelical life and witness.

Evangelicalism is now used to describe a corpus of truths and doctrines, as well as corporate and individual expressions of faith built on those doctrines. Evangelicalism crosses denominational boundaries; it cannot be defined simply by location or ecclesiastical structure.

In 1840 Protestant evangelicals forged an alliance by adopting a common statement of faith. It included belief in the divine inspiration, authority, and sufficiency of the Scriptures; the right and duty of private interpretation of them; the unity of the Godhead and the Trinity; the incarnation of the Son of God and His atonement; justification of sinners by faith; the work of the Holy Spirit as Sanctifier; the immortality of the soul; the resurrection of the body; the final judgment by Jesus Christ; and the divine institution of the Christian ministry.

The publication in 1905 of *The Five Fundamentals* gave further evangelical expression of central beliefs and served to spark the modernist-fundamentalist debate of the early twentieth century. Fundamentalism is one of the nine movements Robert Webber says have contributed to the rise of contemporary evangelicalism: the Protestant Reformation, seventeenth-century orthodoxy, Puritanism, pietism, the pentecostal movement, dispensationalism, the fundamentalist movement, neoevangelicalism, and the charismatic movement.[25]

Evangelicalism, in its simplest definition, describes the biblical position of belief in the person and work of Jesus Christ and the good news of forgiveness of sin. Corporately, it is used to describe those groups that actively promote the truth of Christ's redemptive work on the cross.

The term admittedly suffers from some ambiguity. In reality it is more like a mosaic. Its individual expressions, like chips of glazed ceramic, often do not by themselves fit a full-blown definition. Together, however, they form a picture that points to Jesus Christ and the transforming gospel of saving grace.

Studies of the contemporary influence of evangelicalism are not always thorough.[26] It is almost impossible to describe the multifaceted global work of the Holy Spirit. Neither a focus on western or eastern Christianity will do, for today the power of the gospel in the Southern Hemisphere is off the traditional map, so to speak, of earlier chronicles of church history. Latin American, African, and eastern European churches cry out for attention, as does the dynamic situation in China.

We can segment religious preferences in the world, pinpoint where major religions thrive, and even guess at the unreached peoples of the world, but it is difficult to say how many evangelicals are in the world. Evangelicalism is active, fluid, mobile, and transient in nature. As a pilgrim movement, it stakes few claims on this world as its home. As a political force, however, it lobbies to be heard. At its fringes it reflects a split personality, reflecting both monastic belief and political involvement.

Fresh winds of revival are blowing in the world. For all that the American church represents, with its affluence and seeming capacity to control its destiny, it is being overshadowed by the persecuted churches of our world and the rapidly expanding Latin, Asian, and African churches.

Critics of western Christianity point to the cultural captivity of the church, its theological shallowness, and its antiintellectualism. Numbers of evangelicals are opting for the worship form of Anglicanism. Others are looking back to Rome and Constantinople to give them historic continuity because of their disenchantment with experientialism.

Only a heightened sense of God's power and presence in His church, a recovery of powerful biblical preaching, a visible return to love and caring, and a new focus on unity in the body of Christ will produce a vibrant evangelicalism fit for the twenty-first century. When evangelicals agree that the church is a community of believers living in harmony and in covenant with God and each other, the world may take notice. When others see that we, like the disciples in Gospel times, have been with Jesus, then evangelicalism may shape its character to shape the world.

3
The Church and the Headship of Christ

Let therefore our chiefest endeavour be to meditate upon the life of Jesus Christ.

—Thomas à Kempis

JIM BAKKER. JIMMY SWAGGART. ROBERT TILTON. When the national media reported the moral failures of these TV evangelists, many unsaved people laughed. They mocked Christianity because some of its spokesmen did not live up to the truth they proclaimed. Unfortunately many people still judge the Christian faith by the conduct of its adherents.

True, the consistent witness of Christians is vital to Christianity's reputation and impact. But even so, people should judge Christianity not by its followers but by the character of its Founder. After all, the church is His. Christ founded it and leads it. He said, "On this rock I will build *my* church" (Matt. 16:18, italics added).

When we turn to the Scriptures, we find the focus is clearly on Christ as the Head of His church (Col. 1:18) and as the focus of our faith. In a succession of example and arguments, the author of Hebrews moves from examples of the faithful in chapter 11 to the "author and perfecter of our faith" in 12:2. In clear and compelling language and logic, the Scriptures set forth a series of powerful exhortations: "throw off everything," "run with perseverance," "let us fix our eyes on Jesus," and "consider him who endured" (12:1–3). As noteworthy as the heroes of faith were, they were not to be the objects of veneration. Only Christ is worthy of our faith. Nor is faith in faith to be our focus. It is faith in a person, Jesus Christ our Lord. In this sense, Christianity is indeed Christ. Jesus is the only Foundation of the church (1 Cor. 3:11).

Others in the past have been quick to point out this important point. John Knox may have gone to an extreme by destroying all images of saints at the time of the Scottish Reformation, calling the churches whitewashed sepulchers. However, he scored a central tenet of the Protestant Reformation: Only the Savior, not the saint, is to be worshiped.

German theologian Otto Webber in *Foundations of Dogmatics* emphasized the need to distinguish between faith in the church and faith in its Head. Citing John Calvin, Weber wrote that we are to believe in Christ, not in the church.[1]

With eyes for no one or anything except Jesus, Christians are to live out their faith in obedience to their Lord and with all perseverance and hope.

In studying evangelical ecclesiology, we must steer a clear course between extremes. The church of Jesus Christ is spiritual in nature; yet we need to emphasize its local expression in visible churches. The life of the community of faith is important, yet the presence of Christ in His church is more important. If institutionalism is to be avoided, focus on the headship of Jesus Christ in His church is pivotal. An adequate grasp of this doctrine will serve as a corrective to pastoral or lay abuse of power. Furthermore it may just keep us from giving undue attention to the structure of the church—its buildings and governance—over proper attention to prayer, worship, and guidance by the Holy Spirit.

THE CENTRAL IMPORTANCE OF JESUS CHRIST

The early church fathers described the church as a society formed by Christian believers characterized by faith, discipline, and hope. As a break from the prevailing cults and idolatry of Roman society, Christianity was "faith in the revelation in and through Jesus Christ."[2]

The earliest Christian councils sought to clarify a true and biblical Christology. With the very substance of Christianity at stake, the councils of Nicaea (325), Constantinople (381), Ephesus (431), and Chalcedon (451) clarified the doctrine of Christ. As Christians, we believe in one God the Father and in one Lord Jesus Christ, begotten of (not created by) the Father. This Jesus is the preexistent Son of God. "God always; Son always," was how Jesus was described in opposition to the Arian heresy that the Son had a beginning. Furthermore, this Jesus possesses two natures, divine and human, coexistent and coeternal as one person.

The affirmation that Jesus Christ is truly God and truly man will be all-important to Christian witness in the twenty-first century. At the end of the nineteenth century liberal Christianity denied the deity and even the historicity of Jesus. Denial moved to "myth" in the early twentieth century. Today few biblical scholars deny the reality of the historical Jesus. However, the question still remains as to His nature and deity. Evangelicals affirm faith in Christ, the revealed Head of the church. In the midtwentieth century, neoorthodoxy emphasized the faith experience in Christ. The "death of God" fad—in reality it was the "death of the idea of God"—left only a human Jesus as the object of devotion.

Recovery of a transcendent Christ revealed in the Scriptures as "God in the flesh" is important to the life, vitality, and purity of the church.

The theological and ecclesiastical world is full of confusion today. It looks to philosophy or to the social sciences for direction rather than to the Scriptures. Christianity, however, has a sure anchor and an objective revelation in history. This anchor is Jesus Christ, revealed in the Bible.

The battle of the present and the future will be whether to revise our theology in order to adapt to the changing times or to accept a confessional stance that is countercultural. One approach relies on revising the Scriptures to appear relevant; the other reaffirms faith in the Christ of the Scriptures. As Donald Bloesch wrote, "We must never forget that the hope of the church rests not on its own strategies and wisdom but on the living God alone, who speaks and acts wherever his Word is faithfully proclaimed and wherever the prayers of his children are offered up in faith and repentance."[3]

The affirmation of the most ancient of creeds, "Jesus is Lord," will steady the church in turbulent times. The truth-claims of the gospel, which are the claims of the risen Christ, are basic to orthodoxy. Peter, whom

Jesus called a "rock," pointed to Jesus Christ when he wrote, "The stone the builders rejected has become the capstone" (1 Pet. 2:7).

The headship of Christ is taught in a number of New Testament passages. Paul's words of praise of the Lord Jesus written to the Colossian church show how early believers celebrated their union with Christ. To express the doctrine, Paul employed the rhythmical lilt of what may have been an early hymn. The Christological focus in Colossians 1:15–20 is obvious: "He is the image of the invisible God, the firstborn over all creation. For by him all things were created: things in heaven and on earth, visible and invisible, whether thrones or powers or rulers or authorities; all things were created by him and for him. He is before all things, and in him all things hold together. And he is the head of the body, the church; he is the beginning and the firstborn from among the dead, so that in everything he might have the supremacy. For God was pleased to have all his fullness dwell in him, and through him to reconcile to himself all things, whether things on earth or things in heaven, by making peace through his blood, shed on the cross."

In His deity, Christ is the image or express likeness of God. As to creation, He is the Creator-God, preexistent, supreme in rank, and Sustainer of all creation. As for the church, Jesus and none other is Head. He alone guides and governs the church as its true Chief and Leader.

The concept of headship occurs in other verses, including 1 Corinthians 11:3; Ephesians 1:22; and Colossians 2:19. From these verses, a hierarchical view is evident—but that power is nowhere conferred on bishops or church councils. The issue of the husband's headship over his wife may best be explained as a headship of prior order, modeling the benevolent servant example of Christ and mutual submission of members of the body (1 Pet. 3:7). The fountainhead of a theology of the church—as in all theology—is Jesus Christ. We must stay close to the source.

THE CONCEPT OF CHRIST'S RULE

The 1960s witnessed a revolt against all authority. Bumper stickers and buttons told it all—"Question authority." At the height of the youth revolution, a cartoon appeared in the *New Yorker* which capsulated the ethos of the day. A longhaired hippie was standing in front of the pastor at the door of the church and said, "It is nothing against you personally, Sir; it is just that our generation can't trust anyone over thirty!" This common jibe led some to conclude that they could not trust a God over thirty either.

In our society many are questioning whether there is any absolute truth and final authority. Just as early Christians found their creed, "Jesus is Lord," to be in collision with regal authority of the Caesars, so believers today are facing a culture that refuses to give definitive allegiance to any authority.

The Bible is clear that Jesus is both Lord and King, expressed by the Greek words *kyrios* ("Lord," "Master") and *basileus* ("Ruler," "King").

Evidence of the exaltation of Jesus as Lord springs from the truth of Psalm 110, a royal psalm of David: "The LORD says to my Lord: 'Sit at my right hand until I make your enemies a footstool for your feet'" (Ps. 110:1). This text is repeatedly quoted or used with variation in the New Testament to refer to Jesus (for example, Matt. 22:44; 26:64; Acts 2:34; 1 Cor. 15:25; Heb. 1:3, 13). The lordship of the Messiah is a well-substantiated New Testament truth. By affirming this simple creed, "Jesus is Lord," early Christians confessed Jesus as Ruler of the world (Rom. 10:9; 1 Cor. 12:3; Phil. 2:11) and Ruler of their lives.

God the Father exalted Jesus the Son (Acts 2:36), so that this resurrected Jesus is both Lord and Christ. The lordship of Christ leaves no room for nominal faith. While obedience is unpopular in modern society, it nevertheless is essential in Christian experience. There can be no libertarian Christian stance. The paradox is that through obedience to our Lord we achieve true freedom.

In stirring and inspiring words of worship the prophet Isaiah exclaimed, "My eyes have seen the King" (Isa. 6:5), and John said Isaiah was referring to Christ (John 12:44). In the New Testament Jesus is described as the messianic King of the Jews. His accusers before Pilate falsely charged Him of subversion against the nation: "He opposes payment of taxes to Caesar and claims to be Christ, a king" (Luke 23:2). Jesus was then asked by Pilate, "Are you the king of the Jews?" (23:3). Measuring the unrest in the crowd, Pilate then asked them, "Do you want me to release to you the king of the Jews?" (Mark 15:9). Soldiers mocked Jesus with the words,

"Hail, King of the Jews" (Matt. 27:29). Furthermore, the inscription placed on the cross above our Lord read, "The King of the Jews" (27:37). He was also mocked by the crowd that came to view the Roman execution of a public figure: "He's the king of Israel! Let him come down now from the cross, and we will believe in him" (27:42).

Outside of the Gospels, there is no mention of Jesus as "King of Israel." There is, however, direct reference to the title "King" in Revelation 19:16, where the Rider of the white horse is called "KING OF KINGS AND LORD OF LORDS." These words, which refer directly to our Lord, were included in the great "Hallelujah Chorus" of *The Messiah* by George Handel, first performed in Dublin, Ireland, in 1792.

Christian preachers since John Calvin have proclaimed Jesus' three roles as Prophet, Priest, and King. As supreme Head of the church, Jesus has made us "a kingdom and priests" (Rev. 1:6; 5:10, NKJV) and a royal priesthood (1 Pet. 2:9, NKJV). Our King shares His power with believers without diminishing His own sovereignty. In whatever way human leadership shares in the prophetic, priestly, and kingly rule of Christ in His church, such leadership takes only a secondary role. This fact motivates us to exercise humility, faith, and worship.

The enormity of the truth that Jesus is Lord and King led the fourteenth-century monk, Thomas à Kempis, to write: "It is a great matter to live in obedience, to be under a superior, and not to be at our own disposing."[4]

THE CHURCH AND THE KINGDOM

The Roman Catholic Church views itself as the manifestation of God's kingdom on earth. However, Hans Küng is a major critic of the idea that the church is the same as the kingdom. This Catholic theologian wrote, "In the light of the New Testament message, as it has been rediscovered for us by modern exegesis, it is impossible to speak of Christian society or even of the church as being 'God's kingdom on earth.'"[5] This bold dissenter within Romanism argued that the church is not the glorification of God on earth, that it is called to a pilgrimage and not a rest, and that to equate the church with the kingdom is to blunt the church's mission in the world. Küng also saw the presence of unregenerate people, even secular rulers, in the church as evidence that it could not be the same as God's kingdom. The reign of God, Küng believed, is not the product of the organic development and progress of the church. The glorious reign of Christ on earth is yet to come. The work of the church is to announce something not yet fulfilled. In the words of Küng, the church is not "a fill-in, a compromise solution, an ersatz kingdom for the kingdom of God which was awaited in vain."[6] (For more on the church and the kingdom see chapter 12.)

MODEL FOR THE CHURCH

Do we have a model for church life and governance in the headship of Christ? How are believer-priests to serve in relationship to our High Priest? Within a kingdom of priests, how are believers to relate to each other as well as to their Head? Using the biblical metaphors of sheep and shepherd, are there any guidelines that undershepherds should follow as they serve under the Chief Shepherd of our souls? To what degree do our modern ministries correspond to biblical foundations?

Jesus said that His kingdom was not of this world. This otherworldly dimension of Christian faith has inspired martyrs, led to asceticism, fired the zeal of missionary expansion, and created a burning eschatological hope. Jesus' example of selfless and compassionate service has set a pattern for ministry for all time.

Geoffrey Bromiley has written that "the heart and basis of ministry is the ministry of Christ Himself."[7] The ministry of the church is thus the ministry of the entire body, not just its designated leaders. Each believer in the body of Christ is a participant in His continuing ministry by the Spirit through the Word in the world. Christians are only coworkers and colaborers with Christ (1 Cor. 3:9).

Ultimately the service rendered by the church must mirror the character of Jesus Himself. There is a corporate dimension to Christlikeness that moves beyond a focus on individuals. Who Jesus Christ is shapes who we are to become and how we are to conduct ourselves as members of His body. We, being many, are one body, serving under one Head. There is no such thing as a Baptist ministry, a Lutheran ministry, or a Bible

Church ministry. Christ does not have a bunch of separate bodies. As believers are united to Him in *one* body, they share in *one* ministry. This ministry is to be marked by at least the following:

- the ministry of reconciliation

- the ministry of proclamation

- the ministry of restoration

- the ministry of encouragement and mutual edification

- the ministry of converting the lost

- the ministry of caring, healing, and wholeness

- the ministry of servanthood

- the ministry of love, hope, and faith

- the ministry of offering praise and worship to God

- the ministry of giving

- the ministry of the gifts of the Spirit under the guidance and control of the Spirit

- the ministry of unity and peacemaking

There is no place for arrogance, tension, self-seeking, or resentment in Christ's body. All are to humble themselves under God's mighty hand (1 Pet. 5:6). One of the Bible's benedictions expresses how we are to please our Lord: "May the God of peace, who through the blood of the eternal covenant brought back from the dead our Lord Jesus, that great Shepherd of the sheep, equip you with everything good for doing his will, and may he work in us what is pleasing to him, through Jesus Christ, to whom be glory for ever and ever. Amen" (Heb. 13:20–21).

The grand picture is to understand that Jesus Christ, who is our Lord and King, is the true Minister of the church. Only through faith and obedience can we participate in His work.

SUBMISSION, LORDSHIP, AND HUMAN LEADERSHIP

The domination of the church by clergymen throughout history has produced a spiritually weakened church. The church is not its clergy, but its people. All regenerate, baptized believers comprise the true church. In Christ we are one—one in faith, hope, and love, one in ministry and mission. In the New Testament, distinctions between clergy and laity simply do not exist. All believers serve under one Head, the Lord Jesus Christ, and are to submit to His supreme authority.

The Priesthood of All Believers

The doctrine of the priesthood of all believers emerged in reaction to the sacramentalism that dominated church life and work. Sacramentalism is the belief that in the observance of the sacraments of the church special grace is conveyed to the participants—even saving grace. The priest, according to sacramentalism, has precedence over the laity in exercising the office of the church and particularly in consecrating and distributing the elements in the Lord's Supper (called the Eucharist in some churches).

Luther advocated the priesthood of all believers, which forms a central doctrine of all Protestantism. Priesthood, to him, meant that we stand before God, pray for others, intercede with God, sacrifice ourselves to Him, and proclaim the Word to one another. Universal priesthood never meant "privatism" or religious individualism. Luther believed this right was given to the community of the saints, who are a priestly generation, a royal priesthood. The priesthood of all believers means that believers have the right and duty to share the gospel and teach God's Word. He recognized no community that did not preach the Word and no community that did not witness the gospel.

In his book *Concerning Ministry* Luther spelled out seven rights of this universal priesthood:

- to preach the Word of God

- to baptize

- to celebrate the sacrament (the Lord's Supper)

- to minister the office of the keys (announce divine forgiveness of sins in Jesus' name)

- to pray for others

- to judge doctrine

- to discern spirits.[8]

Luther even went beyond these functions to urge Christians to engage in the mutual encouragement of the Word to each other in the church.

In Luther's day Thomas Münzer of Zwickau, Germany, denounced the immorality and abuse of priests. To Münzer, restoration would come from common people, whom he called "custodians of truth they cannot theologically articulate." These people of God, he felt, should be able to elect their pastors. He also believed that the words that consecrate the elements in the Lord's Supper should be said by the whole congregation as a royal, priestly people.

The Reformation principle of *sola fide* ("faith alone") also led to the doctrine of the priesthood of all believers. Rank-and-file believers throughout Germany, Switzerland, and the Low Countries found in this doctrine new freedoms to express their faith. The Anabaptists, Martin Bucer in Strasbourg, and many others began to address ministerial (magisterial) reform. Some felt that Martin Luther had not gone far enough in his reforms.

Among Radical Reformers the question arose over the legitimacy of any ordination. The nature of the apostolate—apostolic succession—was crumbling. In their yearning to avoid cheap grace and an unholy ministry, the Anabaptists sought to transform the church. They were the true evangelicals calling on a shared ministry in the Spirit of all the people of God.

Their views also extended to interpreting and handling the Word of God. They appealed to the right of the whole congregation, the laity along with the divines (clergy), to judge difficult passages of the Bible together. Baptists later developed this insight into what is known as "soul liberty," the right of individual believers to interpret the truth of the Scriptures under the Holy Spirit's guidance. These Radical Reformers pushed the

Lutheran doctrine of the priesthood of all believers in the direction of a lay apostolate.[9]

The floodgates of the Reformation were thus opened, allowing the common people to engage in full exercise of their spiritual gifts in the church.

Before we leave this doctrine, it may help to look at the importance of the biblical truth on the subject. After all, a central tenet of the Reformation was the centrality of biblical authority.

As stated earlier, the New Testament does not make a distinction between clergy and laity. Both refer to the same people. The word *clergy* comes from the Greek word *klētos*, meaning "the called," and we get our word for laity from the word *laos*, meaning "people." Both words occur in some form in 1 Peter 2:9–10. Believers in general are the called of God (Rom. 8:28, 30; 1 Cor. 1:2; 24; 1 Pet. 3:9; 5:10). The terms *elect, saints, disciples,* and *brothers* all refer to the people of God who have been called by Him.

The church exists in the world as a group of people who have received God's mercy by divine grace. Believers are ordained to carry out good works, both in a personal way and in a collective way. John Wesley understood this to mean there is no such thing as private Christianity. Believers belong to a fellowship of the called.

Leadership in the Church

What place then should we give to human leaders in the church? Our answer comes from the Scriptures. We have the precedents of Peter, James, and John, who were called "pillars" of the church (Gal. 2:9). Peter took the lead among the early disciples and later Paul, Barnabas, and others rose, by exercise of gifts and calling, to be leaders. Timothy and Titus were singled out for special pastoral training, and other leaders, both men and women, are mentioned by name throughout the New Testament.

Historically, the Roman Catholic, Anglican, and Orthodox churches have espoused "apostolic succession." Catholicism alone argues that the pope is the vicar or agent of Christ on earth. While rejecting any notion of "succession," evangelicals accept the general calling of apostles or "sent ones" (Eph. 4:11). After Matthias was chosen to fill Judas's place (Acts 1:26), there is no biblical evidence of any form of apostolic succession. Legitimate apostolic *ministry* (not succession) is seen in the gifts of the Spirit and not in a particular line of appointment.

Nevertheless the early church did evidence some orders of ministry—overseers, pastors, presbyters, and deacons. The first of the two may refer to the same office. These will be examined later.

New Testament leadership rejected any idea of an episcopacy in making decisions for the entire church. This was evident in the appointment of Paul and Barnabas to missionary duty (Acts 13:1–3). If James was the bishop within an episcopacy, it is strange that there was no reference to him in the decision to send Paul and Barnabas to Jerusalem (15:2–4) or in granting them letters or documents to read in the churches following the Council of Jerusalem (16:4). Any argument from silence may be a weak one, but without any support in the Acts of the Apostles or individual epistles, one is hard-pressed to find support for an episcopal form of church leadership as it is practiced today.

The terms *elder, bishop, overseer,* and *pastor* refer to the same office of leadership. Yet even these leaders are subject to the guidance of the Spirit, collectively determined by prayer within the congregation. The Jerusalem Council may be the exception, revealing a form of congregationalism. At that gathering, the decisions rendered were collective and were not given by a single leader.

A Community of Servants

The New Testament ideal is for leaders and followers alike to live and serve Jesus Christ in humility. Jesus taught this to His disciples in His discourse on greatness in the kingdom (Matt. 18:1–5; Mark 9:33–37; Luke 9:41–48). "If anyone wants to be first, he must be the very last, and the servant of all" (Mark 9:35). The word Jesus chose to use, *diakonos,* means "servant." We get our English word "deacon" from this Greek word.

Another dramatic incident in which Jesus illustrated servant leadership is found in two Gospel accounts, Matthew 20:20–28 and Mark 10:35–45. Two of the disciples asked for privileged positions in the kingdom. Jesus addressed His reply to the two, as well as the other ten: "You know that the rulers of the Gentiles lord it over them, and their high officials exercise authority over them. Not so with you. Instead, whoever wants to become great among you must be your servant, and whoever wants to be first must be your slave—just as the Son of Man did not come to be served, but to serve, and to give his life as a ransom for many" (Matt. 20:25–28).

Martin Luther took the servanthood of Christ very seriously. Taking his cue from Galatians 6:2, he believed that the church should identify with the shame of Christ. Furthermore, believers must feel from their hearts the needs of the poor and the suffering of the innocent. Just as Christ emptied Himself, Luther explained, believers are to sell their goods or possessions.

The power of servant leadership cannot be minimized in effecting change in our churches and world. From the example of Christ (Phil. 2:4–5), we are to make others' weaknesses our own. The church is to be shaped not by the lordly form of power, but by the servant stance of Christ's followers.

The biblical doctrine of justification by faith, so central to the Reformation and to evangelical belief, frees us to love others. The question of our own salvation is settled on the Cross. Now we are free to bear our cross, expecting everything from God so that we can give everything we have to serve others.

As stated earlier, there is no room for pride in the church. Pride dulls the power of the preaching of the cross of Christ. We all stand under grace through no merit of our own, and we stand by our brothers and sisters in the body of Christ to lend encouragement and support. Each of us is capable of falling into sin. Therefore we are strengthened by building solidarity with others. Spiritually washing each other's feet reflects a humility borne by all believers who have been served by Jesus. This is what it means to be fellow servants of Jesus Christ.

A Community of the Forgiven

The message of the bumper sticker, "Christians are not better than others, just forgiven," may be too presumptuous. It may also carry a touch of arrogance. The doctrine of divine forgiveness does not lend itself to clichés and cheap slogans.

Faith in Christ results in the forgiveness of sins and the accompanying imputation of righteousness, and the creation of a new being in Christ. Forgiveness brings a new sense of worth; newness in Christ prompts a new obedience. Being forgiven, believers are free to display confidence in God's grace, while at the same time displaying humble obedience to the One who redeemed us from sin.

Through faith in Christ, believers become freed from the power of sin while taking pleasure in obeying Christ's commandments and walking in the Spirit. Having experienced the love and forgiveness of Christ, we may now freely love and forgive others. "Be kind and compassionate to one another," Paul wrote the company of forgiven Ephesians, "forgiving each other, just as in Christ God forgave you" (Eph. 4:32).

A recovery of a sense of wonder and awe in the church might go a long way in demonstrating Christ's power to forgive. How relieved any of us would feel if, though guilty of a heinous crime, we were forgiven by a judge. When Christians gather in Jesus' name, the same scene is enacted. Forgiven in Christ, we stand tall in grace. English Christians sang of this reality as they gathered to worship:

> Father, again in Jesus' Name we meet,
> And bow in penitence beneath thy feet;
> Again to thee our feeble voices raise,
> To sue for mercy, and to sing thy praise.
> —Lady Lucy E. G. Whitmore, 1824

The practice of confession is essential for Christians. Within some evangelical circles the practice of confession is almost totally absent. Yet the Bible commands us to confess our sins to each other (James 5:16). In Acts 19:18 Ephesian converts openly confessed their sins. Only the unrepentant deceive themselves and, by continuing in their sin, make God out to be a liar. Christ's Word has no place in the lives of Christians living with unconfessed sin (1 John 1:10).

Abuses of confession are easy to document. Early Reformers rejected the ecclesiastical rule that required confession to priests. Under the promise given in Matthew 18:18, announcing divine forgiveness to repentant sinners is a gift. It cannot be made a law, Luther believed, but it is an indispensable form of gospel witness. The whole church, he felt, was to be full of a spirit of forgiveness of sins. Whether private or public, confession is to be made according to biblical guidelines. All sin requires confession to God, and where sin is committed against another believer, confession is to be made to that person in private.

When someone sins against us, the Bible instructs us to go to that person and point out the fault. If the person listens, we win back a friend, and if not, we are to take one or two others along. "If he refuses to listen to them, tell it to the church," Jesus taught (Matt. 18:15–17). The inference here is that unconfessed sin calls for further discipline. Lacking both true confession and true biblical discipline, our churches are weakened in their witness to the gospel of divine forgiveness. Only a restoration of holiness in the church will give it muscle to engage in spiritual warfare against all evil.

THE PURITY OF THE CHURCH—CHRISTLIKENESS

Is the purity of the church too much to hope for? Is the church responsible to aim for purity of faith and doctrine? We will conclude each of chapters 4–6 with summary thoughts on the purity of the church—in Christlikeness, in truth, and in holiness. The headship of Christ in His church prompts Christlikeness. The centrality of the Word of God in the church produces purity in truth. And the confidence of the church in the power of the Holy Spirit promotes holiness.

Imitation of Christ

In fifteenth-century Zwolle, Holland, Thomas à Kempis spent his lifetime copying the Scriptures. He was known as a luminary because of his exquisite work in producing illustrated pages of the sacred text. Long before the invention of the printing press, this godly monk worked a lifetime producing three copies of the Bible. Along with this assigned work, this follower of the Brethren of the Common Life wrote devotional literature. The most famous of his works that remain is *The Imitation of Christ.*

This book is by far the bestseller of all times in devotional literature, next to the Bible. Its thought influenced Martin Luther, John Newton,

John Wesley, and a host of other Christians. Respected by Roman Catholics and Protestants alike, the book still continues to influence the church. In spite of its archaic statements, its simplicity still inspires the faithful.

Thomas à Kempis wrote simply, "The doctrine of Christ exceedeth all the doctrines of holy men; and he that hath the Spirit, will find therein an hidden manna. But it falleth out, that many who often hear the Gospel of Christ, are yet but little affected, because they are void of the Spirit of Christ. But whosoever would fully and feelingly understand the words of Christ, must endeavour to conform his life wholly to the life of Christ."[10] Luther, it is said, reacted to this simple thesis in light of his own interpretation of justification by faith: "It is not imitation that makes sons, but sonship that makes imitations."

We may reject the late medieval Christian viewpoint that emphasized imitation as a high form of purity in the church, but we cannot avoid scriptural teachings on the subject. Only a fine line exists between identification with Christ and imitation of Christ. Our oneness in Christ has been made possible by His sacrifice on the cross. In Him all the fullness of the deity lives in bodily form, and we have been given fullness in Him, the Head over every power and authority (Col. 2:9–10). I take this to mean that while Christ alone is deity, we share in His fullness by our Christlikeness. Yet there are limits. Only Christ can claim for Himself the words found in 1 Peter 2:22: "He committed no sin, and no deceit was found in his mouth." No one can imitate Christ in this. He alone has the honor of being sinless. We may emulate him, but we will inevitably fall far short of the goal.

Since Christ suffered, Peter taught the pilgrim congregation, believers are to arm themselves with the same sacrificial attitude (1 Pet. 4:1). Those whose example is Christ do not live the rest of their lives for evil human desires, but rather for the will of God.

The imitation of Christ, rightly understood and practiced, was commended by the apostle Paul (1 Thess. 1:6; 2:14). "Be imitators of God," Paul wrote, "and live a life of love, just as Christ loved us and gave himself up for us as a fragrant offering and sacrifice to God" (Eph. 5:1).

Believers were also told to imitate other believers: "Remember your leaders, who spoke the word of God to you. Consider the outcome of their way of life and imitate their faith" (Heb. 13:7). The veneration and imitation of saints is a far cry from the teachings of these verses. For lack of gods, some will devise their own, but these verses give no room for undue elevation of godly models.

The Meaning of Christlikeness

To be like Christ means to follow Him, to obey His commands, to live as He lived. Christ is our example and pattern to follow. When we suppress lust and hatred, we imitate Christ. When we flee from sin and all evil, we imitate Christ. When we give, pray, show compassion, or carry out any number of exhortations given in the Bible, we imitate Christ.

It is not a lack of knowledge of Christ that makes believers poor imitators of His virtues. It is a lack of love. "If anyone loves me," Jesus said, "he will obey my teaching" (John 14:23). Christlikeness is exercising a practical obedience to the known will of God. It involves denial of self (Luke 9:23), constant abiding (John 15:5), and maturation in Christ (Col. 2:6–7; Eph. 4:13–16). Christlikeness means loving and obeying Christ, our Head.

The Incarnational Principle

"The kingdom is to be in the midst of your enemies," wrote Luther. Centuries later the German preacher Dietrich Bonhoeffer explained, "It is not simply to be taken for granted that the Christian has the privilege of living among other Christians. Jesus Christ lived in the midst of his enemies."[11] Here is a truth that has largely been missed by American evangelicals. Absence of overt persecution, relative prosperity, and the existence of many professing Christians have lulled believers into thinking that the present situation is normative. But it is not.

We are learning from believers all over the world what it means to live as salt and light in hostile environments. Jesus said, "I came from the Father and entered the world" (John 16:28). Jesus also said to the Father, "You sent me into the world" (17:18). The entire doctrine of the Incarnation inspires a principle of church life in the world.

In this incarnational principle, the church is in the world to reveal

Jesus Christ by both life and word. While it would be theologically pre-sumptuous to speak of this incarnational witness in the same manner as the Incarnation of Jesus, it is possible to speak of the in-fleshing of the message of the gospel. I believe it was the English preacher F. B. Meyer who said that every believer is either a Bible or a libel; a Bible to point men and women to Christ or a libel to the name of Christianity. The whole point of the incarnational principle is to lift up Christ, not to ag-grandize the church.

Today the church needs to adopt a radical stance of penetration into the world rather than a withdrawal from it. Our comfort zone must be set aside, or at least expanded, to allow for the light and liberty of the gospel to impact the world.

4
The Church and the Bible

. . . .

*Among Christians the rule is not to argue or investigate, not to be a smart
aleck or a rationalistic know-it-all; but to hear, believe, and persevere in the
Word of God, through which alone we obtain whatever knowledge we have of
God and divine things.*

—Martin Luther

WHAT IS THE PLACE OF THE BIBLE in the church? No question
is more crucial than this in today's church. In many congregations the Bible
is sorely neglected. This has come about because of the church being placed
under the authority of the state, the abuse of papal power, the influence of
humanism during the Enlightenment, the destructive nature of nineteenth-
century rationalism, and the rise of theological modernism. The
Scriptures—which were basic to all apostolic preaching, and which were
recovered in the Protestant Reformation—are now in even more danger of
becoming peripheral than they were in previous centuries.

Educator-theologian Frank E. Gaebelein wrote, "One of the major
problems of Protestantism today is the biblical illiteracy of the laity."[1] He
cited the absence of great Bible preaching and the neglect of sustained
Bible study in the pews as reflective of the weakening pulse of American
Christianity. Gaebelein wrote his indictment over thirty years ago. One
might marshal a line of evidence to counter his pessimism by citing the
evangelical resurgence in recent years, the continuing popularity of Christian belief at the polls, and the prominence of media preachers. However,

71

these externals may not reflect the inner decay of the truth at the core of even "successful" churches.

Amsterdam theologian G. C. Berkouwer flatly stated a fact of history: "Confessions about the Bible do not always mean the Bible is the center of the Church's attention."[2]

John Calvin, whose Reformed conscience was bound to the Word of God, once wrote that if the church has lost the Word, it is not simply ill, its throat is cut.

Whenever churches give ground to prevailing philosophies counter to God's revelation in the Scriptures, the light of truth becomes eclipsed. There is always danger of defining truth to fit the ethos of an era, whether it be scientism, secularism, humanism, or relativism. The latter is more prevalent today than we want to admit—freedom to hold one's own beliefs about truth even though these beliefs are contradictory to the Scriptures.

In many churches the Bible is given only scant or tacit attention, unless it is part of the liturgy. In evangelicalism, the disappearance of Bible reading in the congregation is alarming. Even the proliferation of paraphrases, versions, and translations has led to a loss of commonality in the use of the Bible for reading, study, and preaching. Sermons, once rich with biblical truth and explanation, have become in some circles only diluted descriptions of truth, rather than strong declarations of truth. When these homilies become little more than self-help remedies and good thoughts about life and society, sermons lose their purpose. The Word in the church then gets shoved further back in the priorities of ministry. When "Wordless" messages are crafted, we part company with the apostles, early evangelicals, and Reformers.

No edicts of emperors, demand of the state, of bishops, or councils, or any other authoritative system can take precedence over the Word of God in the life and work of the church. The church derives its life from the Word. Furthermore, it is charged with holding and guarding the truth as a rare jewel in a safe-deposit box. The words of Paul to Timothy are also the words to contemporary churches: "Guard the good deposit that was entrusted to you—guard it with the help of the Holy Spirit who lives in us" (2 Tim. 1:14).

To answer the question "What is the place of the Bible in the church?" we must examine the fundamental issue of authority, then look again at the foundation of the church, examine its creeds and proclamations, and find practical ways to assure the purity of truth.

AUTHORITY—REVELATION OR TRADITION?

What are the sources of Christian truth? Is there a single authority that determines what is truth? Is it a person, a church, a tradition, or a book?

We begin by looking at the Word of God as our authority in matters of faith and practice in the church.

The Word as Authority

The sufficiency of Scripture rests on the fact that it is the supreme revelation of Jesus Christ, who declared Himself to be the way, the truth, and the life (John 14:6). There is nothing beyond the Scriptures that reveals a sufficient way of eternal salvation.

The Lord and His prophets and apostles gave the Word of God to the church. Church councils did not *make* the Bible the Word of God, they *recognized* it as such.

The Bible is the primary source and the only infallible criterion of truth. All opinions of faith and practice are to be tested by their adherence to the Bible. The Scriptures are the rule of faith and practice for Christians. This doctrine came to be known by the Latin words *sola scriptura*, which formed a central plank in the Protestant Reformation.

The Bible is authoritative because it is the direct result of the breathing out of God (2 Tim. 3:16). As the only source of true knowledge of God, and of salvation and godliness, the Scriptures are also the only judge of what we are to believe about God and His Son Jesus Christ. The winds of human tradition, whether pronouncements by councils, popes, or preachers, are always to be judged by the Scriptures.

The Bible affects life, and its truth is authenticated in life. It is "animated," as older theologians expressed it. "The Word of God is living and active. Sharper than any double-edged sword, it penetrates even to dividing soul and spirit, joints and marrow; it judges the thoughts and attitudes of the heart" (Heb. 4:12).

Accounts of the power and authority of the Bible are many. Two drawn from history illustrate the animating authority of the Bible. The first is the testimony of the sixteenth-century Swiss reformer Ulrich Zwingli. His words attest to a deep conviction that grew out of the text of Romans 3:4, "Let God be true, and every man a liar!" He wrote, "No matter who a man may be, if he teaches you in accordance with his own thought and mind his teaching is false. But if he teaches you in accordance with the word of God, it is not he that teaches you, but God who teaches him. . . . When I was younger, I gave myself over to much human teaching, like others of my day, and when about seven or eight years ago I undertook to devote myself entirely to the scriptures I was always prevented by philosophy and theology. But eventually I came to the point where led by scripture and the word of God I saw the need to set aside all these things and to learn the doctrine of God direct from his own word."[3]

Centuries later, French intellectual Emile Cailliet referred to the Bible as the book that would understand him. Reading the Bible for himself, the philosopher came face to face with its power. "I could not find words to express my awe and wonder," he wrote of the experience. "This *was* the Book that would understand me!" Cailliet continued, "The providential circumstances amid which the Book had found me now made it clear that while it seemed absurd to speak of a book understanding a man, this could be said of the Bible because its pages were animated by the Presence of the Living God and the power of His mighty acts."[4]

The Church and Its Authority

Evangelicals affirm that any authority an individual congregation may have is a derived authority. That is, the authority does not reside in the church, but in the Christ of the church attested to in divine Scripture.

While Christ and His apostles were alive on earth, there was little question about authority. When Paul faced an authority crisis of his own, he defined his apostolic calling whenever necessary. In his epistles, with few exceptions, he referred to himself as an apostle. To Galatian believers, he took extra measures to defend his authority (Gal. 1:11–24).

The Roman Catholic Church views itself as being in direct lineage with the apostles, holding authority in what it calls its *magisterium.* This Latin word conveys the idea of the majesty of the teaching body of the church and its pope.

Protestantism did not question the authority that Christ conferred on the apostles but did object to any direct succession of authority through the apostolate. No central power rests in a *magisterium* or in a single human leader.

Protestants appeal to the Bible and the witness of the Holy Spirit as authoritative, not to the church. The Bible is our *magisterium.* Rejecting the authority of church tradition, Protestants generally believe that even the creeds are not binding in and of themselves. The traditions of the faith, such as baptism and the Lord's Supper, are binding only because of the commandments contained in the Word of God. Jude declared that there were traditions to be passed along or "entrusted to the saints" (Jude 3). These are legitimate expressions of an authority of tradition, but they are different from what Christendom has come to call tradition. One is from the Lord, the other from human authority.

The church is to be subject to the Word of God and the Spirit. How then does it determine the truth of Scripture on any given matter?

The union of Word and Spirit was, for the Reformers, especially important. Calvin, in particular, emphasized that the Holy Spirit is the internal Minister of the Word. This he called the *testimonium.* When the Word is spoken, the Spirit impresses the Word on our hearts. It is the function of the Spirit to enlighten or illumine the believer about the Word (John 14:26; 16:13; Rom. 8:16).

Christians should use care in saying, "God told me." This language wrongly speaks more of revelation than illumination. One is the work of God whereby He left to the church a written record of His divine self-disclosure; the other is the work of the Spirit impressing the truths of that record on our hearts and applying them to us. Apart from the Holy Spirit our minds are incapable of grasping the spiritual wisdom of God and our hearts are too prone to wander and err. Thus the Word and the Spirit come to us as one voice enlightening our minds, transforming our wills, and refining our emotions.[5]

The church needs no imprimatur of councils or popes. It possesses the powerful testimony of the Holy Spirit to the reliability of truth found in the Scriptures.

Discovering the will of God on any matter is not a magical thing. Only through prayer, fasting, Bible reading, and study can the church arrive at appropriate, God-guided decisions. We gain a clue as to how this process works from the account of the selection of Barnabas and Saul for missionary work: "While they were worshiping the Lord and fasting, the Holy Spirit said, 'Set apart for me Barnabas and Saul for the work to which I have called them'" (Acts 13:2). The internal witness of the Spirit is illustrated elsewhere in the words, "It seemed good to the Holy Spirit and to us" (15:28). Another instance demonstrates the role of the Scriptures: "Now the Bereans were of more noble character than the Thessalonians, for they received the message with great eagerness and examined the Scriptures every day to see if what Paul said was true" (17:11). Paul's testimony, "And now, compelled by the Spirit, I am going to Jerusalem" (20:22), illustrates more the fact of Spirit guidance than the process itself.

The Abuses of Authority

The validation of truth by the Spirit and the Word should govern all church actions. However, such is not always the case. Unwarranted dogmatism, self-imposed rules, deceit, and deception have marked the convoluted path of church history. False teachers were active in the primitive church, leading people astray, and they are still active today. Protestants are quick to point to historical papal abuse, but are slow to recognize abuses in their own camp. The charge has been leveled that Protestants have a paper pope.[6] But it is not so much abuse of the power of the Word as abuse of human power that weakens the church.

The Reformers had no particular objection to any rule of faith by the *magisterium* of the Roman Church; so long as it was consistent with the Bible. Luther, for all his virtues, was not a biblical absolutist, for he did accept the authority of history. He believed that one could not easily write off fifteen hundred years of common witness, faith, and doctrine. Because of this, Luther was heavily criticized by the Anabaptists for not completely separating himself from all the teachings of Romanism. What Luther objected to were appeals to tradition and conciliar actions that were contrary to biblical truths.

Power corrupts, and, as the English Lord John Acton once said, "Absolute power corrupts absolutely." The history of the Christian faith is checkered enough by abuse of power. Its existence should warn us of the sinfulness of the human heart, which is prone to wander from the truth, and the pride that lurks beneath the thin veneer of religiosity.

THE FOUNDATION OF THE CHURCH

The Word of Christ

Christians do not look to the Law of Moses for the foundation of Christianity. They look to the Word of Christ on which both a living faith and a community of faith are built. By no means antinomian, that is to say, anti-law, Christianity looks to Christ as the fulfillment of the Law (John 1:17).

Reading the Old Testament is like taking a fascinating journey on a road with many signposts—all pointing to Christ. His incarnation, life, works, death, burial, resurrection, ascension, and future return are all predicted in the Old Testament. When Jesus spoke to the two believers on the road to Emmaus, beginning with Moses and all the Prophets, he explained to them what was said in all the Scriptures concerning himself" (Luke 24:27).

Regarding the Lord's Supper, Paul said he received instructions about it "from the Lord" (1 Cor. 11:23). So it did not result merely from tradition. Established by the Lord's words Himself, the Communion, or Lord's Table, is central to the life of the church.

Christ's words, unlike the record of all human authors, will never pass away (Matt. 24:35). They possess eternal life (John 6:68), are taught by the Spirit (1 Cor. 2:13), and are never to be added to or taken away (Rev. 22:18–19).

Christ calls His church to abide in Him and His words (John 15:7). As a condition of fruitfulness, abiding in Christ and obeying His commands produces the lasting fruit of joy. The highest and most commanding word of Christ is this: "Love each other as I have loved you. Greater love has no one than this that one lay down his life for his friends. You are my friends if you do what I command" (15:12–14).

The church's life, worship, and witness are to be ordered not by the consideration of what is sociologically and psychologically impressive, but by the Word of Christ. It would be a colossal mistake to miss this point. The Bible is thus unique and irreplaceable. It is the sole authority in the church, and Christians therefore are to be people of the Book.

Another Look at the Rock

Earlier in discussing the founding of the church, we commented on Jesus' words to Peter about his confession being like a rock. Here we take another look at the concept of the "Rock." As a redeemed community, the church was built on Jesus, whom Peter confessed to be "the Christ, the Son of the living God" (Matt. 16:16). Debate over who Jesus meant to be the "rock" takes on new meaning when we stay focused on His words and not merely on church traditions.

Traditionally, Peter had been viewed as the "rock" in Matthew 16:18. Paul's statement that the church is built on the foundation of the apostles and the prophets (Eph. 2:20), however, focuses the discussion on a plurality of persons and not on Peter alone. Views on the meaning of the "rock" include Peter, Peter's confession, Christ, or all the apostles. Reformers said the "rock" was Christ or Peter's confession about Christ.

Protestants have sometimes tried to get rid of the problem of Peter being the "rock" by denying that he ever resided in Rome. Oscar Cullmann accepts the possibility that he could have been there, but he rejects any idea of the papacy being built on him.[7]

Because of their polemical stance against Rome the Reformers preferred to view the *faith* of Peter as the foundation of the church. The issue of whether Peter was ever in Rome as a leader or a martyr did not concern them. The authority of Christ was the overarching principle on which they built their doctrine of the church.

Jesus calling Peter a rock is no reason to believe he was a pope. The view that Peter was the first pope came as a layer of tradition after the fact. After the earliest chapters of Acts, the New Testament makes no reference to Peter's leadership. The work and witness of the early church focused on the authority of Christ, and on the message and meaning of His incarnation. The *kerygma,* or preaching of the Cross, dominated the establishment of the church, and not the defense of Peter's authority as "rock."

The Word, which is still the single most important focus in the life of the church, recognizes the primacy of Christ (Col. 1:16–17), not of any human. The prominence of Peter among the Twelve cannot be disputed, nor can his faith be abstracted from his person. Yet his role as confessor of Christ places him, like John the Baptist, as a herald of the One who would build His church. That foundation has stood the tests of time.

The Apostles and the Word

The apostles' authority was received by the Lord's commissioning them. It was a derived authority. Nevertheless the apostles were pillars of the church (Gal. 2:9). It was on their foundational preaching that the church was established. We can rightly speak of primitive Christianity and the apostolic church as being the same thing.

"The apostolic church" refers to the early church built on the apostolic gospel, as Luther liked to call it. Any succession of the apostolic church through its leaders is only a general succession based on the call and commission of Christ. Such a call and commissioning to ministry extends to all believers.

Just as the apostles were under the authority of the Word, so is the church. If by "apostolic authority," we refer to their authoritative message, we can accept the term "apostolate." But if by apostolic authority we mean tradition, that authority is to be rejected as unbiblical.

Frederick W. Faber's hymn "Faith of Our Fathers" rightly places emphasis on the *faith* of the fathers and not the *fathers* of the faith. A Roman Catholic, Faber may have mixed his doctrine to combine scriptural authority and the traditional authority of the church, but his words are still powerful.

Faith of our fathers! living still
In spite of dungeon, fire and sword,
O how our hearts beat high with joy
Whene'er we hear that glorious word!
Faith of our fathers, holy faith!
We will be true to thee till death.

Jesus is building His church on the revelation given to the apostles. This colorful bunch left a deposit of faith, as Faber's hymn described. The apostolic foundation has been laid. We need not replace it, nor indeed can we. It is the foundation of the house that Jesus is building.

THE CHURCH AND ITS CREEDS

Late nineteenth-century rationalism led to modernist-fundamentalist conflict in the early twentieth century. Throughout the twentieth century, questions relating to revelation, eschatology, and the inspiration and inerrancy of the Scriptures stirred the pot. At the same time, worldwide advances were made in Bible translation work and church growth. Western civilization has experienced a significant religious shift. The continents of Africa, South America, and Asia have experienced phenomenal church growth. The epicenter of faith is shifting from the north and west to the south and the east. America, Canada, and western Europe, long seen as areas vital to missionary expansion, have experienced a factious, divided Christianity, unsure of its roots. In particular, this uncertainty relates to the crumbling foundations of scriptural authority.

The twenty-first century may be a repeat of the second century. Second-century Christianity had to determine the role and place of Scripture in the church. The establishment of the canon of Scripture, so vital to the life and witness of the emerging church, provided the undergirding necessary to do battle with paganism in the second century. Today's climate of an emerging paganism in western society finds a church weakened and uncertain of itself. At the very time when faith needs clarity of definition, many in the western church are abandoning the Bible as *the* sourcebook of faith for the church.

Within contemporary evangelicalism the need for a clearly defined role and use of the Bible is clear. The growing gap between religiosity and knowledgeable faith is widening. "A part of the church is succumbed to the allurements of secularism," Bloesch says, "but another part is resisting their appeal and is confessing the historic faith anew, though quite properly in the language of our age."[8]

In the name of seeker-sensitive services, there is sometimes an attempt to downplay the supposed scandal of the gospel. The public reading of the Scriptures has all but disappeared. Few people these days carry Bibles to church, knowing they won't need them during the sermon or even during a Bible-study hour. Building Scripture-based communities will demand more than tacit attention to the Bible in our church services.

To define the doctrine of the church in relationship to the current scene, we do well to look back at the major affirmations in history that relate directly to the doctrine of the church. Earlier we saw that the early church felt little need for creedal formulation of an ecclesiology, yet one was being developed from early times. Only when it came under attack did the emerging church develop doctrinal statements relating directly to its ecclesiology.

Early Formulations

The texts of Scripture themselves contain evidence of the earliest of the creeds. These, however, were chiefly Christological. Paul, in particular, emphasized the lordship of Christ in his writings. To the Corinthians he set the ground rules of an effective creed: "No one can say, 'Jesus is Lord,' except by the Holy Spirit" (1 Cor. 12:3). As a confession, "Jesus is Lord" was singled out as essential to salvation, according to Romans 10:9. Furthermore, in the great Christological passage of Philippians 2:5–11, the confession "Christ is Lord" will ultimately be on everyone's lips (2:11).

There is evidence of early creedal or hymnlike expressions in 1 Timothy 3:16. Paul wrote Timothy specific instructions so that he and others would know how they ought to conduct themselves in the church. He called the church the pillar and foundation of the truth (3:15) and then stated (in 3:16) a tightly worded Christology. Paul also offered a simple profession of faith in 2:5: "There is one God and one mediator between God and men, the man Christ Jesus."

Historic Creeds of the Church

The church has historically and publicly confessed its convictions in creeds. Our English word *creed* comes from the Latin word *credo*, which appeared as the first word of the Apostles' and Nicene creeds. In the creeds Christians gave credit to God for what He had done, just as the psalmists composed hymns affirming faith in the Lord.

The creeds are treasures, monumental victories of the Christian faith over inner and outer enemies. Formulated over a period of time and out of great struggle, the creeds provide foundational expression of the faith.

The creeds said relatively little about the church; instead they focused on the Trinity, humankind, sin, and salvation. We do, however, find some statements that describe the church.

The earliest of the creeds, the Apostles' Creed, refers to the "holy church." In later years the word "catholic" was added to the expanded creed recited or read in churches today. This creed existed as early as A.D. 150.

The Nicene Creed of A.D. 325 might rightly be called the Chalcedonian Creed, for it was in A.D. 455 that the original text of the Nicene Creed was expanded and finally accepted. It included the words: "And I believe in one Catholic and Apostolic Church."

The Athanasian Creed came after the fall of Rome to the Goths. By the fifth century a majority of Christians were disillusioned with a crumbling world. While the creed is named after the fourth-century Christian leader Athanasius, it probably served more as a statement of faith in his memory than anything else. This creed labored over an accurate Christology and was mainly Trinitarian in nature. It made no reference to the church. Calvin considered it only a hymn. It may have been written primarily to teach the clergy. Augustine felt that trying to address the vast subject of the Trinity was like trying to empty an ocean with a shell.

A profession of faith by a rich merchant in Lyon, France, has come to us as the Waldensian Declaration of Faith. Valdes, or Waldo, as English-speaking people knew him, led a twelfth-century separatist movement in

France. His followers became known as the Waldensians. This profession of faith adhered to Christian dogmas: the unity of the Trinity; God as Creator and Orderer of all things visible and invisible; Jesus Christ as truly God and truly Man; and the one, holy, apostolic, and catholic church. Other doctrines were also included.

Biblicalism gave a unique character to the Waldensian movement. Abandoned by the pope, this group was branded heretical and many adherents were burned at the stake. It was the only medieval separatist movement with a clear Christian orientation that lasted until the Protestant movement. Waldo introduced a new type of preaching based purely on a personal knowledge of the Bible and not on church law and ethics. Rejecting the apostolic succession of the Roman Church, Waldensians claimed to have received their call to ministry directly from God.

Sixteenth-century Waldensians formulated a declaration of faith in 1532. The Waldensian ecclesiology included a statement that said Sunday is a day of rest in order for people to apply themselves to the hearing of the Word of God. It also spoke to the "great good of the church" by forbidding ministers of the Word of God to transfer from one place to another unless it fulfilled the needs of that particular church.

Out of the Protestant Reformation came the Lutheran Confession of Augsburg in 1530, which stands today as the principal confession of the Lutheran Church. Its confessors, originally Luther and Melanchthon, made it clear that they wished to transmit to posterity no other teaching except what conforms to the pure Word of God. Article 7 reads, "One holy Church is to continue forever. But the Church is the congregation of saints, in which the Gospel is rightly taught and the Sacraments rightly administered. And unto the true unity of the Church, it is sufficient to agree concerning the Gospel and administration of the Sacraments. Nor is it necessary that human traditions, rites or ceremonies instituted by men should be alike everywhere."[9]

Luther and Melanchthon also included lengthy confessions about the church's sacraments, order, and practices. Within the Reformed tradition there were other confessions that indicated a departure from Romanism. The Anabaptists formulated the Schleithim Confession in 1527 under the guidance of Michael Sattler.

The Church of England, in its Thirty-Nine Articles of Faith, placed the focus on the Word and the sacraments in virtually the same way as the Augsburg Confession. Article 19 defines the church as "a congregation of faithful men in which the pure Word of God is preached, and the sacraments duly administered according to Christ's ordinances, in all those things that of necessity are requisite to the same."[10]

The Scottish (1556) and Saxon (1592) confessions were similar, although the Scottish Confession introduced the words, "This church is invisible, and known only to God." In Switzerland the first and second Helvetic Confessions (1536 and 1566) emphasized the "gathered" nature of the church: "The church is a community of believers, or saints, gathered out of the world, whose distinction is to know and to worship, through the Word and by the Spirit, the true God in Christ the Savior."[11]

Three other historic confessions expanded on the doctrine of the church over earlier formulations and formed the basis of other denominational confessions. The first is the Belgic Confession of 1561. In article 29 the authors built on former creeds by appealing to diligence and circumspect discernment of the Word of God. They sought to identify the true church in contrast to sects that adopted the name "church." In part the confession reads, "The marks by which the true Church is known are these: If the pure doctrine of the gospel is preached therein; if she maintains the pure administration of the sacraments as instituted by Christ; if church discipline is exercised in punishing of sin; in short, if all things are managed according to the pure Word of God, all things thereto rejected, and Jesus Christ acknowledged as the only Head of the Church."[12]

A second important confession that has influenced a great number of contemporary doctrinal statements of churches is the New Hampshire Confession of the Baptists (1833). The significance of this confession is that it grew out of early confessions by Baptists during a period of persecution. While many Protestant groups suffered greatly under the tyranny of Rome or of the later, oppressive state of Protestant churches in Europe, the English Baptists developed a cohesive doctrine for the church that has set the pattern for many non-Baptist churches that followed.

In 1644, during a volatile period in the English Civil War, members of the seven Baptist churches in London met to respond to charges and accusations. In the confession they produced there, they wrote, "Christ hath here on earth a spiritual kingdom which is the church, which he purchased and redeemed to himself, as a peculiar inheritance: which church ... is a company of visible saints, called and separated from the world by the Word and Spirit of God, to the visible profession of the faith of the gospel; being baptized into that faith, and joined to the Lord, and each other, by mutual agreement, in the practical enjoyment of the ordinances commanded by Christ their head and king."[13]

A concise statement in the New Hampshire Confession of 1833 emphasizes the visible nature of the church: "A visible church of Christ is a congregation of baptized believers associated by covenant in the faith and fellowship of the gospel; observing the ordinances of Christ, governed by his laws, and exercising the gifts, rights, and privileges invested in them by his word."[14]

Finally, the important Westminster Shorter Catechism of 1647 included the Apostles' Creed with its wording "holy Catholic church; the communion of the saints."[15] Beyond that, the larger confession addressed the issue of the Sabbath day and Christian worship. In the latter, the reading of Scripture, sound preaching, and hearing of the Word with understanding, faith, and reverence were prescribed.

As mentioned before, many other documents give insight into an evangelical doctrine of the church. Baptists and others of free, or non-state-church tradition built their statements of faith on these creeds.

What good is it to rehearse the liturgy of heavy prose affirming the faith of churches and believers long dead? I faced this in a personal way in 1966 while defending my doctoral dissertation. Among the group of professors assigned to the task of examining me was a Lutheran who was a professor of speech and semantics. He and the others wondered if it was possible to hold to a confessional faith and still grant freedom to investigate the faith. Before I could reply, the question was quickly taken up by the group, who began arguing among themselves. The Lutheran had the final say. He made a distinction between valid tradition and "traditionalism." "Tradition," he said, "is the living faith of the dead, while traditionalism is the dead faith of the living." That man's wisdom has stuck with me ever since, and I have used his line many times with people struggling with their beliefs and the dogma of the church.

The Place of Doctrinal Statements of Belief

Evangelicalism includes members of noncreedal groups outside of mainline denominations. "Our only creed is the Bible," some say, while others dogmatically proclaim, "We have no creed but Christ." On closer examination, however, these groups have some fairly definite statements of faith. While they may not formally be called creeds, in reality they are. There is biblical justification for confessions of faith, if not creeds. Matthew 10:32 and 33 acknowledge a link between faith and confessions of faith: "Whoever acknowledges me before men, I will also acknowledge him before my Father in heaven. But whoever disowns me before men, I will disown him before my Father in heaven."

Those who resist formal creeds find their justification from the Anabaptists, who felt that Luther, Melanchthon, and others did not go far enough in their Reformation movement. But it must be remembered that Menno Simons and others developed rather full statements of doctrine. John Hus had earlier done the same and was burned alive for it. There is no avoiding responsibility for delineating belief. It is an illusion that any church body can exist long without forming clear statements of belief for purposes of identification.

The more serious, and perhaps proper, question is, Why do we need a statement of faith? Among the several uses, the following might be considered:

- Basis or standard for calling a pastor

- Requirement for membership in the church

- Basis for interchurch cooperation

- Statement of incorporation for state records

In each case, there is ample evidence of abuse. Groups can draw the lines so tightly and narrowly that they exclude rather than include. Churches need to be clear, as were the Reformers, in recognizing the dangers of mixing belief and unbelief in the church and in its leaders. Lax standards lead to a weakened fellowship, while, on the other hand, tight standards may lead to spiritual pride and a divisive spirit.

We must avoid the extremes of taking too lightly matters of faith on one hand and, on the other hand, trampling on our brothers and sisters in Christ who through honest prayer and searching of the Scriptures arrive at conclusions differing from our own. Where do we draw the line? How can we avoid sectarianism while affirming in a unified way commonly held beliefs based on the Word of God?

Today a number of churches are dropping denominational wording in their names, choosing rather to use "nonoffensive" labels to attract the unregenerate. Time will tell if this practice is beneficial. Meanwhile, how do we know if this or that community church or any "visible" church really teaches the Bible? The churches' names do not always tell us. Building churches that conform to the headship of Christ and to the Word of God as taught by the Holy Spirit, and that affirm oneness of belief in the one true and triune God, should occupy our energies.

Freedom of Conscience and the Word in the Church

From emperors, popes, pastors, and bishops, to denominational associations and local church councils, churches have lived under authority of one kind or another. There have been three primary sources: the Scriptures, traditions, and hierarchies. Defining what is God's and what is Caesar's has been a tension throughout history. Churches need to exercise humility, prayer, study, and reflection to resolve the conflict between conscience and authority.

Since the Reformation there has emerged the doctrine of "soul liberty." No one single doctrine more forcefully and effectively demonstrates the freedom of Spirit-guided conscience under the governance of the Word of God than this. Baptists alone cannot take credit for this, although it is one of the marks of their historic distinctiveness.

Luther appealed to the liberty of the soul before God in matters of truth. Every believer, he said, is a priest and a prophet. Calvin and other Reformers affirmed the same truth. The Act of Supremacy, passed by the English Parliament in 1534, established the Church of England, or Anglicanism, with the king as its supreme head. In time, this led to a revolt by congregationalists and the Puritans. In America the nonconformist colony Rhode Island was another revolt against the establishment. Differing with the Massachusetts Bay Colony leaders, Roger Williams refused to sign an "oath of fidelity" to the colony. He was viewed as a troublemaker. A defender of Native American rights and an advocate of the separation of state and church powers, Williams established a colony on land purchased from the Narragansett Indians. By 1644 the separation of state and church became law in that colony. In a bit of inflammatory writing, Williams spelled out differences between worship and civil liberty. In 1644 he wrote *The Bloody Tenet of Persecution*, in which he explained his view of absolute religious freedom. Rhode Island became a haven for dissenters, even anarchists. Williams never viewed his colony as a new Zion, as did the Puritans, although he articulated remarkably well the meaning of freedom of conscience within the civil laws of the state or colony.

The doctrine of soul liberty has kept some churches from becoming creedal communities. This concept means that a church cannot dominate the faith or conscience of its members. Those churches for whom the doctrine of soul liberty is a distinctive foundation stone must grant liberty to one another and to others beyond their local fellowship. The ultimate, binding authority is God alone, who judges the conscience. In a voluntary association, members are covenanted to one another and may agree on truths of behavior and expression.

The doctrine of soul liberty flies in the face of a statement adopted by the Roman Church on April 8, 1546, at the Council of Trent. The council was called to answer issues raised by the Reformers. The council issued a decree "Concerning the Edition, and the Use, of the Sacred Books." It began with strong, authoritarian language: "In order to restrain petulant spirits, it decrees that no one relying on his own skill, shall . . . presume to interpret Scripture contrary to that sense which the holy mother Church—whose it is to judge of the true sense and interpretation of the holy Scriptures—hath held and doth hold."[16]

Freedom of the soul means that Christians are to search the Scriptures prayerfully. It does not mean that any person's idea of truth goes. How then does this work itself out in the life of the church? F. S. A. Hort characterized proper interpretation of the Scriptures and the stance of soul liberty when he wrote: "Our faith rests first on the Gospel itself, the revelation of God and His redemption in His Only begotten Son, and secondly on the interpretation of that primary Gospel by the Apostles and Apostolic men to whom was Divinely committed the task of applying the revelation of Christ to the thoughts and deeds of their own time. That standard interpretation of theirs was ordained to be for the guidance of the Church in all after ages, in combination with living guidance of the Spirit."[17]

THE CENTRALITY OF PROCLAMATION

When the French mathematician and physicist Blaise Pascal died in 1662, his friends discovered a scrap of paper sewn into the lining of his clothes. Laced with Bible references, Pascal's written testimony of faith revealed a profound respect for the Scriptures. The tersely worded account of his conversion concluded with the text of Psalm 119:16, "I will not neglect your Word."

Our need of clear and powerful Bible preaching is evident today. Churches must not neglect the Word. To do so courts ruin, for the Word gives us guidance (119:105). John Burton put it well in the words of a hymn:

> Holy Bible, book divine,
> Precious treasure, thou art mine;
> Mine to tell me whence I came;
> Mine to teach me what I am.

Burton's hymn is rarely sung today, but the preaching of the Word must command a central place in evangelical church worship. Luther never missed an opportunity to engage in proclaiming the liberating power of the Scriptures. For him, preaching was the dynamic act of proclaiming Christ. Christ cannot be known without the Word, and the world cannot hear the Word without "someone preaching to them" (Rom. 10:14).

The Word and the Ordinances

As already noted, for the Reformers the Word and the sacraments marked the true church of Christ. What relationship do the two have with each other? The precursors of the Reformation recognized the vital role of preaching. Lollards and others moved about the English countryside preaching the Word wherever they could gather a crowd. Christian humanists like Erasmus in the fifteenth century gave prominence to preaching, and that emphasis (of the Word over the sacraments) has today been adopted by many churchmen of independent tradition.

The linkage of Word and sacraments, or, preferably, ordinances, weds two kinds of proclamation. One is verbal and expositional; the other is symbolic and powerfully spiritual. In baptism we see the enactment of death, burial, and resurrection, and in the Lord's Table we engage in worshipful communion with the Lord. However, in preaching we explain the ordinances based on exposition of the Word of God. Then to observe the ordinances is an act of obedience. In the Lord's Table, believers declare the Lord's death until He comes again (1 Cor. 11:26).

Preaching is public proclamation, and the ordinances are forms of public witness. Baptism, in particular, demonstrates a radical break with the world. The Lord's Table demonstrates the intimacy of celebrating the presence of Christ in the act of communion with other believers. Through the centuries the debate has centered more on the meaning of the Lord's Table than on the Lord of that table. Is it a real presence or spiritual presence? Do the bread and the cup represent Christ's body and blood, or do they become such in actuality with the blessing and pronouncement of priests? These questions will be visited again later, as will questions about the ordinance of baptism. Public preaching of the Word is indispensable if the ordinances are to mean anything at all.

THE CHURCH AS DEFENDER OF THE TRUTH

A brief word is in order here on the function of the church as the watchdog of truth. Repeatedly, the New Testament warns of false teachers and urges believers to be on guard against error and the attack of Satan.

Believers individually and corporately must seek the mind of Christ on all matters of truth. Christ warned against false Christs and false prophets in the last days (Matt. 24:24). He also warned about sheep stealers (John 10:1) and wolves that would attack the flock of God (10:11–13). Similar warnings also occur in the Epistles (2 Cor. 11:1–6; Col. 2:4–23; 2 Tim. 3:1–13; 2 Pet. 2:1–3, 12–22; Jude 8–19).

The apostle John warned believers to test the spirits. Explicit instructions were given, including the fundamental test of orthodoxy: "This is how you can recognize the Spirit of God: Every spirit that acknowledges that Jesus Christ has come in the flesh is from God, but every spirit that does not acknowledge Jesus is not from God" (1 John 4:2–3).

In the early centuries of the church the many conflicting interpretations of truth and contrary doctrines forced the church to centralize its interpretive authority in the bishops, councils, and the pope. But the church is in full possession of the Word and the Spirit, and need not turn to human authorities. Like the early Bereans, who checked everything out with the Scriptures (Acts 17:11), the church today must constantly be on guard against error. It must school itself in the truth, know its Lord intimately, prayerfully study the Word, and, above all, live in the light of its truths. As Paul wrote to Timothy, the church is responsible to handle the Word "correctly" (2 Tim. 2:15). As exegete, or interpreter, of the truth, a church faces a major crisis if it does not give its members help in knowing how to study the Scriptures. If its leaders pass along only predigested spiritual food, then the people perish for lack of the meat of the Word.

A believer once told me he no longer had any need to study the Scriptures for himself. "The church determines the truth of God for me," he said. This individual happened to be a follower of the Eastern Orthodox faith, but he could just as well have been one of any number of church members who passively sit week after week, only listening to another person's views of truth.

All the confessions about the Bible and its truths do not mean that the Bible is the center of a church's attention. I believe it was Carl Henry who once remarked, "I fear the loss of the use of the Bible by the common people in the pew."

THE PURITY OF THE CHURCH—TRUTH

Wherever the light of truth shines, the enemy seeks to extinguish that truth. But truth has always had its faithful defenders. They are in every corner of the globe where the gospel has taken root.

Through trials the church is refined, and through the truth the church is purified. George Keith's hymn, "How Firm a Foundation," penned in 1787, expresses the purity of the Word and the refinement of faith through trials:

> How firm a foundation, ye saints of the Lord,
> Is laid for your faith in His excellent Word!
> What more can He say than to you He hath said,
> To you who for refuge to Jesus have fled?
>
> "Fear not, I am with thee; O be not dismayed,
> For I am thy God, and will still give thee aid;
> I'll strengthen thee, help thee, and cause thee to stand,
> Upheld by My righteous, omnipotent hand.
>
> "When through fiery trials thy pathway shall lie,
> My grace, all sufficient, shall be thy supply:
> The flame shall not hurt thee; I only design
> Thy dross to consume and thy gold to refine.
>
> "The soul that on Jesus hath leaned for repose
> I will not, I will not desert to its foes;
> That soul, though all hell should endeavor to shake,
> I'll never, no, never, no, never forsake!"

John Calvin said that every church should be a school of Christ. The church has only one curriculum, which is Christ, and only one book, which is the Bible. All other themes and books have value only in relationship to Christ and His Word. The Word births the church's members (1 Pet. 1:23), and feeds, edifies, and purifies the flock (2:2).

Whenever a church operates independently of the Word and seeks its success by espousing the concerns of this world, it becomes a false church.

Furthermore, when the tyranny of individualism, selfism, and privatism hold sway, it is a false church. But when the church is under its Head, Christlikeness purifies the church; and under the Word, truth purifies the church. We must guard the truth by proclaiming the Bible.

The greatest enemies of the Bible are not those who persistently attack its veracity but those who ignore it. In our postmodern age it just isn't taken seriously by many. Jesus, however, took the Scriptures seriously, and so must we. Almost as an aside, Jesus gave endorsement to the Word of God: "The Scripture cannot be broken" (John 10:35). By this he meant it cannot be set aside as irrelevant, inaccurate, or nonauthorative. It has to be reckoned with.

Public worship must be awash in Scripture. The Word must be used for more than describing the current cultural scene or in prescribing therapy for the needy. Only by rediscovering norms outside and apart from our culture can we avoid becoming enslaved to the self-image of this age. Only the Bible gives us those norms.

A theology grounded in Scripture is the only theology by which a church can judge the secular world. It is precisely the Bible's claim to speak truth that separates the gospel from a mere story. The Bible is not just a word from the past, but the living voice of God speaking to our present condition.

Reclaiming the Bible for the church will free us from slavish demands of fads and cultural trends. It will allow us to imitate Christ rather than the latest whim of a fragmented culture.

Those who spend their careers translating the faith into terms that can be understood by moderns are in danger of flirting with heresy. According to Stanley Hauerwas and William Willimon, this very approach doomed theological liberals in pre-World War II Germany.[18] They domesticated theology to the point of not being able to say no to Hitler.

Sociologist Peter L. Berger delivers a scathing analysis and critique of the cultural accomodationists: "Each time that one has managed, after an enormous effort, to adjust the faith to the prevailing culture, that culture turns around and changes. . . . Our pluralistic culture forces those who would 'update' Christianity into a state of permanent nervousness."[19]

Today the Scriptures have become subservient to the needs and requirements of a fragmented society. It should be the other way around.

Only then can we save our churches from a slow and painful starvation. When we fail to teach and preach the Word, we render the ministry a comic spectacle to the world. When we think we have to adjust the Bible to the world, our churches will die.

The whole point of the Scriptures is to point people to Christ, the living Truth of God. We have the words of Jesus Himself: "These are the Scriptures that testify about me" (John 5:39). If we are to display faith in a faithless era, then we need the hearing of the Word, as Paul declared in Romans 10:17. Only that produces faith.

5
The Church and Holy Spirit Power

The Church is in an excellent state when it is sustained by God only.
—Blaise Pascal

ISSUE-DRIVEN PEOPLE create firestorms that are difficult to control. Like arsonists with tinder-dry lumber, they start conflagrations that sometimes get out of control. On the other hand, they may just hit on a winning strategy. Early Christians were just like that—spiritual arsonists spreading the unquenchable fire of faith.

In the summer of 1972, when Sargeant Shriver accepted the nomination for vice president of the United States, he quoted Pierre Teilhard de Chardin: "But some day . . . after mastering the winds, the waves, the tides and gravity, we shall harness for God the energies of love: and then, for the second time in the history of the world, man will have discovered fire."[1]

The church has everything to do with fire, not the kind that consumes forests and destroys lives, but the kind that ignites passion for truth, that converts and transforms the landscape of a life to enable it to be lived in the power of the Holy Spirit. The Lord asked, "Is not my word like fire?" (Jer. 23:29). From the moment of his call, Jeremiah experienced a white-hot passion for spreading God's Word. "I will make my words in your mouth a fire," thundered the Lord (5:14). Later the prophet responded, "His word is in my heart like a burning fire" (20:9).

When the fire of Pentecost fell on the disciples, they were transformed from timid, reticent learners into bold, courageous witnesses to the truth of the resurrection of Christ. Speaking of angels, God said He makes them winds and flames of fire (Heb. 1:7). Quoting from Psalm 104:4, the writer to the Hebrews marshaled imagery of powerful natural elements to illustrate the execution of mighty power.

Earlier, the disciples on the road to Emmaus had been touched by the fire of the truth given to them by Jesus: "Were not our hearts burning within us while he talked with us on the road and opened the Scriptures to us?" (Luke 24:32)

Throughout history, from Pentecost to the present, God's messengers have faithfully drawn on the truth of Holy-Spirit power to fire the church. In 1495 Girolamo Savonarola was forbidden to preach in Florence, Italy. Out of obedience to the Word of God, he defied Rome and in 1498, at the age of forty-six, was burned at the stake in the Piazza della Signorina. Martin Luther, in his own defiance of Rome, praised the boldness of Savonarola, whose words revealed implicit confidence in the Holy Spirit: "The message of the Lord has been a consuming fire within my bones and my heart; and I have not been able to endure it, but constrained to speak, for I feel all burning and all inflamed by the Lord's Spirit."[2]

Four hundred fifty years later Christian martyr Jim Elliot wrote of his desire to be a flame for God. His July 7, 1948, entry in his diary read, "'He makes his ministers a flame of fire.' Am I ignitable? God deliver me from the dread asbestos of 'other things.' Saturate me with the oil of the Spirit that I may be a flame. But flame is transient, often short-lived. Can'st thou bear this, my soul—short life? In me there dwells the Spirit of the Great Short-Lived, whose zeal for God's house consumed Him. 'Make me Thy Fuel, Flame of God.'"[3]

The story of the advance of the gospel is a story of fire—God's fire on earth. In reality, the establishment of the church is a story of spiritual power at work—the Holy Spirit's power convicting, transforming, baptizing, and filling believers. Our attempts to understand this spreading flame and to develop a doctrine of the church must account for the power issues that set the church apart from any human institution. What distinguishes the church from merely an organization is the Holy Spirit in its life and witness in the world. Today the church needs fresh power from God through His Holy Spirit.

"Do not leave Jerusalem," Jesus instructed His followers, "but wait for the gift my Father promised, which you have heard me speak about" (Acts 1:4). Luke recorded Jesus' words based on the earlier teaching of John 14:16: "I am going to send you what my Father has promised, but stay in the city until you have been clothed with power from on high" (Luke 24:49).

The hymn, "Rise up, O Church of God," written in 1909 by W. P. Merrill, declares the need for spiritual power in the church. Stanza three rings out a rousing call to action:

> Rise up, O men of God!
> The Church for you doth wait,
> Her strength unequal to her task,
> Rise up, and make her great.

The greatness of the church does not depend on us, however. "Strength unequal to the task" aptly describes the reality of our dependence on God's power.

POWER, POWERS, AND THE HOLY SPIRIT

One of the marks of the twentieth century was an obsession with power. We witnessed the rise of Nazi power, to see it subsequently wane and be destroyed. The totalitarian state, epitomized by Marxist collectivism, had its seventy years in the sun before it toppled, as surely as the Berlin Wall crumbled. Yet we can turn the compass in almost any direction and still see the quest for power being played out on planet earth. Aspirants to godlike power are a dime a dozen. It is part of the sinfulness of humankind.

The apostle Paul understood the nature of spiritual battle when he wrote the Ephesian believers: "For our struggle is not against flesh and blood, but against the rulers, against the authorities, against the powers of this dark world and against the spiritual forces of evil in the heavenly realms" (Eph. 6:12). The church of Jesus Christ must disassociate itself from every power base but God. The temptation is always present to rely on political and military strength. We tend to forget Jesus' words, "My kingdom is from another place" (John 18:36).

CHRIST'S GIFT OF THE HOLY SPIRIT

Jesus Christ is the Giver of supernatural power to His church. While still on earth He repeatedly alluded to another "coming"—the coming of the Holy Spirit (John 15:26; 16:7). When the Holy Spirit comes, John wrote, "he will convict the world of guilt in regard to sin and righteousness and judgment" (16:8). Jesus described this "coming" as a gift, the promised presence and power of the Holy Spirit. The gift of the Counselor (14:16), unaccepted by the world, was promised to His disciples as from the Father sent in Jesus' name (14:26).

The one who was "with" the disciples would soon be "in" them. "The world cannot accept him," Jesus taught, "because it neither sees him nor knows him. But you know him, for he lives with you and will be in you" (14:17). The Holy Spirit is more than a power or an impersonal force. As the third person of the Trinity, He comes from the Father and is a gift from the Son, ever living, filling, and empowering believers in the body of Christ.

Christ's gift of the Spirit is a rare jewel, worthy of lofty praise. Anglicans sing an old hymn on Whitsuntide commemorating the coming of the Spirit at Pentecost.

> Hail thee! Spirit co-eternal,
> Love omnipotent, supernal;
> Honour meet to thee we render,
> Veneration deep and tender;
> Hail, LORD GOD, the HOLY GHOST!
>
> —S. J. Wallis (1934)

The Threat of Worldliness

Are churches taking their directions from the living God or from the fading fads of modernity? More churches seem to be leaning more toward popular culture than toward the timeless Word and the powerful Spirit to empower the church.

Worldliness is a word that has fallen out of use today. Most recently it got trapped in the garb of twentieth-century separatism. And so it also did in the second century among desert fathers, in the fourth century onward in monasticism, in later centuries by the Hutterites and the Amish, and in contemporary movements organized for withdrawal from society. Unfortunately worldliness is very much alive and well in our churches.

The devaluation of the church as a shaper of culture proceeds unabated. Os Guinness calls our times something akin to a black hole in the universe: "At a certain point the dissolution of faith's authority and the disappearance of any positive force for truth and godliness turn into a high-density, negative, and devouring force for evil—in short, nihilism."[4] In an attempt to be contemporary, many churches have a look-alike church culture, little different from the cultural setting of our world.

The decline of personal standards of holiness indicates that the church is engulfed by worldliness. As defined by the apostle John, worldliness is "the cravings of sinful man, the lust of his eyes and the boasting of what he has and does" (1 John 2:16). The worldly practice of sinful desires, lustful looks, and arrogant boasting all too often characterize believers.

A corrective to the corrosion of the prevailing culture is a return to preaching and teaching the doctrine of the Holy Spirit. If we only sing our one-line jingles praising the Spirit, we engage in worship without understanding how the Spirit and the Word work in unison. If we only spread a thin layer of religious experience, even ecstatic experience, over our unrepentant proneness to sin, we endanger the life and vitality of church witness. If the church desires the blessing and power of God, then conformity to Christ alone must become the standard.

The very survival of the church is at stake. The gates of hell may not overcome the church, but letting down our guard against worldliness certainly weakens the church and seriously damages its testimony. We should put no confidence in the flesh, Paul wrote (Phil. 3:3).

The Temptation of Power

Following the Watergate scandal, American politics witnessed the exposure of raw power wielded by a handful of the president's men. Whether in society or in the church, the temptations of power are great.

Two New Testament incidents reveal the use of power for personal gain. The deception of Ananias and Sapphira in Acts 5 and the deviousness of Simon the sorcerer in Acts 8 amply illustrate sinful quests for power.

The case of Ananias and Sapphira stands in stark contrast to the generosity of Barnabas. While Barnabas sold property and contributed all the profits to the church (Acts 4:36–37), the two sold a piece of real estate and pretended to give all the money away when actually they kept some of the proceeds for themselves (5:2).

This was no slight offense or incidental event. In the chronicles of the Holy Spirit this deceit was labeled a sin, not only a sin within the community but a sin against God. Lying to the Holy Spirit is synonymous with lying against God (5:3–4). Ananias and Sapphira violated the trust of the church and also sinned against God, the Holy Spirit. Luke summed up the effect on the church: "Great fear seized the whole church and all who heard about these events" (5:11). In recording this incident Luke used the word *ekklēsia* ("church") for the first time in Acts (see also 7:38; 8:1; 9:31; 11:22; 13:1; 14:23; 15:22, 41; 16:5; 19:32, 40; 20:28).

Philip's preaching in Samaria, which was accompanied by miraculous signs, caught the ear and eye of a local sorcerer known in Samaria as the "Great Power" (8:10). He had a following because of his magic, but when Philip preached the gospel, many believed. Even Simon became a baptized follower, astonished by the great signs and miracles done by the apostles.

When Simon saw that the Spirit was given by the laying on of hands by Peter and John, he devised a scheme to merchandise the situation. "Give me also this ability so that everyone on whom I lay my hands may receive the Holy Spirit," he appealed to the apostles (8:19).

Simon's sin was in offering money to buy spiritual power. Rebuking

Simon in strong language, Peter told Simon to repent of his wickedness (8:22). The story did not end there. Justin Martyr, who died around A.D. 165, labeled Simon the first heretic of the Christian faith, and Irenaeus wrote of Simon as the father of Gnosticism. The Simon Magus of later legend may have been the same devious man whose conversion was disingenuous.

Simony, the sin of gaining a church position by deception or purchase, rears its ugly head in the church from time to time. Luther charged Rome with being party to it, and modern charlatans of the faith mar the witness of the gospel. Religious quackery is as old as Acts 5 and 8. Sin, which is any act of rebellion against God, is something God hates. It may express itself in willful arrogance, egotism, or moral decadence. All sin is sin against the Holy Spirit.

Spiritual power can neither be purchased nor faked. The great task of the Christian church is to live out the gospel in genuine fashion, relying only on God and His power. We are to reject any deceptive method or illusory tricks aimed at gaining converts to Christ.

BAPTISM INTO ONE BODY, THE CHURCH

The Bible teaches that believers in this church age are baptized by one Spirit into the body of Christ. "For we were all baptized by one Spirit into one body—whether Jews or Greeks, slave or free—and we were all given the one Spirit to drink" (1 Cor. 12:13). In God's grand design for His church, this baptism is differentiated from water baptism. Admittedly, Christians have differed over the interpretation of Spirit baptism and water baptism. Those who espouse a sacramental view equate the two. Charismatics, on the other hand, view them as separate, but insist on baptism of the Spirit as a work of God in the human heart subsequent to conversion. Advocates of believers' baptism view the Scriptures as teaching water baptism as a requirement for believers in obedience to Christ. Others say water baptism is essential for conversion.

Our purpose in this chapter is not to expound in detail each of these views; rather it is simply to present the differences between the two uses of the term *baptism* and to show the significance of the baptism of the

Spirit. Care must be taken not to confuse this teaching with other ministries of the Spirit, such as His regenerating, indwelling, and filling.

At the moment of salvation every believer is baptized by the same Spirit which places him or her into the body of Christ. Three distinct things mark this work of the Spirit:

1. It is universal in the sense that all Christians experience this baptism.

2. It is inclusive. Unlike circumcision for the Jewish male, this action of God cuts across all ethnic and gender boundaries. Furthermore, this work of the Spirit is classless in nature.

3. It is not a repeatable work of God. It occurs at the moment of salvation; nowhere are Christians urged to be baptized by the Spirit.

At Pentecost a unique thing happened. For the first time Christ baptized His disciples and many others into His body, the church. Ever since then, the moment a person turns to Christ for salvation he or she is baptized by the Holy Spirit, that is, placed into the church, Christ's body. At Pentecost the church began, and the Holy Spirit and the church became inseparably linked. This baptism sets the shape for the unity of the church. No other doctrine emphasizes this more: "We were *all* baptized by *one* Spirit into *one* body . . . and we were *all* given the *one* Spirit to drink" (1 Cor. 12:13, italics added). All other doctrines of the Spirit flow from it— regenerating, sealing, indwelling, filling, gift-giving. It is the foundation for fruitful service in the church. To be a Christian is to be baptized by the Holy Spirit.

Baptized and indwelt by the Spirit, believers become a "holy temple in the Lord . . . a dwelling in which God lives by his Spirit" (Eph. 2:21–22).

The baptism of the Spirit is not experiential, that is, the experience of it at Pentecost is not normative today. God continues to do His quiet work by His Spirit through Christ, placing people into His body. One by one, multitudes are regenerated and baptized by the Spirit. The church, not the Holy Spirit, is God's footprint left on earth. Only a spiritually minded church, however, gives room for the Holy Spirit, who anoints with power. "The possession of the Holy Spirit is a gift not an achievement," wrote William Barclay.[5]

THE DIVERSITY OF THE CHARISMATA

As already noted, the Holy Spirit is a gift of Christ to His church. In turn, the Holy Spirit gives gifts to the church. We call these the *charismata*, from *charis*, which means "grace." The spiritual gifts are evidence of God's grace, but they differ from the gift of salvation or the gift of the Holy Spirit. God's grace in giving us salvation grants us entrance into glory, whereas God's grace in giving us spiritual gifts brings glory to Christ in the church.

The Purpose of Spiritual Gifts

In 1563 the Heidelberg Catechism was drawn up, named after the German city in which it was framed. It includes an important statement about spiritual gifts: "Everyone must know it to be his duty readily and cheerfully to employ his gifts for the advantage and salvation of other members."[6]

Where did these evangelicals of a bygone era get their convictions about the existence and purpose of spiritual gifts? The answer is obvious: from the Word of God, which to all Christians is the infallible Word of truth.

"Now about the spiritual gifts, brothers," Paul wrote the Corinthians, "I do not want you to be ignorant" (1 Cor. 12:1). Paul then stated that there are different kinds of gifts, but the same Spirit; different kinds of service, but the same Lord; and different kinds of working, but the same God, who works all of them in all believers (12:4–6). And in Ephesians 4:7–8, the other major "gifts" passage in the New Testament, Paul quoted part of Psalm 68:18: "But to each one of us grace has been given as Christ apportioned it. This is why it says: 'When he ascended on high, he led captives in his train and gave gifts to men.'"

From these verses on spiritual gifts we can draw several conclusions about God's grace-gifts for the church.

- Spiritual gifts are God's grace-gifts to all believers ("to each one," 1 Cor. 12:7; see also Rom. 12:3–8).

- These gifts are for the church as a whole, not merely to enrich individuals ("for the common good," 1 Cor 12:7).

- Spiritual gifts serve their purpose only if the body is built up into unity in the faith and in knowledge of Jesus Christ, in short, if they promote spiritual maturity in Christ's body (Eph. 4:7–13).

- Exercise of these gifts is for the edification (encouragement and comfort) of the church (1 Cor. 14:3–5, 12, 26).

- In the service of Christ and through proper use of spiritual gifts, men and women are led to believe in Christ and obey God (Rom. 15:18).

- What constitutes a *charisma* is not the form of the particular action of service, but the blessing of God ("We have this treasure in jars of clay to show that this all-surpassing power is from God," 2 Cor. 4:7).

- Spiritual gifts are for the praise and glory of God (1 Pet. 4:11).

We conclude then that a spiritual gift is a divinely given ability, empowered by the Holy Spirit to be used in the ministry of the church to accomplish the spiritual purposes for which it was intended.

The Gift of Gifts to the Church

When I was a child, I would try to rank the wrapped packages under the Christmas tree. Which one would be my favorite? Which was of the greatest value? At our home, we had a "no-touch" rule, but my parents had difficulty enforcing it. By the time Christmas morning arrived, I had, or thought I had, figured out all the gifts.

One year, to my great surprise, what I had thought was the gift of least value turned out to be the gift of greatest worth. It's that way with God's gifts of service to His church. We have already seen that Christ Himself with His gift of eternal salvation is the greatest gift. When the church values Christ above all else, then blessing is in store.

Furthermore the gift of the Holy Spirit is another treasure of the church. When my wife and I were visiting a sixteenth-century Swedish parish church, a sexton took us into a room where a huge metal and wooden chest was stored. Using a key as old as the church, she pulled out a small, gold-plated crown used in wedding ceremonies for centuries. My

Swedish wife stood in awe, realizing that her great-grandmother may have worn that very crown on her wedding day. However, of far greater value than a gold wedding crown is the Holy Spirit.

Charles Haddon Spurgeon is known for his preaching, but few know that he also wrote hymns and spiritual songs. In the *Baptist Hymnal* Spurgeon's hymn, "The Holy Ghost Is Here," appears, along with a section of other hymns about the Holy Spirit. Many of these hymns express a thin theology, but not Spurgeon's hymn.

> The Holy Ghost is here,
> Where saints in prayer agree,
> As Jesus' parting Gift is near
> Each pleading company.
>
> Not far away is He,
> To be by prayer bro't nigh,
> But here in present majesty,
> As in His courts on high.
>
> He dwells within our soul,
> An ever welcome guest;
> He reigns with absolute control,
> As monarch in the breast.
>
> Obedient to Thy will,
> We wait to feel Thy pow'r;
> O Lord of life, our hopes fulfill,
> And bless this hallowed hour.

This One sent by Christ Himself in turn grants gifts to the church for productive service. Among the diversity of gifts, there is one that is rarely treated as a spiritual gift. I speak of the gift of love. In 1 Corinthians 12 Paul listed a number of spiritual gifts. All were necessary and honorable, and all came from God. However, for church people known for a divisive spirit there was one gift that was needed above all others: love.

Love is the path of power in the church. All other endowments are good for nothing if love is missing (13:1–3). It is this greatest of gifts that points others to the love of God in Christ Jesus. To the degree that believers display genuine love for each other, for the world lost in unbelief, and for their enemies, the power of God will be displayed.

Gifts of the Holy Spirit

In recent years much attention has been focused on the various spiritual gifts. Seminars, spiritual-gifts inventories, specialists in determining gifts, and a general preoccupation with ministry skills each reflect a revival of interest in the subject.

In the small-town church where I met my Savior, there were a number of choice saints whose diversities of Christian service influenced my conversion. I am quite sure that some of these godly people knew little of their special gifts. But because of their humble service, people were blessed. In their acts of mercy people were shown the mercy of God. Those who taught the Scriptures actually helped people learn things from their stumbling lessons. The preaching of many sermons resulted in people believing in Christ. Even though they knew little about spiritual gifts, these gifted people accomplished the work of Christ. From the women who canned fruit for Navajo Indians, to farmers who witnessed in the local rescue mission after long hours in the fields, these giants of the faith worked their way into the fabric of my soul, and I placed my faith in Christ.

How many gifts are there? The New Testament gives us several lists which, to some degree, vary. There is some indication in Romans 12, 1 Corinthians 12, and Ephesians 4, that the gifts are treated from at least two differing vantage points. In some cases, the gift itself is listed; in others, the persons who are exercising the gifts appear to be central. Beyond these texts we read from 1 Peter 4:11 that there may be another way to group them—"speaking" or verbal gifts and "service" gifts.

Some Bible expositors attempt to categorize the gifts in several ways: prophetic gifts, priestly gifts, kingly gifts, knowledge gifts, gifts of power, and gifts of speech.[7]

A partial list of spiritual gifts in the Bible might look like this:

Prophecy	Miracles
Serving	Faith
Teaching	Distinguishing spirits
Encouraging	Tongues
Giving money	Interpretation of tongues
Leadership	Apostle
Mercy	Prophet
Word of wisdom	Teacher
Word of knowledge	Evangelist
Gift of healing	Pastor-teacher

Not every believer possesses every gift, nor is any one single gift possessed by all believers. They are variously given "according to the measure of faith God has given" (Rom. 12:3). And they are apportioned as God wills (1 Cor. 12:11). Nowhere are believers instructed to seek a particular gift, other than the "greater gifts" (12:31).

Were we to search the New Testament for the many activities in which Christians are to be engaged, the list might grow. Why does the Bible not mention gifts of hope, prayer, or patience? The point is that these are qualities to be exercised by all believers.

Do some gifts outlive others? Is there a temporal quality to certain gifts? For sure, the gift of love will endure, as Paul stated in 1 Corinthians 13:13. Arguments for no differentiation between temporal or permanent spiritual gifts are posed by proponents of tongues-speaking, healing, prophetic utterance and miracles of healing in particular, while others hold the view that some gifts ceased in the early church. The "cessationists" base their arguments on the nature of the process of divine revelation. While the canon of Scripture was incomplete, certain gifts attested to the prophetic teaching and evangelistic work of the apostles. The miraculous gifts, they say, were "signs" that verified the Word. "When the perfection comes, the imperfect disappears," Paul wrote in 13:10. Most cessationists say this refers to the closing of the canon of Scripture, so "sign" gifts are not necessary. Others say the words "the perfect" refers to the Second Coming, so that all the gifts, not just most of them, are to be exercised until Christ returns. Also cessationists point out that the sign gifts were needed only in the apostolic age to confirm the message of the apostles (2 Cor. 12:12).

How do Christians resolve these and other related differences between charismatics and noncharismatics? We must remember that this is a debate within the body, where every part of it, foot, ear, eye, and hand, to use the analogy of 1 Corinthians 12:14–27, is valuable.

A proper appeal for either tolerance or intolerance of various viewpoints should not rest on experience alone. Our faith must rest on the firm truths of Scripture. All experience should be measured ultimately against truth.

Our appeals, conclusions, and judgments of one another's views and ministry must aim for the unity of the body. Granted, the present intemperate nature of feelings and divisions do a disservice to our evangelical witness. Nevertheless we must continue to seek the mind of Christ in all humility.

There have been miraculous epochs in history—the times of Moses, the prophets, and Jesus Christ and the apostles. Do we live in such an era or epoch? Can God work miracles and display unique signs? Certainly. God's power is unlimited. But the larger question is, *Should* He display His power in these ways today, and, if so, for what purposes?

The preaching and teaching of the Word must remain central. Every believer is to exercise the gifts God gave him. If there is abuse, the scriptural caution that "everything should be done in a fitting and orderly way" is to be heeded (14:40). Appealing to the text, "For God is not a God of disorder but of peace" (14:33), believers are to work out differences prayerfully and civilly.

We must laud the scholars who study the Scriptures, we must honor our elders who minister the Word, and we must pray for one another, holding our differences in the bonds of love. Above all, we need to return again to the truths of Scripture.

THE PURITY OF THE CHURCH

René Pache, the Swiss lawyer who turned theologian and founded InterVarsity Fellowship in Switzerland, wrote, "The touchstone of all doctrine concerning the Holy Spirit is the question: What place does it give to the Lord Jesus Christ?"[8]

The purity of the church springs from its Christcenteredness, its reliance on divine truth through the Scriptures, and its holiness growing out of life in the Spirit. In essence, this is the summary of the teaching of Christ's headship, the Word, and the Spirit (as discussed in chapters 3–5).

Holiness and God's Peculiar People

The apostle Peter wrote of the uniqueness of Christians: "But you are a chosen people, a royal priesthood, a holy nation, a people belonging to God, that you may declare the praises of him who called you out of darkness into his wonderful light" (1 Pet. 2:9). Peter's use of terms moves us beyond mere individual Christianity. He used collective terms: chosen people, royal priesthood, and holy nation. And drawing on Old Testament imagery, Peter painted a picture of the uniqueness of the church.

In 1 Peter 1:15 Peter quoted from Leviticus (Lev. 11:44, 45; 19:2; 20:7) to clarify and define the character of Christians as holy. Holiness is the hallmark virtue of people "set apart" and belonging to God. Called to a new life in Christ, the chief Cornerstone, the church is "a *holy* temple in the Lord" (Eph. 2:21, italics added). Called "saints," believers are to display moral character consistent with their God. They are called to a holy life (2 Tim. 1:9).

A unique vocabulary of holiness describes the people of the church: elect, beloved, holy and beloved, faithful, and saints. Built on the foundation of "holy apostles" (Eph. 3:5), they are to give heed to the "Holy Scriptures" (Rom. 1:2).

Holiness flows from the church's relationship to the Trinity: the "Holy Father" (John 17:11); Christ, the "holy one" (Luke 1:35; also called the "Holy and Righteous One," Acts 3:14; and the "Holy One of God," Mark 1:24), and the "Holy Spirit" (the most frequent title of the third person of the Trinity).

There is no escaping the persuasiveness of the term "holiness." This mark of the church cannot be masked. The church must be holy, reflecting the holiness of God. In sanctification the ministry of the Holy Spirit helps Christians grow in Christlikeness, that is, holiness.[9]

Holiness has little to do with a particular style of dress, how a person combs his or her hair, endless lists of trivial do's and don'ts, self-righteousness, peculiar mannerisms, or unattainable perfection. It has everything to do with one's relationship with God, an ethic based on divine revelation, an inner and outward devotion to God, genuine worship in spirit and truth, and dedication to doing the will of God on earth.

The doctrine of holiness may be approached in numerous ways. One is theological, studying the doctrine of sanctification and its related topics of the Spirit's filling, and our walking or living in the Spirit.

Another way is to study it historically. American Protestantism reflects various branches of religious confession and belief that have their roots in the past. The "holiness movement" is reflected today in the modern charismatic movement as well as among traditional Pentecostals, but its roots go back to the rise of Methodism in England and to the Azusa Street revival of the first decade of the twentieth century. Not all Christian groups who identify themselves with the holiness movement are charismatic. Various denominations espouse perfectionism, the so-called second work of grace, and neo-Pentecostalism, which Peter Wagner calls the "third wave of the Holy Spirit."[10]

Also holiness may be studied experientially. The very use of the term is suspect, but such need not be the case. A proper biblical orientation to the character and ethical dimensions of holiness should serve as both a guide and a guard. Merely claiming to have an experience of the Holy Spirit does not in itself lend credibility to the purported experience. Every area of church doctrine, life, and experience must be brought within the domain of scriptural authority and not authenticated by experience alone.

The study of holiness may also be approached from a combination of the various threads of life and thought under what has come to be called "spirituality." Christian spirituality can be defined simply as life in the Spirit. The devotional life of the church grows out of the roots of pre-Reformation thought, the Reformation, the pietistic movement, quietism, the various evangelical revivals of the eighteenth and nineteenth centuries, and contemporary quests, including the ongoing Keswick movement in England.

With the Wesleys and their "Holy Club" and with George Whitefield,

William Booth, D. L. Moody, R. A. Torrey, A. J. Gordon, A. W. Tozer, and a host of others, modern exponents of holiness reflect a blend of various interpretations and understandings regarding the doctrine of the church. All would agree, however, to the need to give prominence to the person and work of the Holy Spirit.

A Holy Priesthood

The priesthood of believers reflects the two dimensions of life: immediate access to God and service to others. In the believer-priest model, prayer and worship are wed with servanthood and ministry of the Word.

The concept of the believers' church[11] is very evident in Baptist and Anabaptist traditions, Brethrenism, Free churches, and Bible churches. Common threads of conviction include believers' baptism, congregationalism, individual liberty, voluntarism, separation from the world, mission and witness, church discipline, acceptance of a secular government, and denial of priestly or apostolic succession.

Members of this "royal priesthood," to use Peter's designation (1 Pet. 2:9), view the church primarily as a spiritual fellowship ("a holy priesthood," 2:5). Thus godliness, openness to the Spirit's guidance, ministry of the laity, rejection of external creeds and nonsacramental views of the ordinances mark this movement.

Overarching all this is a profound desire to restore the church to apostolic patterns of faith and practice. Again believers differ on how to attain this purity of form and life. Even Martin Luther, who at first resisted separation from the Roman Church, later espoused a form of simple Christian service for the devout, which included meeting devoutly in homes, studying Scripture, baptizing in faith, sharing the Lord's Table, and singing psalms.

Practicing Holiness in the Church

The church consists of a pilgrim people. Its allegiance is to the Lord, whose methods are not of this world. Yet the church's witness is in and to the world. The church seeks to make Jesus Christ known through the lives of believers and by the message of the gospel. Therefore character consistent with the message of truth is paramount.

The church, living in obedience to the Word, works for harmony and unity. Peacemaking is its pattern, unity its goal, and holiness its style.

Holiness is not mysticism, nor does it consist of a thin overlay of behavior on an inherent Pharisaism. Holiness calls for a genuine purity of life, for living in reverence to God (2 Cor. 7:1), obedience to the Word, and perseverance in service. "Train yourself," Paul wrote Timothy, "to be godly" (1 Tim. 4:7).

Weakened by the lack of holiness, many churches are searching in vain for artificial means of doing the Lord's work. Rather than seeking power from secular sources—political, societal, or corporate structures—believers must recognize that power rests ultimately in God and is mediated to the church by Christ its Head, by the Word of God, and through the Holy Spirit.

In 1544 John Calvin delivered a defense of his Reformed ideals before the Holy Roman Emperor Charles V at what is known as the Diet of Speyer. The emperor had convened the gathering to attempt reconciliation between quarreling factions. Here, in part, was Calvin's eloquent defense of spiritual power and true holiness: "Since, therefore, in our churches, God alone is adored in pure form, without superstition, since his goodness, wisdom, power, truth, and other perfections, are there preached more fully than anywhere else, since he is invoked with true faith in the name of Christ, his mercies celebrated with both heart and tongue, and men constantly urged to a simple and sincere obedience; since in short nothing is heard but what tends to promote the sanctification of his name, what cause have those who call themselves Christians to take us up so ill?"[12]

I recall seeing a cartoon in the *New Yorker* years ago. It had only a picture of a rocky island, a lighthouse, and a lighthouse keeper holding an extension cord with a puzzled look on his face, searching the open sea for somewhere to plug it in. That picture describes the contemporary scene quite well. Without spiritual power the church is incapable of reflecting the holiness of God.

6
The Church and Commitment

Having received this preaching and this faith, as I have said, the Church, although scattered in the whole world, carefully preserves it, as if living in one home.

—Irenaeus

SHEILA LARSON SPOKE for a lot of Americans when she described her personal faith: "I believe in God. I'm not a religious fanatic. I can't remember the last time I went to church. My faith has carried me a long way. It's Sheilaism. Just my own little voice."[1] University of California sociologist Robert Bellah included her testimonial in his book *Habits of the Heart* with his own comment that naming one's own religion opens up the possibility of 220,000,000 "faiths."

Early Christians would have had difficulty accepting the "privatism" of Sheila Larson. The Christian church came into existence because of God's intervention in history. Unlike the New Age movement of recent decades, which focuses on divinity within the individual, early Christianity emphasized the historicity of the Incarnation, the Cross, the Resurrection, and the descent of the Holy Spirit. Pentecost, and the church that grew out of it, was a corporate experience.

The multitude of those who believed were not a crowd of self-centered individuals. They were "one in heart and mind" (Acts 4:32). In their commitment to the Lord and each other they even pooled their possessions for the common good of all.

Life in the community of faith involves commitment. This includes obedience to Christ, the faithful observance of His ordinances of baptism and the Lord's Supper, and what the Reformers insisted was a distinguishing mark of the church, namely, discipline.

SALVATION AND THE CHURCH

"Outside the church there is no salvation" Cyprian of Carthage wrote. He also said that a person "cannot have God as his father who has not the church for his mother." These axioms were challenged by the Reformers because they viewed the Church of Rome as an apostate church, incapable of dispensing salvation. The idea of an apostate mother church was too much for Luther, Calvin, and their fellow Reformers.

The Reformers questioned the whole system of mediation of the gospel by the church and the accompanying viewpoints of the primacy of the pope, the powers of bishops and priests, the authority of tradition, the priesthood, and the sacraments. Protestantism, according to Catholic theologian Karl Rahner,[2] concentrated on the definition of the church as a visible reality in the world. This differed from the Catholic view that the church is a mystical body. The church, according to the Reformers, is to announce the gospel of eternal salvation found in Jesus Christ alone. Rather than a priest mediating between God and humankind, Jesus Christ is the Mediator (1 Tim. 2:5).

The certainty of faith lies in inward confirmation by the Holy Spirit. This is "soul-certainty," not "self-certainty." Our theology rests on the Word of God, illuminated by the Spirit of God. Faith in Christ places our salvation completely in God's hands and frees us from anxieties over our eternal destiny. And this certainty of faith frees us to serve others.

The reality of faith rests on the objective reality of Christ's atonement. Jesus Christ is both Reconciler and Redeemer. Justification is by faith alone. Luther said that if we lose this doctrine, we also lose Christ and the church. He saw the doctrine of justification as the summary of all Christian doctrines.

The idea that the church is the means by which individuals achieve salvation is a distortion of the truth. Sharing in the community is the result of salvation, not its cause. The church does not dispense grace; for grace comes from God alone. No amount of human works can achieve salvation. It is God who effects salvation, not the church. "I will not listen to the Church or the Fathers or the apostles," Luther once wrote, "unless they bring and teach the pure Word of God."[3]

Calvin stated that all controversies concerning doctrine in his day related either to the legitimate worship of God or to the ground of salvation. To him, the whole of salvation was attributable to the grace of our Lord Jesus Christ.

Only those who have experienced spiritual rebirth are true members of the church, the body of Christ. To understand the church as a believing people carries with it emphasis on Christian discipleship. To affirm "I am a Christian" starts one on a journey. There is no instant perfection other than the imputed righteousness of Christ. Pilgrims together, we and other believers everywhere in the world are to submit willingly to Christ's headship, the authority of the Word, and the guidance of the Holy Spirit. Fellow saints on the way to heaven, we band together with others of like faith in the fellowship of Christ's suffering, becoming like Him in his death (Phil. 3:10).

CONDITIONS FOR MEMBERSHIP IN THE CHURCH

What are the requirements for membership in the church? I believe there are essentially four: a regenerate heart, a credible confession of faith, voluntary baptism in obedience to Christ, and an exemplary Christian life.

Conversion of sinners is essential to assure a converted membership in the church. For evangelicals this would appear to be the normal way of looking at things. However, after the Edict of Milan (A.D. 313), entire populations were declared Christian, and this blurred the distinctions between believer and unbeliever. In pre-Reformation Europe the concepts of the kingdom, church, and state had merged.

A regenerate membership is essential if the church is to maintain purity. Churches cannot tolerate a two-class membership of the regenerate and unregenerate. While God alone judges the heart, some measure of judgment is necessary to assure that only believers whose sins are forgiven and who in good conscience can give a clear testimony of their faith comprise the church.

Another requirement is the public act of believer's baptism. The Scriptures teach that this is a public confession in obedience to Christ. While baptism is commanded, it must be entered into voluntarily. That is, a person should submit to the waters of baptism by willing assent.

The early church took great pains to explain the meaning of baptism to its catechumens (learners of the catechism). In early times baptism was administered only at Easter and Pentecost so as to ensure a knowledgeable consent to this public act of confessing Christ as Lord and Savior. Appropriate portions of the Bible were to be explained before the ordinance was observed.

In time the church moved from observing the ordinances in compliance with the commands of Christ to a sacramentalism in which the sacraments supposedly bestowed grace and remission of sins. We ought to steer church practices away from abuse and toward a recovery of the original, biblical intent of the ordinances.

Church membership also called for regenerate baptized believers to be walking in fellowship with the Lord, not in deliberate sinful disobedience to the Word.

ORDINANCES OF THE CHURCH

Our Lord commanded His church to perform two ceremonies, or ordinances: baptism and the Lord's Supper. The word *sacrament,* from a root word meaning "sacred," has generally been avoided by Baptists and other evangelicals, whereas many mainline denominational groups use the word. The word *ordinance* comes from the fact that Christ "ordained" these acts of worship. *Sacrament* denotes an act of divine grace.

Christians differ over the meaning of the sacraments or ordinances, although outside of Roman Catholicism, there is agreement on the number. Reformers of the church universally agreed that the Scriptures teach that only two ordinances or sacraments are to be observed in the churches.

Jesus warned against observance of mere traditions, thus making the Word of God of no effect. "You have let go of the commands of God,"

Jesus charged the Pharisees and teachers of the Law, "and are holding on to the traditions of men" (Mark 7:8). We have been warned by Christ not to honor God with our lips while our hearts are far from him. Such worship is labeled "vain" (7:7).

Both ordinances are for believers only. And both are channels of blessing to the church, from God alone. While these gracious acts of obedience reflect the inner grace of God at work, they do not dispense grace as a pharmacist dispenses medicine.

In 1920 the Church of England issued an appeal for unity between the Church of England and other Protestant bodies. Six years later, on May 4, 1926, Baptist churches of England and Ireland gave their reply. Associating themselves with the Anglican Christians in faith, the Baptists nevertheless asserted cardinal doctrines that reflected their differences. In our age of religious pluralism and accompanying relativism of truth, this response may sound to us narrowly sectarian. Such was not the case, since Baptists from the time of John Bunyan onward have rarely polemicized against the Church of England, choosing rather to minister quietly in association with other free, non-state churches. Here, in part, was their response: "Because we hold the Church to be a community of Christian believers, the ordinance of baptism is administered among us to those only who make a personal confession of repentance and faith."[4]

Baptism was commanded by our Lord in His commission of the disciples: "Therefore go and make disciples of all nations, baptizing them in the name of the Father and of the Son and of the Holy Spirit" (Matt. 28:19). Instituted by Christ, baptism is linked in Matthew 28:19–20 to the work of evangelism and teaching. Thus it is not peripheral to the gospel work of the church.

Baptism, as practiced in the early church, reflected the commitment of believers to Christ and to the community of faith.

The mode and meaning of baptism are significantly bound together. The Greek word *baptizō* means "to immerse" in water. Followers of John the Baptist were baptized "in" the Jordan River (Mark 1:5). And in the case of Jesus' baptism by John, words were carefully chosen to explain that He came up "out of" the water. Twice the New Testament refers to baptisms that took place because there was "plenty of water" there (John 3:23; Acts 8:36). In Philip's encounter with the Ethiopian eunuch, they went down into the water and came up out of the water (8:38–39). This clearly implies immersion.

The believer's identity with Christ is best symbolized by immersion. It was in the name of Jesus (Acts 2:38; 8:16; 22:16), and it was symbolic of a burial in death (Col. 2:12; Rom. 6:4). Baptism is also symbolic of cleansing from sin and participation in a new life. By submitting oneself to baptism in full witness of the church, a Christian is saying, "I have believed in Jesus, and I am putting to death the old life and will live the resurrected life of union with Christ." Baptism pictures a cleansing from the past and identification with the new supernatural life in Christ.

Baptism was viewed in New Testament times as symbolic of the inner work of the Holy Spirit in regeneration, a "washing and renewal." Death, burial, and resurrection to newness of life pointed to one's identification with both Christ and His church. As Robert Saucy has pointed out, "One is not united to the Head without at the same time being united with the body."[5]

Baptismal regeneration is held by Roman Catholics and a few Protestant groups but is not supported by Scripture. Since baptism is a symbol of the beginning of life in Christ, it follows that only those who have begun the walk with Christ are to be baptized.

This point is very significant because the New Testament places emphasis on a proper sequence of baptism following conversion (Acts 2:41; 8:12; 10:44–48; 1 Cor. 1:16). To make the rite an act of faith itself is to introduce works into our salvation, which the Bible precludes (Eph. 2:8–9).

Christians who avoid baptism miss a great blessing. They also miss an opportunity to testify to others their identification with Christ. Faith is strengthened both in the life of the believer and in those who witness the event.

Quite aside from the sacramental view of Roman Catholics, some Protestant groups espouse the practice of infant baptism. Lutherans, Methodists, Episcopalians, Presbyterians, and members of many Reformed churches view the baptism of infants of believing parents as a covenantal act. These groups link baptism with the Jewish rite of circumcision as a sign of the covenant community. Citing household conversions, as well as Colossians 2:11–12, they feel they are on good ground to baptize infants. The practice of infant baptism in the churches, however, is a later tradition than that of the New Testament, and we find no direct command in the Bible to baptize infants.

Proponents of infant baptism say that it symbolizes future regeneration of the child and places responsibility on the believing parents to bring up the child in the nurture and admonition of the Lord.

Several arguments speak against the idea of infant baptism. One is that infant baptism was introduced *after* the apostolic period of the church. Furthermore, when proper emphasis is placed on the importance of repentance and faith, the maturity of the one being baptized becomes important. Another point raised is that baptism in one's infancy creates a false sense of security. Paedobaptism (baptism of infants) can lead to an unregenerate church membership, because people may presume they are regenerate when they are not.

The English Baptists, in response to the archbishop of Canterbury's call for union, included reference to children and faith: "In our judgment the baptism of infants incapable of offering a personal confession of faith, subverts the conception of the Church as the fellowship of such believers. We recognize that those concerning whom Jesus said 'Of such is the Kingdom of Heaven' belong to God, and believe that no rite is needed to bring them into relationship with Him. But many of our churches hold services at which infants are presented, and the duties, the privileges and responsibilities of parents emphasized, and the prayers of the Church offered for children and parents."[6] The issue, then, is clearly one of a personal confession of faith. Baptism should follow when a child understands its meaning and the responsibility of church membership.[7]

As a pastor, I have confronted this over the years. People who were baptized as infants have sometimes thought themselves to be Christians, but when confronted with the gospel, these same people come to faith in Christ. They often ask, "Why didn't someone tell me this before, that personal faith in Christ is essential for eternal salvation?"

Proponents of believers' baptism have to face a serious question: When is a child accountable for personal faith in Christ? This is often referred to as the "age of accountability." Baptists and others have faced this but without fixed conclusions. Salvation indeed is of God; He is the ultimate judge. But if the Scriptures issue a clear call to repentance, we must reckon with that as well. It is safe to say that the age of accountability will vary from child to child. So we commit them and ourselves as parents to the mercy of God.

Throughout this discussion I have assumed the value of a committed membership as vital to church health and discipline. I fully acknowledge that there is a current de-emphasis on these issues. In the first days of the church, converts were "added to the church." One might argue for this being a universal body without local or regional responsibility, but there are no grounds for such a view in the Bible. The church, after all, is not a company of the uncommitted.

Fellowship in the body of Christ does not hinge on particular views of baptism. The Christocentric nature of our faith would rule in only one direction. Our fellowship, as John wrote, is with the Father and with His Son (1 John 1:3). Churches, however, should agree to conditions of membership, while also upholding the unity of the body of Christ.

The Lord's Supper

The highest point of Christian worship is the observance of the Lord's Supper or Communion. "This do in remembrance of me," Jesus said. The principal biblical texts which elevate this beautiful service are found in the Gospels (Matt. 26:26–28; Mark 14:22–26; Luke 22:17–20) and in 1 Corinthians 11:23–25.

Attempts by the Reformers to make a complete break from the Mass left their marks on the way Communion is observed today. Luther viewed the observance as a sacrament, while resisting the transubstantiationist view of the Roman Church, which taught that Christ's death is reenacted in the sacrament and that the elements actually become the body and blood of Christ in the taking. Luther's view is known as "consubstantiation," meaning Christ's body and blood is actually *present* in the elements along with the bread and wine. Calvin taught a "spiritual presence" is in the elements. Zwingli and the Anabaptists preferred to view the observance as a memorial act of devotion to Christ in which the elements are viewed as symbols of His death.

On Maundy Thursday, April 13, 1525, in the Grossmünster Cathedral of Zurich, Switzerland, Zwingli and two assistants led a new kind of service. The cathedral was packed. The Mass was abandoned, and in its place an ordinary table was placed in front, with the leaders facing the congregation. Zwingli insisted that the bread be passed while participants remained in their seats. Wine was passed to everyone in simple wooden chalices to avoid the appearance of pomp.

Though the observance was limited to four times a year, this revolutionary action by Zwingli altered the landscape of the Reformation. This memorial view of the ordinance prevails in most evangelical churches today.

Primarily, the Lord's Supper symbolizes the Lord's death. In the taking of bread we remember His body given for us: "Take, eat: this is my body" (Matt. 26:26, KJV). Christ is not present in the bread, for He gave His life only once on the cross. He cannot be sacrificed again and again, as the Mass portrays nor do we literally eat His flesh and drink His blood: Furthermore, the whole substance of the bread cannot be translated into the real body of Jesus, validated by a consecrated priest. We are incapable of reenacting the incarnation of our Lord. "Unlike the other high priests, he does not need to offer sacrifices day after day, first for his own sins, and then for the sins of the people. He sacrificed for their sins once for all when he offered himself" (Heb. 7:27).

Furthermore, the Lord's Supper allows believers to give thanks for Christ's gracious sacrifice on the cross. The word *Eucharist* comes from a Greek word that simply means "thanksgiving." Our ultimate gratitude for our Lord's gift of grace is shown when we partake of the elements of bread and wine at the Lord's Table. Also our participation affirms the unity we share in Christ. One of the words for the service is "Communion." The table is the Lord's Table, not the property of any one church. Each time we observe the Lord's Supper, we make a bold statement to the world that we are one in Christ. "Because there is one loaf," Paul wrote, "we, who are many, are one body, for we all partake of the one loaf" (1 Cor. 10:17).

In taking communion, Christians participate in the blessings of salvation. Though Christ is not present in the elements, there is a sense of His presence among the faithful. Communion thus gives the church a great opportunity to worship God and to give thanks for the gift of salvation.

The bread and wine signify the Lord's death on our behalf. His death on the cross, He said, is the basis of the New Covenant (Mark 14:24). By perpetuating the remembrance of Christ's death, the church dramatically recalls the past while declaring a present reality. The potency and vitality of a past act are carried over into the life and experience of the present. In remembering our Lord, the vitality and worship of the church is continually renewed. Commemoration is a compellingly vivid act. We need not settle for mere formality or perfunctory service to God. Paul's use of the word "participation" in 1 Corinthians 10:16–17 places the proper emphasis on the spiritual meaning of the Lord's Supper.

Furthermore the observance of the Lord's Table is a precursor of our future feast with our Lord in heaven (see Matt. 22:1–14; Mark 14:25; Luke 14:24; Rev. 19:9).

CONFESSION OF SIN

The confession of sin is a necessary condition for receiving divine forgiveness. This is true for sinner and saint alike. We are all guilty sinners, and our merciful heavenly Father extends His mercy and forgiveness to us.

At the end of the Middle Ages, sacramental confession was firmly in place in Christendom.[8] Every Christian who had reached the age of discretion was required to confess at least once a year. Later, Christians were required to confess during the season of Lent, during times of peril or imminent death, before the Eucharist, and before the Mass. Pointing to John 20:22–23, the medieval church claimed that Jesus Himself instituted the sacrament of confession and penance. Confessing one's sins to a priest became essential for reconciliation with God. In penance a person was also to carry out deeds of contrition, such as giving money or land, making a pilgrimage, or reciting "Hail Marys." Absolution by a priest was necessary when a Christian engaged properly in confession. "Let the confession be simple, humble, pure, faithful, and frequent, unadorned, discreet, willing, ashamed, whole, secret, tearful, prompt, strong, and re-proachful, and showing readiness to obey."[9]

This pithy statement with its sixteen conditions or qualities of confession became standard motivational fare for sacramental confession, which came to be a comprehensive and organized system of social control. It affirmed a priest's dominance and the church's authority in discipline, and it ensured guilt as the means of perpetuating penance. No wonder the Reformers objected! They viewed sacramental confession as a means of torment rather than consolation for the sinner. Attacking hypocritical contrition, Luther called for more than "gallows sorrow," the kind of confession engaged in by a thief facing execution. He said that absolution comes from God alone, even when a minister of the gospel announces forgiveness in Jesus' name.

Protestant Reformers of the sixteenth century did not agree on what kinds of discipline should replace sacramental confession and penance. However, Luther and Calvin retained the practice of private confession of sin as essential to church discipline. Zwingli and the Anabaptists viewed obligatory confession of sins to a priest as useless. Confusion still remains today in the church as to the place of confession.

Reformers chose the doctrine of Christian liberty to effect transformation in people's lives. Justification of sinners by faith was the dominant teaching in their abandonment of sacramental confession. It is faith that merits forgiveness, not the works of penance. In light of the consoling truth that God forgives sin and sinners, believers are to be sensitive both to the consequences of sin and the consolation of grace (James 5:16).

But is there room for private or public confession in the church? Doesn't the Bible teach we are to confess our sins to God and our faults to each other? The common notion that a Protestant does not confess is faulty.

Today our churches are missing an important dimension of discipline—godly sorrow that leads to confession of sin and repentance (2 Cor 7:10). Peter wrote of purification by obeying the truth (1 Pet. 1:22), and John wrote of our hope that purifies us (1 John 3:3). Confession of sin is the only antidote for the pride of Christians who claim they have no sin (1:8–10).

Unfortunately the word *sin* is outdated today. Yet its various forms remain—racial oppression, injustice, alienation, manipulation, selfishness, moral corruption, deception, pride. These are symptoms of a cancer of the soul. The only way to enjoy the remedy for sin is not to deny the disease, but to confess it. Salvation is available only to those who acknowledge (confess) their need as sinners. Our sins involve us in guilt, forgiveness is offered to us by God, and confession is necessary to receive divine forgiveness.[10]

The words of John Stott are helpful: "God is willing to forgive sinners through Christ. We must forgive one another. The Church has absolute authority to forgive and to restore to its fellowship those who have offended against it and been suspended, but have subsequently repented and confessed their sin. We need to demonstrate the forgiveness of God to a world burdened with guilt, and to a world torn by bitter animosities the way in which the disciples of Jesus are taught to forgive one another. We need more faith in the promises of God to rejoice in divine forgiveness; more love for each other to rejoice in human forgiveness."[11]

The church is a fellowship of the rescued and the rescuing. We are all in the same boat, sinners who have been rescued by divine grace, liberated in Christ to rescue others, even wayward fellow believers. Confession of sin ought to be part of our Christian privilege and duty.

THE COMMUNION OF THE SAINTS

One of the compelling concepts of the church is the doctrine of the communion of the saints. The Apostles' Creed included this designation as a platform of belief. Earlier we looked at Christian fellowship in light of the marks of a true church. The reality of a common bond in Christ between Christians regardless of race, gender, or class should be an obvious mark of the church. But the *koinōnia*, unique to the essence of the body of Christ, is more than a binding element. It carries with it responsibility and accountability. The fellowship of the saints should corporately display our unity in Christ and our accountability both to the Word and to other believers. "For none of us lives to himself alone," wrote Paul, "and none of us dies to himself alone" (Rom. 14:7).

The weak and the strong are together in the bonds of love. We must do all we can for mutual edification (14:19), making every effort to do what leads to peace within the fellowship. "We who are strong ought to bear with the failings of the weak and not to please ourselves. Each of us should please his neighbor for his good, to build him up. For even Christ did not please himself" (15:1–3). Our oneness in Christ forms the basis of church unity, which manifests itself in fellowship and love. True caring flows from this unique communion. It cannot be contrived. It is born of God, for "whoever lives in love lives in God, and God in him" (1 John 4:16).

The Scriptures clearly spell out the obligatory dimensions of this communion. The following are some of the obligations God has given to believers:

- do not judge others (Matt. 7:1 Rom. 14:13)

- carry each other's burdens (Gal. 6:2)

- edify one another (1 Thess. 5:11; 1 Cor. 14:4–5)

- rescue the wayward (James 5:19–20)

- confess sins to those we have offended (James 5:16)

- pray for the sick (5:15)

- do good to all, especially other believers (Gal. 6:10)

- work for unity (2 Cor. 13:11)

- be hospitable to others, including strangers (Heb. 13:2)

- spur one another toward love and good deeds (10:24)

- be faithful in meeting together with other believers (10:25)

- support ministers of the gospel (Gal. 6:6)

- generously give to others in need (1 Cor. 16:1–2; 2 Cor. 8:1–15)

- rejoice with those who rejoice (Rom. 12:15)

- mourn with those who mourn (12:15)

- serve others (Matt. 20:26)

- look out for the interests of others (Phil. 2:4).

Having received God's grace in salvation, believers in turn are to be gracious in every respect toward others, bearing the fruit of the Spirit and thus preserving the unity of the body.

DISCIPLINE WITHIN THE CHURCH

Early theologians were obsessed with concern for the purity of the church, often a missing dimension today. Emphasis on evangelical expansionism has replaced ethical and moral purity in the church. The nature and essence of God Himself, not human rules, set the standard for purity and discipline.

Why do many people not accept the gospel? Often it is because of the undisciplined, sinful lives of professing Christians. While there is no perfect church, or for that matter no perfect saint, the church is responsible to maintain a pure testimony.

While the church is a great missionary agency in the world reaching out to sinners, it must not forget that it is first of all an assembly of the saints. We dare not mix faith with unbelief, truth with error, or for that matter, believers with unbelievers in the membership of local churches. "Do not be yoked together with unbelievers. For what do righteousness and wickedness have in common? Or what fellowship can light have with darkness? What harmony is there between Christ and Belial? What does a believer have in common with an unbeliever? What agreement is there between the temple of God and idols? For we are the temple of the living God. As God has said: 'I will live with them and walk among them, and I will be their God, and they will be my people. Therefore come out from them and be separate'" (2 Cor. 6:14–17).

Seriousness of Sin in the Church

All sin is sin against God. When purity of life and doctrine are disregarded, discipline must be exercised, as painful as it may be. In Paul's travels he often faced disorderly congregations. Not every congregation he planted flourished. In the Corinthian church, for example, he faced the following disorders: schism (1 Cor. 1:10–17; 3:1–9), spiritual arrogance (4:18–21), incest and immorality (5:1–13), Christians taking other believers to court (6:1–11), sexual impurity (6:12–20), abuse of Christian freedom (8:1–13), abuse of the Lord's Supper (chapters 10–11), abuse of gender (11:1–16), disorder in the exercise of spiritual gifts (chapters 12–14), misunderstandings about the Resurrection (chapter 15), easy acceptance of false teachers (2 Cor. 11:1–15), quarreling and unrepentant sinners in the church (12:20–21), and rejection of apostolic authority (13:1–10). This is a formidable list of problems in only one church! Are churches today much different?

Purposes of Church Discipline

Only two purposes exist for church discipline: to expose sin and to restore the sinner. In the face of an unrepentant believer, dismissal from the local church may be necessary. Within the history of the church such dismissal has been called excommunication. Before such drastic action is taken, however, every effort must be made in love to restore the sinner to the fellowship. Membership in the local church is a privilege, not a human right. Thus every measure needs to be taken to respect privacy laws, laws that govern defamation of character, and any other civil, state, or federal laws governing discrimination. Submission to governing authorities, both within and outside the church, is to be the norm.

The need for proper church discipline is taught in numerous passages: Matthew 18:15–18; Romans 16:17; 1 Corinthians 5:2, 9–13; 2 Corinthians 2:5–11; 2 Thessalonians 3:6, 14–15; Titus 3:10–11. The right to exercise discipline is given only by authority of the Word. At the very least, the unrepentant sinner is forbidden to participate in the Lord's Supper and at the extreme, excommunication is declared. The latter should rarely be exercised in view of the patience, kindness, and mercy of God. We are to bear others' sins and burdens, that is, to forbear them as our Lord has shown patience toward our own sins. Such radical action as giving one over to Satan in order to save the soul (1 Cor. 5:5; 1 Tim. 1:20) was done only by apostles, and is not considered part of regular discipline today.[12]

Self-centered clashes of the human will, pride on the part of both ministers and congregations, and human pettiness often color church discipline efforts. Instead the meekness and gentleness of Christ must govern all disciplinary actions. "For though we live in the world, we do not wage war as the world does" (2 Cor. 10:3). We all live under the judgment of God.

THE CHURCH AND THE STATE

It may be thought somewhat odd that a chapter on commitment includes a discussion on the church's relationship to the state. After all, our commitment is to Christ and His Word alone. Such commitment binds believers together under the overarching will of God. However, the words of Jesus must be considered: "Give to Caesar what is Caesar's, and to God what is God's" (Matt. 22:21). Here Jesus was speaking about paying taxes, a duty the apostle Paul also clearly taught: "If you owe taxes, pay taxes; if revenue, then revenue; if respect, then respect; if honor, then honor" (Rom. 13:7).

Today, however, the issue of separation of state and church is a much broader issue than the simple duty of paying taxes and meeting our financial obligations. It extends to everything from the use of tax money, to the support of religion, to taking up arms in war.

State-enforced religion is common in Muslim, Hindu, and Buddhist nations. Under state-sponsored atheism, communist countries denied the basic right of freedom of religion to Christians and adherents of other religions, which is still true in China and Cuba. In the Middle Ages Roman Catholics linked up with the state. Even today, state-sponsored religion is prevalent in many countries, favoring either Protestantism, Orthodoxy, or Roman Catholicism. This, however, is disappearing as secularism takes over.

Is it right for Christians to persuade governments to make laws consistent with biblical standards of morality? This is entirely acceptable so long as the laws do not favor one religious body over another. However Jesus did teach us to pray, "Your will be done on earth," (Matt. 6:10). Paul urged Timothy to make requests, prayers, and intercession for everyone, especially kings and all those in authority, that we might live "peaceful and quiet lives in all godliness" (1 Tim. 2:1–2).

Several principles should be noted (1) Christ's kingdom is not of this world (John 18:36); (2) the weapons of our spiritual warfare are not carnal (2 Cor. 10:4); (3) civil governments are ordained by God to maintain order and to punish evil (Rom. 13:1–7); (4) faith, including matters of internal church doctrine, cannot be forced by governmental power; (5) and each sphere—church and state—must respect the other's sphere of authority. Dominion theology or theonomy—the view that God's laws are to be adopted by the state in a kind of restored theocracy—is to be rejected.[13] The same is also true of abuse of civil or governmental power requiring religious conformity or abridging freedom of worship.

By exercising restraint in the present world, Christians can nevertheless do what godly prophets have always done. We are free, like them, to denounce paganism, unbelief, immorality, and all abuses of God's law. Our method should be persuasion, not coercion by law.

A sober fact of history is that Christian faith has survived under all forms of human government, but when granted special favors, the church's testimony is weakened. The health of true religion does not depend on any power other than that exercised by God. Recognizing that God's power is greater than all human powers liberates the church to live and witness resurrection power through the message of the Cross (1 Cor. 1:18–25).

The knowledge that God and God alone works in everything has tremendous significance for our faith. This fundamental platform of Luther's ruled his theology. God is present everywhere, among our enemies and in creation. He has created everything and rules everything. "We should therefore fear and trust only in God and most certainly believe that nothing can destroy us; for God is Lord of all the powers that threaten us," wrote Luther. "We are in his gracious hand, no matter what happens. This is the believer's royal freedom and joy."[14]

Luther's views on the separation of powers created in time a conquering church. State-church Lutheranism persists today in various degrees throughout Scandinavia and in Germany. Opposed by Anabaptists and Zwingli, Luther's replacement of Roman power with a purged government prompted continued struggle. Calvin also sought to wed the spiritual and secular kingdoms in the city of Geneva. Throughout the centuries following the Reformation, the tides and crosscurrents of ideas have tended to enforce a separation of the secular from the spiritual. As a result some Christians have been attracted by quietism, a seventeenth-century teaching that minimized human activity, sublimated the human will and responsibility, and stressed withdrawal from worldly affairs. However, this practice never received a wide following. Molinos of Spain, its chief proponent, was branded a heretic in November 1687 by Pope Innocent XI. The writings of Madame Guyon, François Fénelon, Brother Lawrence, and others continue to draw followers. The two worlds in which we live— Caesar's and God's—call for engagement rather than withdrawal. Holding all things in balance, believers must resolve the seeming polarities and forge a world-view that places God's kingdom above all kingdoms, while still recognizing the realities of human governmental authority.

A committed Christian cannot afford to withdraw from the real world.

7
The Church and Its Ministry and Organization

The long painful history of the Church is the history of people ever and again tempted to choose power over love, control over the cross, being a leader over being led. Those who resisted this temptation to the end and thereby give us hope are the true saints.

—Henri Nouwen

THE NEW TESTAMENT gives evidence of an organized church. Like any developing institution, the church reflected the dynamism and spark of a revolution. This was not a revolution in the usual sense of total disruption, for Christianity, when it emerged, blended with its Jewish setting. However, as resistance to the message of the Cross grew in intensity, the new shape of an incendiary fellowship developed. Under apostolic care and direction, organization emerged in response to necessity. This point must not be missed. From the vantage point of two thousand years later, it may seem easy for us to define the organizational structures of the early church in tidy ways. Though that organization was far from tidy, patterns arose immediately after Pentecost.

In the light of early Christian expansion, believers devoted themselves to the apostles' teaching or doctrine (Acts 2:42). In this regard the apostles played a central role in organizing the meetings of believers. Such gatherings were marked by an intense fellowship and bonding with one another around a core of Christian truth. The faith of the expanding church was far from static; it fairly vibrated with life and vitality.

Overwhelmed by duties of oversight, the apostles appointed elders in each church and in every city where the gospel spread (14:23). These stewards of the faithful were to keep watch over the flock. Paul declared that their designation as overseers was by appointment of the Holy Spirit (20:28).

Earlier and out of necessity, the twelve apostles had gathered the disciples together (a term now used to describe all followers of Christ) and said, "It would not be right for us to neglect the ministry of the word of God in order to wait on tables. Brothers, choose seven men from among you who are known to be full of the Spirit and wisdom. We will turn this responsibility over to them and will give our attention to prayer and the ministry of the Word" (6:2–4).

Other evidences of organization became obvious as the number of disciples grew in number. Christianity became more than a spontaneous happening. It evidenced an orderly pattern and yet gave indication of great flexibility, something that is missing today in some church circles. The leaders apparently knew the number of converts (2:41; 4:4). They organized smaller groups for fellowship, Bible study, and prayer, and believers shared meals together, practiced the ordinances of baptism and the Lord's Supper, and gathered money for communal and compassionate causes (2:42-47).

Organization in the apostolic period was ministry-driven. That is, only such organization emerged as was necessary to help fulfill Christ's commission and to provide compassionate care for and instruction of the flock. This is a key principle. Later the status of officers in the church became fixed. The Pastoral Epistles reflect the growth of the organizational aspects of the church.

AN ORDERLY FAITH

The Pauline dictum "Let all things be done decently and in order" (1 Cor. 14:40) became an overarching principle for first-century Christianity. It is also an apt word for all times. Rather than fitting the faith to the organization, organization was established to fit the faith.

Church elders and deacons could be found wherever Christianity took root. Specific mention is made of overseers and deacons in Philippians 1:1, thus raising a question over the legitimacy of an episcopacy. Clarifying the meaning of terms can help straighten out misunderstandings about titles and numbers of officers in the church. From the clear record of the Pastoral Epistles we discover the qualifications and general duties of these officers. Furthermore the nature and function of ministry emerged from Pentecost onward. Issues that are divisive today were also faced early on. Ordination, exercise of spiritual gifts, the role of women in ministry, forms of governance, church discipline, and membership were issues encountered in the early years of the church.

The Protestant Reformation brought a radical new way of looking at the church. It shifted emphasis from sacramental relationships to the Word of God. Thus Scripture, not tradition, was to govern all church organization. It was desirable that in church organization uniformity should prevail. In time this visible unity was supposedly secured by an "established" religion. Dissenters from this view, however, established "free" churches separate from state-church religion. Thus various patterns of organization have been passed down to us. Honed by dissent, revivalism, and just plain pragmatism, church organization today reflects considerable diversity. Where the Scriptures do not clearly spell out organizational patterns, it is perhaps wise to dogmatize less and respect diversity more than is commonly practiced. Our tendency is to become sectarian, but emphasis on the unity of the church should draw Christian groups together rather than divide them over organizational matters. This unity should be based on genuine Christian principles, not on a quest for ecumenical union.

CHURCH MEMBERSHIP

Some Christian groups shun the idea of specific membership in local churches. They prefer to place attention solely on membership in the invisible or universal church that is assured by personal faith in Jesus Christ. Some groups of this persuasion do not even insist on water baptism. They would prefer to accept a membership in the body that is known only to God.

The bulk of Christian churches, however, maintain that membership in a local church is vital to assure the purity of the faith and discipline.

In the accounts of early conversions, the language indicates that people were "added" to the church (Acts 2:41, 47; 5:14). While one may argue that this "addition" was to an invisible body, the fact is that there was also a visible unity of believers who met together. Believers were not to forsake the assembly of Christians (Heb. 10:25). On the first day of the week believers met to break bread (Acts 20:7). In Paul's instructions regarding orderly exercise of spiritual gifts in the church he wrote, "So if the whole church comes together . . . if an unbeliever or someone who does not understand comes in . . ." (1 Cor. 14:23–24). This indicates more than a vague "spiritual" or invisible gathering of believers. These words indicate a gathering in a designated place.

Furthermore, it appears from the case of the Corinthian church member caught in an incestuous relationship (1 Cor. 5) that churches were able to exercise some control over wayward individuals. First Corinthians 11:18–20 also refers to believers coming together in one place to observe the Lord's Supper. In the New Testament, "church" meant a visible group of believers banded together in Christ, subject to the disciplines of the Word of God, the rebuke and correction of elders, and the encouragement of other Christians. Church membership obligates the local church as a whole to minister to its members, and it obligates each member to serve the whole.

The central issue of membership is that a "qualified" membership is taught in the Bible. Some would argue for an open membership to allow seekers to feel comfortable. Their motivation is noteworthy so far as the comfortable part of it goes, but this practice invites a mixed multitude of regenerate and unregenerate persons. As noted in the previous chapter, regeneration is an absolute requirement for church membership. Paul's Corinthian letters focus clearly on church membership, consisting of "those sanctified in Christ Jesus and called to be holy, together with all those everywhere who call on the name of our Lord Jesus Christ—their Lord and ours" (1 Cor. 1:2). At Ephesus and Philippi, believers were called "saints" (Eph. 1:1; Phil. 1:1). Colossian Christians were addressed as "holy and faithful brothers" (Col. 1:2), and Peter wrote to the "elect" (1 Pet. 1:1) and to "those who through the righteousness of our God and Savior Jesus Christ have received a faith as precious as ours" (2 Pet. 1:1). The epistles to the Thessalonian church uniformly referred to "the church of the

Thessalonians in God the Father and the Lord Jesus Christ" (1 Thess. 1:1; 2 Thess. 1:1). Those in the believing body of the faithful at Rome were addressed as ones "loved by God and called to be saints" (Rom. 1:7). Clearly members of these churches were believers.

A genuine fraternal (brotherly and sisterly) love is implied in the New Testament church. Even the letters to the seven churches of Asia (Rev. 2–3) reflect a standard of membership which, when violated, incurred the rebuke of our Lord. In these letters, calls for repentance were made to the unfaithful, the lukewarm, and the apostate within the church.

Membership in the New Testament church was exclusively for "baptized" believers (see chapter 6). The ordinance or rite of baptism as a requirement for local church membership is substantiated in the New Testament. In Romans 6:4, Paul taught that a believer's union with Christ through participation in his death and resurrection is pictured by the ordinance of baptism.

Infant baptism is a practice dating from the third century, although its proponents feel that it was assumed from the earliest of times. To make this assumption, they link the practice to household conversions and to viewing infant baptism as Christian circumcision. However, as noted in the previous chapter, infant baptism is not mentioned in the New Testament.

Baptism is not necessary for salvation. To say that it is essential is to deny that we are justified by faith alone. Just as circumcision was not viewed by Christians as necessary for salvation (Gal. 5:1–12), so baptism is not viewed that way either. The example of the dying thief whom Jesus promised would be with Him in paradise (Luke 23:43) refutes those who insist on baptism as essential to salvation. He could not have been baptized, but he was saved.

Those who point to Mark 16:16 as proof of baptismal regeneration ignore the fact that this ending to Mark is not found in the earliest and best Greek manuscripts. In any case this verse, "Whoever believes and is baptized will be saved, but whoever does not believe will be condemned," does not say people were condemned because they were not baptized. It is meant rather as a general statement linking baptism close to the act of believing.

When one is baptized on confession of faith in Jesus Christ, he or she joins a distinguished crowd of converts—the three thousand at Pentecost

(Acts 2:41), Samaritan believers (8:12), the first African convert (8:38), and Cornelius (10:48). In the New Testament it was simply a matter of fact that baptized believers were added to the church. These references and the importance of baptism show that church organization in the New Testament called for membership in the local church.

TYPES OF GOVERNANCE IN THE CHURCH

Churches have historically chosen different kinds of governance. Because practices vary and the Bible does not require one form, we cannot be overly dogmatic as to which type is biblical and which is not. Certainly in administering governance, churches may err and even reflect corruption. The Reformers pointed this out in the sixteenth century. Each form of church government has strengths and weaknesses, though, as discussed later, I think congregationalism is to be preferred. Of course, when it is unclear in the Bible what particular model of governance should be chosen, we do well to allow differences of persuasion.[1]

Episcopalian

The Episcopalian system in Protestantism—which is most common in Anglican circles, Methodism, and to some degree among Lutherans, Assemblies of God, and other groups—emphasizes the role of the bishop. The system is not directly found in the New Testament, although some groups have found it beneficial in establishing order in the churches. Government by bishops is also present in Roman Catholicism and the Greek Orthodox Church.

The word is derived from the Greek term *episkopos*, meaning "overseer," and the word *episcopal* is an Anglo-Saxon form of the Latin *episcopus*. Bishops appoint other bishops and ordain priests (presbyters) and deacons. Episcopalians differ over the apostolic succession of bishops. Methodists, for instance, have a bishopric form but do not believe in direct apostolic succession.

Proponents of episcopalian forms of government point to the central role James played in Jerusalem. He gained prominence as the presiding leader of the church at the Jerusalem Council mentioned in Acts 15. Paul recognized him as an apostle and a pillar in the church (Gal. 1:19; 2:9). Returning from Europe, Paul went straight to a meeting with James and all the elders in Jerusalem (Acts 21:17–18). No doubt James was a central figure in the church at Jerusalem.

Within this form of government, bishops are considered the chief pastors of the church. Together with the priests and deacons within their own spheres of influence, they embody the unity of the church. Their responsibilities include ordaining local-church leaders and consecrating churches. After the Reformation the title "bishop" was maintained by Lutheran churches in Denmark, Norway, Sweden, Finland, and Romania. Not all these churches, however, claim apostolic succession of bishops.

Central to the episcopacy is the concept of succession of office. However, the absence in the New Testament of explicit instructions on succession speaks against the episcopal form of government. In our Lord's commissioning of the apostles He gave no instruction about apostolic succession (Mark 3:14–19).

History reveals no clear succession of bishops, or in the Roman Catholic tradition, of popes. Luther pointed this out in his own polemic against the Roman Church.

The episcopalian form fails to account adequately for the priesthood of all believers. This is perhaps its chief weakness. Dependent on a clerical form of ministry, laity may assist in ministry but may never fully engage in the New Testament ideal of every believer using spiritual gifts for the work of ministry (Eph. 4:12).

Presbyterianism

Presbyterianism bases its governance style on elder rule, which stems from the Greek word *presbyteros*, "elder." The present-day Presbyterian pattern involves a hierarchy of four interrelated bodies: the session, the presbytery, synods, and the general assembly. The session is usually composed of ministers and lay elders who are the elected representatives of a congregation. The presbytery consists of ministers and representative elders from a prescribed region overseeing sessions, ministers, and congregations. The synod represents a larger geographic area and includes the presbyteries. The synod serves as a court of appeal in church matters. The general assembly, the church's highest court of appeal, is responsible for the denomination's mission. Elected officials to this body generally meet annually. Within each of these four levels, ministers and elders have equal voting privileges.

Elder rule was based originally on John Calvin's concepts of church organization. He said the church has four offices—pastors, elders, teachers, and deacons—and he based this representative style of Presbyterianism on Romans 12:8; 1 Corinthians 12:28; and 1 Timothy 5:17.

The only Presbyterian state church is the Church of Scotland, although Presbyterian churches are found around the world in great strength, particularly in Hungary, Northern Ireland, Korea, and Switzerland. In the United States, Presbyterians are divided into a number of groups, the largest body being the United Presbyterian Church, which became the Presbyterian Church (USA) in 1983.

Proponents of the Presbyterian form of government point to its orderliness, allowance for limited local church autonomy, its confessional strength, and its insistence on high qualifications for ministers. However, Presbyterian churches may vary considerably in doctrine. Ministers are elected by the congregation and are thus subject to its discipline, as is any member of the church. Ordination of ministers enables them to carry on in a full-time manner what trained laypersons can do only part-time.

The Scriptures include no evidence in support of a church authority over several local bodies of believers.[2] Theologian Louis Berkhof, a proponent of Presbyterianism, recognizes this fact. He wrote, "Scripture does not contain an explicit command to the effect that the local churches of a district must form an organic union. Neither does it furnish us with an example of such a union. In fact, it represents the local churches as individual entities without any external bond of union."[3] Autonomy was evident in the selection of deacons (Acts 6:3–5) and in exercising church discipline (1 Cor. 5:5; 2 Thess. 3:6, 14–15). While Paul, Barnabas, and Titus apparently appointed elders (Acts 14:23; Titus 1:5), there is no scriptural support for a hierarchical form of ordination. Individual exceptions in later church history may have related to pioneer church-planting efforts where congregations had not yet matured in the faith and where outside appointment was necessary.

Nowhere in the New Testament do we have elders exercising authority over churches beyond a local assembly. The council called in Jerusalem included apostles and elders, but this was probably an exception. The "whole church" decided to choose some of their own leaders to go with Paul and Barnabas to Antioch (Acts 15:22) to deliver a letter to Gentile believers. While *apostles* had authority over all churches, there does not appear to be any precedence of *elders* governing beyond their own local congregations.

Critics of Presbyterianism point to its failure to enforce evangelical doctrine because of its somewhat remote and cumbersome style of debate and discussion at the general assembly level without lay representation. This alone, however, need not disqualify Presbyterianism. These churches have given the world some of the finest evangelical leaders of this century.

Congregationalism

Congregationalism is a form of governance based on the independence and autonomy of the local church. All members of the church, being believers, are viewed as "priests of God." Congregationalism "represents the earliest form of Church order."[4] Congregationalists claim only Jesus Christ as Head and place emphasis on a democratic form of governance by the people of God.

Congregationalism as practiced after the Reformation has evidenced several patterns that may differ from New Testament patterns. In certain churches, such as in Ephesus, there may have been a plurality of elders. Baptists and other Congregationalists view the titles of bishop, pastor, and elder as referring to the same office. Generally a single elder or pastor is selected in congregational churches, although in recent practice, churches have tended to expand church staffs to include several pastors or elders. In such cases there is usually a "senior pastor" who assumes leadership over other leaders.

Pure Congregationalism is rarely practiced. In this system, every decision is brought to the congregation for action.

Some newer congregations claim to have no form of church government. Investigation, however, shows that leaders in such cases are evident either by self-appointment or by common congregational agreement and appointment to preach and teach the Word.

Criticism of Congregationalism usually centers around the abuse of independence to the neglect of broader church unity. Also leaders without accountability to the larger body of Christian churches may exercise authoritarian power without adequate checks and balances. Usually churches with this type of government form associations of churches, and those associations set general standards for ordination and missionary appointment.

Congregationalism, while practiced by many independent groups, is represented as a denomination in the present United Church of Christ, which was formed in 1957, and in the Conservative Christian Congregational Churches. Throughout history, separatist congregations have emerged within national church bodies, administering the ordinances and preaching the Word. Most of these tend to be congregational in polity. Many of these resist denominational labels, choosing to remain completely independent from other local congregations.

BIBLICAL DISTINCTION OF OFFICE

The preaching of the Bible, service to believers, and obedience to Christ the Head are essential to the work of the church. Thus we must look at the biblical teachings about office and officers in the church in light of foundational principles. The church does not exist for its leaders; leaders exist to fulfill the purposes of the church.

The New Testament stresses two central themes that form the basis of church office. One is inward and the other outward—service to the body of believers and outreach to the world. The first theme is seen in the essential unity of the church from Acts 2:1 onward. The care and feeding of the flock were inward ministries. The second theme is implied in the wording used in the selection of Judas's successor: "For one of these must become a witness with us of his resurrection" (1:22). The situation in the developing church, however, was far from static. It was dynamic and fluid.

In a real sense every office mentioned, from deacons in Acts 6:3 to apostles, prophets, evangelists, pastors, and teachers in Ephesians 4:11, reflected a kind of functional diversity. Deacons, from the example of Philip and Stephen, served not only within the church but also as evangelists outside the church. It is proper to refer to the "church gathered" and the "church scattered" as one and the same.

Paul outlined the purposes of church offices as follows: "To prepare God's people for works of service, so that the body of Christ may be built up until we all reach unity in the faith and in the knowledge of the Son of God and become mature, attaining to the whole measure of Christ" (Eph. 4:12–13). In three verses the first offices mentioned are apostles and prophets (1 Cor. 12:28; Eph. 2:20; 4:11). They were the original guarantors of the revelation of the mystery of the church. Furthermore they were noted as foundational to the church (Eph. 2:20). I believe the Scriptures teach that these two offices are not to be perpetuated in the church. However, their functions are to continue, as seen in the meaning of the words: Apostles were messengers or "sent ones," and so are we; and prophets were proclaimers of the gospel ("forth telling" rather than "foretelling").

It is not crystal clear whether the leaders mentioned were offices or whether they were functions in which the leaders used their spiritual gifts without having an officially appointed status. These could have been merely examples of gifts given without designation of ecclesiastical office. Yet even if they were only specific gifts, we know from the biblical record that certain individuals fulfilled these functions and were undoubtedly recognized in the churches.

Elders, Pastors, and Overseers

Bible scholars have generally agreed that there are but two offices in the church, elders (or pastors/overseers) and deacons. In the first of these, however, there is some confusion of titles. As a designation, the term *elder* was interchangeable with *pastor* and *overseer*, the latter also sometimes being called *bishop*. Generally this first designation is of leaders who were appointed to keep watch over the souls of church members (Heb. 13:7). In the New Testament we see a pattern of churches governed by elders

(Acts 20:28; Heb. 13:17; 1 Pet. 5:2–3). These elders were undershepherds of the flock, sometimes called pastors or pastor-teachers (Eph. 4:11). The English word *pastor* comes from a Latin word meaning "one who cares for sheep." We recall Jesus' words to Peter in John 21:15–17: "Feed my lambs"; "Take care of my sheep"; "Feed my sheep." Peter later wrote to fellow elders, "Be shepherds of God's flock" (1 Pet. 5:2). While the word *pastor* is used only once (Eph. 4:11), it seems interchangeable with the term *overseer* (Acts 20:28) and *elder* (20:17). In the Pastoral Epistles Paul uses the term *overseer* to refer to the same function as a pastor (1 Tim. 3:1–2; 5:17). In a similar fashion Paul instructed Titus to appoint *elders* (Titus 1:5), but in 1:7 he referred to these same individuals as *overseers* (or *bishops*, 1:7). The idea of a bishop having responsibility for several churches dates from the second century and was not in the New Testament documents.

Elders have three general duties as outlined in the New Testament: managerial or administrative, pastoral, and instructional. They were to "rule" the church, according to 1 Timothy 3:5; 5:17; Titus 1:7; Hebrews 13:7, 17, 24. The word *rule* means "to stand before" or "to take care." This clearly does not mean "lording it over" the church (1 Pet. 5:3). Elders also were to be caregivers. This is the shepherding or pastoral function of the elder. This entailed exhorting, admonishing, helping the weak, encouraging the timid, and disciplining the erring with tenderness. Also elders were to teach (1 Tim. 3:2). Here we see a linkage between Ephesians 4:11 and the Pastoral Epistles. Placing the terms *pastor* and *teacher* after one Greek article (as in Eph. 4:11) denotes a single office or function. "Those who set their heart on being an elder desire a noble task" (1 Tim. 3:1), which carries immense responsibility for leading, caring for, and feeding a body of believers.

The seriousness of the office is revealed in the imposing combined list of requirements in 1 Timothy 3:1–7 and Titus 1:6–9:

- above reproach, blameless, upright, holy

- husband of one wife[5]

- temperate, not quick-tempered

- self-controlled

- respectable, not overbearing

- hospitable

- able to teach, able to encourage others, able to refute those who oppose sound doctrine

- not given to drunkenness, not given to much wine

- not violent

- gentle

- not quarrelsome

- not a lover of money, not pursuing dishonest gain

- able to manage his own family well; a man whose children believe and behave

- not a recent convert

- one who loves what is good

- of good reputation with outsiders.[6]

Deacons

The office of deacon emerged from the church problem described in Acts 6. Grecian Jews complained against Hebraic Jews because their widows were being overlooked in the daily distribution of food (6:1). In response the Twelve gathered all the disciples (here implied as all members of the church), and they approved a proposal to select seven qualified servants (from the Greek word *diakoneō*, "to serve"). The Twelve prayed and laid hands on them, implying an official appointment to service.

The wisdom of this proposal was evidenced by the result: "So the word of God spread. The number of disciples in Jerusalem increased rapidly" (6:7).

In the Pastoral Epistles the office of deacon is specifically mentioned (1 Tim. 3:8–13) with appropriate duties and requirements. In addition, as stated in Acts 6:3, deacons were to be full of the Spirit and wisdom. First Timothy 3:8 and 12 states that they were "to be men worthy of respect" and husbands "of one wife." Bible scholars disagree on whether women were appointed as deaconesses. Some prefer to translate *diakonos* in Romans 16:1 as "servant" and not "deacon" or "deaconess."

As for specific duties, deacons may have had considerable latitude in the early church. They apparently had some ruling duties, perhaps financial, as well as caregiving (1 Tim. 3:8, 12). Deacons and their wives were viewed as serving together, as implied in 1 Timothy 3:11. It is noteworthy that this teaching did not extend to the wives of elders, although the same truth may apply. The requirements of a deacon listed by Paul in 1 Timothy 3:8–13 are as follows:

- worthy of respect

- sincere

- not indulging in much wine

- not pursuing dishonest gain

- able to hold the deep truths of the faith in clear conscience

- experienced ("they must first be tested")

- husband of one wife

- able to manage his children and household well.[7]

Deacons who serve well gain "an excellent standing and great assurance in their faith in Christ Jesus" (3:13). My own experience bears this out. Deacons I have known, notably my own father, were good people in the right use of the term. In my travels I have met deacons within Anglicanism and nearly every other form of church government who command great respect for their servanthood. A godly deacon in Hong Kong, who single-handedly convinced the English government to create rooftop schools for refugees from mainland China in the 1950s and 1960s, taught me much about the grace of humble servanthood. In his declining years he reflected the godly radiance of one on the threshold of receiving great reward for fulfilling the servant role of a deacon.

It is wrong to suggest that deacons need not be as highly qualified as elders. Deacons are not second-class citizens, compared with first-class elders. Nor, for that matter, are missionaries and evangelists, who may also qualify as officers but who are rarely considered as such. As long as we keep Christ central, observe servant attitudes, and adhere tenaciously to the truth, matching character with competence, the church will remain strong.

CHURCH AND THE MINISTRY

In 1973 I met a young Marine who had been wounded in Vietnam. Without knowing I was a minister he told me of his faith in Christ. When I asked him what he planned to do when he got out of military service, he replied, "I may go into psychiatry, but then again I may go into the ministry." This comment led to a healthy discussion of the word *ministry.*

What is the ministry? Is it a calling and a profession? Or is it a term used for a common life of service shared by all believers? To answer these and related questions we must first return to a definition of the church. The *ekklēsia* is aptly named because it calls everyone out and assembles them together under the headship of Jesus Christ. "The church," as Karl Barth correctly wrote, "is the community instituted by God himself, the community of faith and obedience living from the Word of God, the community of the faith and obedience of sinful men."[8]

The Reformers rejected a hierarchical or monarchical form of the church and recovered the doctrine of the priesthood of all believers. Not all, however, accepted a radical view of ministry which denied the existence of priests or special ministers. Both Calvin and Luther accepted the special calling of ministers in churches but also affirmed a general priesthood of all believers. Luther put it best when he wrote, "The priesthood means: we stand before God, pray for others, intercede with and sacrifice ourselves to God and proclaim the Word to one another."[9] Such a universal priesthood points to the collective service or ministry of all the saints.

Every believer participates in the full ministry of Christ because every believer is a priest. Ministry as a unique, sacramental, professional, or leadership "caste" is to be rejected. By the third century the church had moved worlds away from the ideals of the New Testament. Instead of being a community of saved servants, it became a community of clerical authorities.

The Reformers rejected *clericalism,* meaning they objected to the church being ruled by a separate class of clergy. They also rejected the dualism of lay and clergy, one being secular and the other spiritual. Christian tailors, cobblers, stonemasons, carpenters, innkeepers—these bold Reformers taught—have all been consecrated like priests for the work of ministry. They viewed vocations as callings as much as a separate priesthood. The Puritans carried the idea to an even greater extent. A shepherd in keeping sheep, a judge in giving sentence, a magistrate in ruling, or a preacher in preaching—each represents a good work before God.

Ministry, then, needs to be defined if it is to incorporate both a general and a special calling. Six affirmations may be useful.

CONCEPTS OF MINISTRY

1. All Christians without exception are called to the ministry. It is not the privilege of an elite corps of "holy" people, although elders and deacons are mentioned in the New Testament.

2. Spiritual gifts determine ministry of the congregation.

3. All ministry, regardless of its diversity, is based on servanthood.

4. Ministry has its source in the pattern of Jesus Christ Himself.

5. Ministry in the church rests on the ministry already fulfilled by Jesus Christ in His incarnation, sacrificial death on the cross, and triumphant resurrection.

6. By recognition of gift, some individuals may be "ordained" to a more full-time exercise of their gifts and be worthy of church support.

Geoffrey Bromiley, respected church historian and Anglican scholar, has written a succinct description of ministry. "This serving of Jesus and fellowmen is not restricted in the New Testament to any one group, for example, the twelve disciples within the first community of believers. All Christians may not be called to minister in the same way, so that we need not be surprised if a special commission and task of ministry are assigned to particular men. Yet all those who are associated with Jesus are equally called to serve Him and their fellows according to their differing opportunities and capacities. The women minister to the wants of Jesus no less than the disciples."[10]

While a special responsibility was originally placed on the apostles with their special commissioning (Mark 3:13–19), different men and women within the body of Christ are called to fulfill different functions. The whole body is called and committed to ministry. Bromiley concluded that we corrupt the ministry by focusing on certain ministers of the gospel. "The ministry instituted by Christ and fulfilled in the New Testament church is not what we popularly describe as 'the ministry' today, and we pervert the whole conception if we isolate certain aspects or functions of ministry and regard them as if they were the whole. The ministry instituted by Christ is . . . discharged in the power of the Holy Spirit in and through His people according to their varying endowments and opportunities. It is the ministry of the church."[11]

Requirements for Ministry

The Scriptures set forth general qualifications for ministry. They are essentially few in number, though all-encompassing in magnitude. Elders and deacons were not appointed at random, as noted earlier, nor is ministry a right to be claimed. It is a privilege to be discharged in obedience to Christ and His Word.

The first requirement for ministry is identification with the cross of Christ. This is the principle of Luke 9:23: "If anyone would come after me," Jesus said, "he must deny himself and take up his cross daily and follow me."

Elevating self above the Savior is a current heretical practice of many believers. The self-affirmation movement has run its destructive course. While self-preservation is instinctive, self-aggrandizement is sin. Self-esteem is normal and healthy, but self-love is detrimental to the spiritual life. The self must come under God's gracious and liberating governance. "No one can serve two masters" (Matt. 6:24).

Those who know God but do not know themselves in relationship to God become proud. On the other hand, those who despair of themselves and do not know God end in hopelessness. Only when a believer views himself in relationship to the loving rule of God can he or she experience true freedom. Jesus taught, "Whoever finds his life will lose it, and whoever loses his life for my sake will find it" (Matt. 10:39). These words inspired Jim Elliot, the Christian martyr, to write in his journal, "He is no fool who gives up that which he cannot keep to gain that which he cannot lose."

The Cross calls for denial—not gain; for humility—not arrogant pride. To those who are perishing, the message of the Cross is utter foolishness, but to those who are saved, it is the power of God (1 Cor. 1:18). When we identify with the Cross in ministry, we throw in our lot with all those whom the world counts as losers.

In the fourteenth century godly monk Thomas à Kempis wrote these convicting words about the Cross: "All desire to rejoice with him, few are willing to endure anything for him. Many follow Jesus into the breaking of bread, but few to the drinking of the cup of his passion. Many reverence his miracles, few follow the ignominy of the cross. Many love Jesus so long as adversities do not happen. Many praise and bless him, so long as they receive comforts from him; But if Jesus [should] hide himself and leave them but a little while, they fall either into complaining, or into too much dejection of mind."[12]

Few today are scandalized by the Cross. We have domesticated it, obscured its message in the church, and reduced it to an architectural artifact or a piece of jewelry. To Thomas à Kempis, however, it meant everything. "In the cross is salvation, in the cross is life, in the cross is protection from our enemies, in the cross is infusion of heavenly sweetness, in the cross is strength of mind, in the cross is joy of spirit, in the cross is the height of virtue, in the cross is the perfection of sanctity."[13]

In the Incarnation, in which God condescended to our level, we have the supreme example of humble ministry. No one can deny that the life and death of Christ were one great offering of unselfishness.

Christ's call to ministry is not so much by appointment as by association. Our identification with Christ and the Cross in discipleship comprises our credentials for service.

A second requirement for ministry is a close walk with God. Cultivation of the spiritual life is one of the highest activities of the Christian. No quest for the inner experience of devotion to God should ignore the ultimate dimension of the Father-child relationship. True spirituality involves aligning our human will with the will of the Father. Jesus exemplified this devotion to the Father: "For I have come down from heaven not to do my will but to do the will of him who sent me" (John 6:38). By example and in deep humility, Jesus prayed in Gethsemane, "My Father, if it is possible, may this cup be taken from me. Yet not as I will, but as you will" (Matt. 26:39).

Growing in Christ implies many things, but fundamentally it means doing God's will. "Do not be foolish," Paul wrote the Ephesian church, "but understand what the Lord's will is" (Eph. 5:17). This verse is immediately explained by adding the requirement to be "filled with the Spirit" (5:18).

The spiritual life is nothing more or less than life in the Spirit, which is a life of faith. We are to live by faith and not by sight (2 Cor. 5:7). Our service is to be according to the faith given us (Rom. 12:3, 6). We are to exercise faith in the Giver of faith, not faith in faith itself. In his closing benediction the writer to the Hebrews longed for believers to be equipped with everything good for doing his [God's] will (Heb. 13:21). I take this to mean full exercise of the gifts of Christ received by faith.

To minister effectively we must lead lives of prayer and dependence on God. We are to "pray continually" (1 Thess. 5:17). Prayer is a sacred expression reflecting the inner serenity of the soul. Prayer for the Christian and the church is not merely one more technique in an arsenal of human endeavor. It is the heart and soul of ministry. Effective prayer reflects the intimate and trustful approach to God modeled and taught by our Lord. Prayer is drawing near to God. How good of our God to invite us to pray![14]

A close walk with God seeks to bring glory to God. Johann Sebastian Bach took his music and his theology seriously. The abbreviations found at the beginning and end of many of his manuscripts indicate a deep personal faith in God: "J. J." at the beginning meant *Jesu Juva* ("Jesus, help us") and "S. D. G." at the end meant *Soli Deo Gloria* ("To God alone be glory"). This humble servant understood the essential nature of Christian ministry: bringing glory to God. All our service for Christ is to be done to magnify Him. "To him be glory in the church," prayed the apostle Paul (Eph. 3:21).

On August 27, 1531, Martin Luther preached a sermon from the parish church at Wittenberg on 2 Corinthians 3:5, "Not that we are competent to claim anything for ourselves, but our competence comes from God." Luther claimed there were only two kinds of ministers—those who qualify themselves and those who are qualified by God. Our sufficiency is from God, therefore, and we are to honor His name in every act of service.

A third requirement for ministry is compassion and caring. Again, we take our cue from Christ. From His announced messianic mission recorded in Luke 4:18–19, to His final words on the cross, Jesus modeled this essential requirement of ministry. Preaching good news to the poor and proclaiming freedom for prisoners, recovery of sight for the blind, release for the oppressed, and forgiveness to His executioners were only part of Christ's ministry on earth. Jesus, who wept at the tomb of a friend and cried over a city, revealed His compassionate heart, compassion that ought to characterize every believer as well.

The phrase "cure of souls" has historically been used to apply to the Christian ministry. Jesus' healing ministry, which touched the soul, mind, and body, exemplifies His work as the Good Shepherd. As His undershepherds we, too, are to display compassion and care for people's souls.

Our Lord taught, "Be merciful, just as your Father is merciful" (Luke 6:36). Quoting Hosea 6:6, Jesus defended His actions on the Sabbath by explaining the essential requirement of ministry: "I desire mercy, not sacrifice" (Matt. 12:7). This quality of mercy should be obvious and visible in our work of ministry.

A caring ministry includes carrying others' burdens, thus fulfilling the law of Christ (Gal. 6:2). Since the church possesses the "keys," or message of divine forgiveness, this spiritual requirement of ministry should be broadly applied. No priest has power to forgive or to cure the soul. This is the work of the church in Jesus' name.

On December 4, 1655, Richard Baxter, the Puritan minister at

Kidderminster, England, published *The Reformed Pastor*. This enduring classic explained his vision of a renewed ministry. Ahead of his time, he saw the need of pastoral counseling in churches. The care and comfort of souls was his primary concern. He held strong convictions that churches should not grow beyond the capacity of pastors and leaders to oversee the flock. Richard Halverson, former chaplain of the U.S. Senate, whose own fruitful ministry at the Fourth Presbyterian Church, Washington, D.C., was centered on care and nurturing, called Baxter's work a welcome, wholesome prescription for the contemporary church. "The love of God," Halverson wrote in the introduction to the 1982 edition of *The Reformed Pastor*, "is characterized by a longing for the eternal welfare of every living soul."[15]

Ordination to the Ministry

Ordination denotes installation in office by the laying on of hands. The English word *ordain* may be traced to the Latin *ordo*, "order." The practice is accepted by almost all churches. It represents recognition of a special call to ministry in contrast to a general call to salvation and to ministry applicable to every member of a church. Ordination is a human rite in recognition of a divine call. As such, it finds precedence in Scripture, but it is not essential for the work of the gospel.

Early in the church, laying on of hands accompanied baptism and symbolized the bestowal of the Holy Spirit. Though such a practice has now disappeared, its biblical roots are found in Acts 8:17.

Ordination for ministry finds its biblical roots in the word *commit* in Acts 14:23, which states that Paul and Barnabas committed elders to the Lord's service. Some form of ordination or commissioning is mentioned six times in Acts: the choosing of deacons (6:1–6), the Samaritan baptism case (8:17), the conversion of Saul (9:17), the commissioning of Paul and Barnabas (13:2–3), the appointing of elders in churches in Asia Minor (14:23), and the ordination of Ephesian believers (19:6). The Pastoral Epistles refer to the act in 1 Timothy 4:15; 5:22; and 2 Timothy 1:6. Those who see a special conveyance of grace (sacramentalism) in the act find little support except from tradition. Unbiblical, hierarchical patterns are unfortunately often perpetuated by ordination, so churches must take great care. Christian ministry requires competent leadership, but not an unbalanced clericalism.

Ultimate authority in the church resides with Christ. Even if a church ordains its leaders, it must understand that authority to minister is not limited to a select few. Shared authority is always to be in the spirit of *diakonia*, "service."[16] It is possible to view ordination quite properly and with historical precedents as an act of commissioning without conveying the idea of apostolic succession or designated authority.

8
The Church and Worship

You have made us for yourself, and our hearts are restless till they find their rest in you.

—Augustine

See to it that you be the worshiper which you persuade your learners to be.
—Richard Baxter

N○ SINGLE WORD in the vocabulary of evangelicals divides generations more than *worship*. What was intended to be a foremost spiritual activity of the church now separates people. We have even segmented our services of worship to God. One form of service we call "traditional," and the other we label "contemporary." Depending on where one sits in the pew, one style of worship is viewed as irrelevant.

English novelist Samuel Butler once wrote that a *definition* is "the enclosing of a wilderness of an idea within a wall of words."[1] *Worship* is one of those words that qualifies as a wilderness yet untamed.

As long as Christians focus on the style of worship, there will be misunderstandings, division, and little common ground for communication. When Jesus confronted the Samaritan woman at the well, He gave her the required focus and parameter of worship: "God is spirit, and his worshipers must worship in spirit and in truth" (John 4:24). The style is peripheral to spirit and truth.

Currently the worship of many congregations stands at an uncertain crossroad. Are we to stick with tradition? If so, which tradition? Or are we to adopt a contemporary style? Again, which contemporary style or styles? Or do we blend both old and new? Through all the current debate is it possible to regain a central focus? Is it too idealistic to hope for a recovery of the prophet Isaiah's vision and worship experience: "I saw the Lord seated on a throne, high and exalted, and the train of his robe filled the temple" (Isa. 6:1)? Or is it hopelessly archaic to recover in our worship the words of David, quoted by Peter at Pentecost, "I saw the Lord always before me" (see Ps. 16:8; Acts 2:25)?

CONFUSION IN THE CHURCH

Confusion over worship clusters around the words *style* and *substance*. Our world is shaped more by the first than by the second. Advertising and marketing appeal to what people want and like. The whole point of marketing is to discover a need and to fill it by shaping people's wants and wishes. Advertising creates cravings. It molds our preferences into ostensible necessities, compelling us to buy more products.

Worship, however, is not a product to be advertised or marketed. It is the supreme activity of the redeemed, intended to bring glory to God. It is to be God-focused rather than person-centered or, to use a term currently in vogue, "user-friendly."

Purpose of Worship

The purpose of worship is to bring glory to God. *Worship*, from an Anglo-Saxon word meaning "worthship," is essentially ascribing "worth" to God, that is, acknowledging that He is worthy of our adoration. It is our human response to the presence of God among His people. Worship, the corporate responsibility of the entire church, involves a cluster of attitudes and activities designed to help us focus and concentrate on God. In the "ritual" of worship we are not engaged in meaningless and repetitive patterns of religious duty. Instead, ritual in the right sense incorporates artistic and aesthetic freedoms (within the boundaries of biblical truth) that encourage us to worship with heartfelt devotion.

Today the dogma of worship relates much less to truth than to form and style. "These people honor me with their lips," Jesus charged the formalists of his day, "but their hearts are far from me. They worship me in vain; their teachings are but rules taught by men" (Matt. 15:8–9). Even churches today that pride themselves on creative freedom in worship reflect patterned ritual in their style, without recognizing its traps.

The simple truth is that God alone is to be worshiped. Jesus confronted the devil with strong words: "Worship the Lord your God, and serve him only" (4:10). Only at that point did Satan leave Him. A clear focus on God in our worship will afford no room for the tempter. Worship is one-directional—Godward. Worship in the house of God is where we are to get in touch with God—not ourselves. In fact, God is *seeking* worshipers (John 4:23).

It may be difficult for some evangelicals to accept the fact that the goal of a church is the adoration and worship of God. Mission-driven and success-oriented, some would even claim that a worship emphasis is detrimental to church growth. They contend that the church service must not offend outsiders to the faith. Those who hold to the view that a service of worship must be "seeker sensitive" view the worship service as outreach, not primarily as a service for the saints. The old motto, "Enter to worship; depart to serve," may be trite and somewhat dated, but it speaks worlds to the purpose of Christian gatherings. If our worship is missing or off target, then our service is futile and fruitless. Paul's question to the Galatian church should be asked by every minister or worship leader: "Am I trying to please men? If I were still trying to please men, I would not be a servant of Christ" (Gal. 1:10).

To give glory to God is to believe in Him and to regard Him as the only wise, righteous, merciful, and almighty God. It means acknowledging Him as the only Source and Donor of every good and perfect gift. "Worshiping God," Luther believed, "is nothing else than glorifying God,"[2] and glorifying God is to be the chief aim of Christians.

Loss of Transcendence

Loss of the sacred in our churches is serious. In our therapeutic society, emphasis on ourselves and how we feel has often replaced genuine worship of God. True worship, however, has little to do with us; it has everything to do with our great God and Lord. Worship is for His benefit and not ours. It is to magnify and bring glory to Him, not us. Self-focused worship blurs the distinction between the lofty Creator and us, His humble creation. Worship of our lofty God fulfills our humanity, which in salvation has been made new in Christ. But sharing in His divine life does not make God our casual friend. Knowing that God is with us and indwells us is no invitation to overlay a lofty God with a thin layer of popular culture in hopes of making worship palatable to unbelievers.

Form and Style

Not everyone agrees on what worship should look like in a Christian church. Yet for many, worship involves a blending of silence, prayer, praise, music, confession, adoration, and the proclamation of the Word. For an increasing number of evangelicals, it is a free-flowing collage of celebration, drama, praise, and preaching, all in a spirit of outward joy.

Edmund Clowney wrote about this current confusion: "For centuries, nothing was more fixed in Christendom than the form of worship. Priests recited the Latin Mass to uncomprehending parishioners assembled to receive the body of Christ. Today, nothing seems fixed: the varied styles of Christian worship reflect the patchwork of world cultures and the kaleidoscope tastes of current entertainment. The church of your choice is the church that styles its worship to your beat. Evangelism drives change, wishing to make services 'seeker friendly,' yet it can clash with the desire to make worship more participative, and strangers may demur at the handclapping exuberance of incantational choruses."[3]

This well states the present-day confusion over what constitutes biblical worship.

THE CENTRAL ELEMENTS OF WORSHIP

Worship is a spiritual activity. It is a Christian response to knowing God. It involves both a quest and a rest; silence and outward expression; attitude as much as action. To try to codify a liturgy from the New Testament is unsuccessful. But the New Testament does reveal a number of facts about the worship of the early church.

We learn from Acts 2 that believers in Jerusalem continued to meet in the temple courts (2:46). For a time at least, worship in the synagogues and in the temple constituted Christian church worship. From the beginning the reading and exposition of the Scriptures were key parts of Christian worship. To these activities were added observance of the *agapē* love feast and the Lord's Supper. Praise and singing were also prominent. Sunday, the day of resurrection, was the day of their highest acts of worship (Acts 20:7; 1 Cor. 16:2). The observance of the Lord's Supper also included acts of giving. William Maxwell, in his outline of Christian worship, cites seven elements with scriptural support to illustrate what a worship service may have included in the early church.

1. Scripture lessons (1 Tim. 4:13; 1 Thess. 5:27; Col. 4:16)

2. Psalms and hymns (1 Cor. 14:26; Eph. 5:19; Col. 3:16)

3. Common prayers (Acts 2:42; 1 Tim. 2:1–2)

4. People's amens (1 Cor. 14:16)

5. A sermon or exposition (1 Cor. 14:26; Acts 20:7)

6. A confession of faith (1 Cor. 15:1–4; 1 Tim. 6:12)

7. Almsgiving (1 Cor. 16:1–2; 2 Cor. 9:10–13; Rom. 15:26)[4]

All of these would have come from worship patterns in the synagogues. To these forms or elements of worship we may add the following:

1. Celebration of the Lord's Supper (1 Cor. 10:16; 11:23)

2. Prayers of consecration and thanksgiving (Luke 22:19; 1 Cor. 11:23–26; 14:16; 1 Tim. 2:1)

3. Singing songs and hymns unique to the apostolic faith (Phil. 2:6–11; 1 Tim. 3:16;)

4. The kiss of peace (Rom. 16:16; 1 Cor. 16:20)

Over the centuries, layers of tradition have been added to these elements of worship. From the late first century came the *Sanctus*, "Holy, Holy, Holy, Lord of Hosts, every creature is full of Thy glory." Later, formal salutations or greetings and prayers were added, as well as the observance of Easter and special days commemorating martyrs. Responses such as "Lord, have mercy" appeared by the third or fourth centuries. Even a church order attributed to Hippolytus of Egypt in the third century became a standard form with translations into Latin, Coptic, and Arabic. The fluid rites of the primitive church eventually rigidified into set rituals and liturgical forms with terms foreign to many evangelicals—collects, lections, antiphonals, and secrets (prayers and responses inherited from the period of Roman persecution). East and West developed their own traditions, many of which persist today in Orthodox and Roman Catholic circles.

The Reformers changed many but not all of the worship forms of their day. The Mass became a service in the common language of the people (vernacular) rather than Latin. Vestments were abandoned, images of the saints were destroyed, and new music forms became common. Luther, Zwingli, and Calvin all agreed on the central role of the Word in worship, but, as noted earlier, they differed on whether the Lord's Supper represented a memorial service or a means of grace. In some instances radical groups abandoned music in their churches and substituted antiphonal recitations of psalms. By the end of the sixteenth century, however, congregational songs were introduced.

In Scotland and England the *Forms of Prayers* and the *Book of Common Prayer* became accepted guides to worship. Separatists and Puritans each developed their own forms of service. Each innovation tended to come from honest attempts to do justice both to biblical essentials and revered tradition. The rise of eighteenth- and nineteenth-century evangelicalism, certain sects, and separatists, marked a departure in form.

The Great Awakening and revivalism influenced evangelical churches by introducing gospel singing, emotional response, testimonials, and altar calls. Many churches have now abandoned tradition in favor of entertainment, extended praise singing (often while standing for long periods), and lengthy preaching or teaching. Public use of the Bible in some instances is disappearing, with the preacher narrating the text for the audience in the sermon.

At the same time, there appears to be a countermovement akin to the Oxford Movement of nineteenth-century England. Some call this present-day phenomenon a new catholicity. Disenchantment with the free-form worship of independents and parachurch movements has led some to turn to Eastern Orthodoxy, Anglicanism, or the mysticism of Romanism. These efforts tend to reflect a desire to recover a worship style and form separate from the world. They reveal a conscious need for inner purity and less concern over a seemingly outdated formalism.

What common elements of Christian worship can serve as foundations of biblical worship? Are there shared attitudes and actions in worship that may serve to unite rather than divide? I think so. True worship, in whatever form—word, song, prayer, response, silence—must ascribe worth to God.

Ministry of the Word

In true worship the Bible will be prominent. From as early as the third century, believers stood in reverence while the Scriptures were read. Furthermore they sang many of the psalms. Both the reading and singing of the Scripture were seen as essential elements in worship. In a worshiping congregation the Bible will be preached. While there were powerful examples of preaching in the Middle Ages, it was only after the Reformation that the pulpit recovered its prominence in worship. Even architecturally, the centered pulpit, which began to appear after the sixteenth century, silently stressed the power of the Word of God.

Preaching is part of worship because God addresses His people through the Word. Paul charged Timothy, "In the presence of God and of Christ Jesus, who will judge the living and the dead, and in view of his appearing and his kingdom, I give you this charge: Preach the Word; be prepared in season and out of season; correct, rebuke and encourage—with great patience and careful instruction" (2 Tim. 4:1–2).

"The world needs still to be told of its Saviour," explained Charles Haddon Spurgeon in a lecture on preaching, "and of the way to reach him."[5]

The Bible teaches that we are not to despise the preaching of Christ and the Cross (1 Cor. 1:18–25; 9:16). If preachers believe that people today only need to hear about how to succeed in the corporate world, how to have fit bodies, better marriages, beautifully behaved children, and more romantic sex, they are wrong! As ambassadors of Christ, preachers are called on to address life-and-death issues, questions of the human soul and of human destiny. In worship the role of preaching is not to play to the galleries, so to speak, but to be faithful to Christ and His Word.

Some people today say because the church is irrelevant, we should give people what they want to hear. Above all, they would say, steer clear of doctrine and theology. After all, a generation scared away from church by dullness has the right to set its own agenda for entrance back into the pews.

All this sounds appealing. Admittedly, dullness has left its trail of destruction. The flip side, however, is that the church's primary call is to be faithful to Christ and His Word. This is precisely what the apostle Paul had in mind when he warned Timothy about people who ignore biblical preaching. "To suit their own desires, they will gather around them a great number of teachers to say what their itching ears want to hear" (2 Tim. 4:3).

Confession and Profession

Public Christian worship is in itself a powerful confessional statement of faith in God. Worship involves confession of two kinds—acknowledgment of sin and acknowledgment of God and His divine revelation of truth.

All true confession of sin by the believer is to be made to God, as David acknowledged in Psalm 51:1–6: "Have mercy on me, O God, according to your unfailing love; according to your great compassion blot out my transgressions. Wash away all my iniquity and cleanse me from my sin. For I know my transgressions, and my sin is always before me. Against you, you only, have I sinned and done what is evil in your sight, so that you are proved right when you speak and justified when you judge. Surely I was sinful at birth, sinful from the time my mother conceived me. Surely you desire truth in the inner parts; you teach me wisdom in the inmost place."

Confession is essential for abiding continuously in Christ. The Word calls us to repentance and faith, and thus confession should always follow as a response to the Word. This is what it means to "walk in the light" (1 John 1:7).

160

A proper time for confession of sin is before serving the Lord's Supper. The Scriptures teach that believers are to examine themselves as they come to the table of our Lord (1 Cor. 11:28, 31). In services where the Ten Commandments are recited (a disappearing habit), it is only natural that confession from the heart be given to God, detailing one's sin or sins (1 John 1:9). The whole point of confession in worship is to ask for cleansing and then to forsake the sin. God gives His grace to overcome, and He gives His divine forgiveness to remit or remove judgment of sin.

We dare not presume on the mercy of God. Right relationships with God, our neighbors, and our brothers and sisters in Christ call for confession of sin (James 5:16).

The second and most significant type of confession is acknowledgment of Christ as Lord: "No one can say, 'Jesus is Lord,' except by the Holy Spirit" (1 Cor. 12:3). The Greek word *homologeō* means "to promise, confess, declare or praise." The word *confess* is most often used in the Bible to refer to public and open confession. For example, Paul made a good confession before Felix (Acts 24:10–16). In doing so, he kept his conscience clear before God and man.

In a confession of faith one recognizes that it is God alone who has provided salvation through Jesus Christ. It seems certain that an early confessional formula is behind Romans 10:9–10: "That if you confess with your mouth, 'Jesus is Lord,' and believe in your heart that God raised him from the dead, you will be saved. For it is with your heart that you believe and are justified, and it is with your mouth that you confess and are saved." Furthermore, the believer confesses God through acts of service (2 Cor. 9:13). Timothy made a "good confession" before "many witnesses" (1 Tim. 6:12). Jesus is our model in His own "good confession" before Pilate (6:13). Paul referred to every tongue confessing Jesus as Lord (Phil. 2:11).

Room should be made in the worship service for this form of confession. It usually comes in reciting a creed. The Apostles' Creed, still used in many worship services, was one of the earliest doctrinal formulations surrounding the simple confession "Jesus is Lord." In Hebrews 13:15 the link between offering "a sacrifice of praise" to God and confession is very significant. Praise and confession are called the fruit of our lips.

Confession of faith usually accompanies the public service of baptism.

This too is an act of worship. We should not minimize the importance of open declaration of church beliefs and personal faith in Christ as Lord.

Offering

In worship the *offering* takes on double meaning: giving ourselves to God and giving money for the assistance of others. The first is clear from the gift of life by our Lord on the cross. The "collection" for the saints is a tangible, ongoing act of sacrifice that embodies the grace gift of Calvary, as well as compassionate service to the poor and needy (Rom. 15:27–29; 1 Cor. 16:1–4; 2 Cor. 8:1–15). Jesus warned against ostentatious acts of giving and taught that the sincere motive of the heart is what counts. Greed and possessiveness are two vices to avoid (Luke 12:13–21). In the spiritual act of giving, believers worship the Lord and, as a result, become "rich toward God" (12:21).

Prayer

Prayer is an essential part of worship. When Jesus overturned the tables of the moneychangers in the temple, He quoted Isaiah 56:7: "My house will be called a house of prayer" (Matt. 21:13). Synagogues were also places of prayer (Acts 16:13), and in the early church they were gathering places for the preaching and teaching of the gospel (18:7, 11; 19:8–10). Eventually believers met in homes. It was to a home where people were gathered in prayer that Peter went when he was miraculously released from prison (2:12–13).

After the Reformation, ministerial prayers in the common language of the people became part of the worship service. Dissent from state-church liturgies led to separatists forming small groups for prayer. Prayer, both within the church service of worship and outside the Lord's Day circle of the faithful, became common.

Patterns for praying have come to us from our Lord Himself, who regularly prayed to the Father, taught His disciples to pray, and poured out His heart in prayer in the Garden before His arrest, trial, and crucifixion. Early believers regularly prayed together and the Epistles exhort us to pray. Prayer is to be no peripheral exercise voiced out of mere habit.

The prayer that Jesus taught His disciples serves as a model for Christian worship. The Gospels record two accounts of the Lord's Prayer, one in Matthew 6:9–13 and the other in Luke 11:2–4. In the Matthew account the Lord's Prayer was given in contrast to ostentatious and empty prayer. In Luke the prayer was given by our Lord in response to the disciples' request "teach us to pray." Jesus' prayer habits were known to His followers (Luke 3:21; 6:12; 9:18). Perhaps because of the differences in how the prayer is presented by the Gospel authors, we should have the freedom to use the Lord's Prayer either as a general guide or as a prayer to be repeated in exact form.

The Lord's Prayer was apparently used in early church worship, for it appeared in the second-century *Didache*. Early church fathers referred to it as a model, and believers considered the prayer so sacred that only members of the church could repeat it. Today its use is disappearing in independent evangelical churches, but it is retained in the more traditional worship services of various mainline denominations.

This prayer is to be distinguished from the prayer our Lord prayed on the way to the Garden of Gethsemane (John 17). Some scholars, however, see similar ties in theological content in both prayers: the glorification of the Father, Jesus' work on earth, the name of God, and the petition to be kept from evil. These, however, may simply reflect the patterns of prayer engaged in by our Lord whenever He prayed.

Paul's instruction to Timothy detailed types of prayers—requests, prayers, intercession, and thanksgiving (1 Tim. 2:1). Prayer in worship is not to be limited to petitions for the faithful; it should be made on behalf of all in authority. And we must pray for the salvation of the lost: "This is good, and pleases God our Savior, who wants all men to be saved and to come to a knowledge of the truth" (2:3–4).

Today in evangelicalism some of the greatest impetus to pray often comes from parachurch efforts of groups with loose organizational affiliations. Interchurch efforts through what some are calling "Concerts of Prayer" unite believers across denominational lines. In some churches formal services of prayer, praise, and intercession are disappearing. On the other hand, praise-group leaders often intersperse prayers in their singing, making prayer seem quite natural. There is always the danger of trivializing prayer by too much repetition, by poorly framed expression, or by the failure to acknowledge that all prayer is to God through Jesus Christ, the only Mediator (1 Tim. 2:5). There is still a place for well-considered expressions of prayer from the pulpit which address our exalted God, who commands respect and awe. A study of the many prayers in the Bible reveals that they are more than a jumble of words thought up at the moment. They often reflected great theological depth.

In corporate worship the leader may be the one praying aloud, but he is praying on behalf of the people of God, and this is a corporate experience.

Several types of prayer may be used in public worship. One is *adoration*. This kind of prayer expresses wonder and gives objectivity to our worship. "Great is your name, O Lord," is a sample of adoration to our lofty omnipotent God.

Thanksgiving prayer is another type. Thanksgiving for our redemption should always be the climax of this kind of prayer.

Intercessory prayers lift us from our personal concerns to those of others. Petitions for our nation, world leaders, all in authority, and those in need may form the structure of this kind of praying.

Confessional prayers are often general in nature. Petitions for pardon, mercy, and divine forgiveness are essential parts of this kind of public prayer. Prayer, in reality, is itself a confession of faith in the God who forgives and grants pardon for sinners. It is a confession of dependence on God.

Whatever the style and wherever the setting, prayer from the heart should have a prominent place in worship.[6]

Music

Music, which played such a prominent role in Israelite history, also has a place in Christian worship. The fact that Psalms, the longest book of the Bible, is a songbook is impressive. The "Psalter," as it has come to be known, has played a vital role in the worship of the saints. The singing of psalms is mentioned in Colossians 3:16 and Ephesians 5:19. In the Western church the earliest Latin Psalters were translated from the Septuagint. By the seventh century they were common. In the Eastern church the psalms have continuously been used. Early forms were translated from the Septuagint and the Syriac Peshitta, which from the fifth century on was the official version of the Bible in Syriac-speaking countries. The word *Peshitta* means "simple."

Beyond the use of a Psalter in worship, a great variety of music forms have accompanied and aided the worship of the saints. Monastic music consisted of more than Gregorian chants, with innovations being introduced by Hildegard of Bingen, Bernard of Clairvaux, and others.

Selected hymns have survived from early times. At the Last Supper the disciples sang a hymn (Matt. 26:30, probably the Hallel). Ps. 136 is called the Great Hallel). Scriptural evidence gives indication of Christian hymns (Eph. 5:19; Phil. 2:5–11; 1 Tim. 3:16; 6:15; 2 Tim. 2:11–13; Rev. 15:3–4; 22:17). The earliest hymn that has survived outside of the Scriptures is a hymn to Christ by Clement of Alexandria (A.D. 150–215).[7]

In England, hymns in the vernacular appeared at the time of Bede (680) and Christmas carols were sung as early as 1521.

The Reformation profoundly affected music styles in worship. Martin Luther, himself a good musician, imitated patterns in medieval secular music. Calvin would tolerate nothing but the words of Scripture in his services. Charles and John Wesley, Isaac Watts, Philip Doddridge, John Newton, and William Cowper have left an indelible imprint on modern worship. Revivalism introduced the experience-based gospel song, but America's favorite "Amazing Grace" came from the pen of John Newton and appeared first in *Olney Hymns* in 1779.

In recent years praise choruses have been introduced and now tend to dominate many worship services. Luther's example of using secular tunes has been copied by modern Christian musicians in an attempt to modernize singing in evangelical churches.

Whatever the style or substance of our use of music, they hold no candle to what is revealed in the Book of Revelation. Numerous angels surround the throne saying, "Worthy is the Lamb, who was slain, to receive power and wealth and wisdom and strength and honor and glory and praise!" (Rev. 5:12).

In Christian worship, music allows believers to speak to each other. This "communion" of the saints is an exercise of the priesthood of believers. In both Ephesians and Colossians (Eph. 5:19; Col. 3:16) ministry in music is couched in the context of exhortations and commands. Exercising spiritual gifts in music include speaking, teaching, and admonishing. Some, however, deny the use of musical instruments in worship services since the New Testament makes no explicit reference to them. Most, however, make wide use of musical instruments. Music in worship aims to fulfill the purpose of making music in the heart to the Lord, always to be accompanied by thanksgiving to God. Early Christian catechetical classes undoubtedly employed music as a way of teaching children.

Whether by speaking, singing, or admonishing, the Word must always be prominent. This may well serve as a guide and corrective to the use of hymns and spiritual songs in worship.

In July 1723, shortly after Johann Sebastian Bach arrived in Leipzig to became the cantor at St. Thomas Church, he wrote a hymn based on a text by Johann Franck, "Jesus, My Friend." Whenever Christians sing the hymn, the excellent words and music rise like an offering to God:

Jesus, priceless treasure,
Source of purest pleasure,
Truest friend to me;
Long my heart both panted,
'Til it well nigh fainted,
Thirsting, after Thee.
Thine I am, O spotless Lamb,
I will suffer nought to hide Thee,
Ask for naught beside Thee.

Only when music is combined with faith and when artistic beauty is wed to truth does music serve the church meaningfully. Only when it brings glory to God does it inspire, teach, and lead us to Him.

DEVELOPING A WORSHIPING CONGREGATION

What makes some churches more "spiritual" than others? There is no easy way to answer this question. Those of charismatic persuasion may wish to claim the label over other congregations. But the Holy Spirit—

not the style—is the One who unites believers through worship. Godly Anglicans with a more structured liturgy can worship with free-style charismatics if the focus is on Christ and not style. Let everyone be fully persuaded in their minds as to what constitutes worship. Baptists, Presbyterians, Lutheran, Methodists, Bible Church, Brethren, and Quaker believers can all find agreement. Our evangelical faith transcends denominational barriers, for all who are in Christ drink from the same well.

Reformers taught us that where the marks of the church are present—the Word, the ordinances, and discipline—there indeed is a church. Developing a worshiping congregation ought to be the aim of every group of believers. Whether a chancel is divided, or whether one music form is preferred over another, the central questions are these: Is Christ preached? Is the Cross uplifted? Is the Holy Spirit reverenced? Is the Word expounded?

A worshiping congregation will evidence two essential qualities—understanding of the spiritual life and expression of thankfulness to God. How a church worships God reveals whether believers are spiritually mature. Giving thanks may be the highest form of worship, especially when expressed in the Lord's Supper. Thankfulness separates Christians from Paul's description of pagans in Romans 1:21: "Although they knew God, they neither glorified him as God nor gave thanks to him." Building a thankful congregation is the same as building a worshiping congregation.

Spiritual devotion and piety will be the results of a well-taught congregation. Pride and legalism are to be avoided. A worshiping congregation will learn to apply the exhortation of Hebrews 10:22, "Let us draw near to God with a sincere heart in full assurance of faith." Within the context of this passage there are exhortations to hold unswervingly to hope (10:23), to consider how to spur one another on toward love and good deeds (10:24), not to give up meeting together (10:25), and to give encouragement to others (10:25).

All these functions contribute to the cultivation of the spiritual life of the church. Drawing near to God takes top priority in the list. Some would relegate this totally to private devotion and worship. Of course, no one would dispute the value of individual growth in knowledge and grace, which can be fostered by means of good literature, Bible study aids, and disciplined approaches to personal spiritual growth. But corporate growth is essential too. I believe this is the thrust of Hebrews 10:22–25. Just as Israel was to see themselves as the people of God, so Christians are to view themselves as growing, thankful Christians in congregations whose chief purpose is to glorify God.

Evangelical attempts to make an awesome God affable are in poor taste. The awesome reality of the exalted God, worthy of being feared, is diminished when He is "downsized" into our buddy system. When God is thus reduced, we misunderstand our humanity, which is dearly in need of mercy and grace. When we celebrate God's transcendence, we measure our own human endeavors for what they are. This calls for a humbling of spirit, a poverty of mind, and a contrition of heart. A world-view that elevates human accomplishment over God's power is wrong.

Worship is a state of awe which stimulates praise and thankfulness, but it presumes understanding something of God's greatness, His redemptive acts in history, and the Holy Spirit's presence in the church. Any recovery of worship must account for a more theological understanding of God and not just offer a thin veneer of praise tantamount to vain repetition.

Is there still a place for the hymns of the church? Nikolaus Ludwig von Zinzendorf (1700–1760) wrote that hymns are "a kind of response to the Bible, an echo, and an extension thereof. In the Bible one perceives how the Lord communicates with mankind; and in the hymnal how mankind communicates with the Lord."[9] Singing the truths of Scripture and responding to those truths are worthy elements of worship. If they are missing, the church is impoverished. Hymns provide a medium for communicating the deep meaning of the Christian faith in artistic form. Admittedly, hymns sometimes reflect theology that may not be biblically sound, so discretion is needed in selecting hymns for congregational singing. Clear teaching of the Word of God in our worship services equips believers to discern good hymns from bad ones. Hymns, as is true in all forms of musical expression, employ poetic imagery, metaphors, and other literary devices to deepen insight and enrich expression. Thus they should not be held to the same scrutiny as the Scriptures themselves.

The aim of hymn singing should be the same aim stated in the Scriptures (1 Cor. 14:15; Col. 3:16)—to sing so that God's Word and Christian teaching may be instilled in the hearts of worshipers.

THE CHURCH AND WORSHIP

Franz Schubert, who died at the age of thirty-one, produced work of such high quality that he gained a position of eminence alongside Johann Sebastian Bach. His final work, "Mass in D Major," included the text of the ancient Nicene Creed. What better way to convey theological substance than in music? Singing only praise choruses limits the church's scope of theological understanding. A contemporary writer calls us back to the use of substantial music in worship:

> When in our music God is glorified,
> and adoration leaves no room for pride,
> it is as though the whole creation cried:
> Alleluia, alleluia, alleluia!
> So has the Church, in litany and song,
> in faith and love, through centuries of wrong,
> borne witness to the truth in ev'ry tongue:
> Alleluia, alleluia, alleluia!
> Let ev'ry instrument be tuned for praise;
> let all rejoice who have a voice to raise;
> and may God give us faith to sing always:
> Alleluia, alleluia, alleluia![9]
> —Fred Pratt Green (1972)

THE LORD'S DAY

A chapter on Christian worship would not be complete without a restatement of the Christian position on the Lord's Day. While some churches retain Saturday worship as observing the true Sabbath, most groups worship on Sunday.

The expression "the Lord's Day" appears only in Revelation 1:10 as a designation of the first day of the week. However, we know that early Christians gathered on the first day of the week to commemorate the resurrection of our Lord. While the earliest records reveal that they were "daily" in the temple and continued to worship on the Jewish Sabbath in the synagogues, Sunday gatherings also took place as early as the midfifties of the first century. Such a Sunday service is described in Acts 20:7–12.

The Lord's Day is the celebration of the resurrection of our Lord. Paul sanctioned this in his letters to the Corinthian and Galatian churches (1 Cor. 16:1–2). There is ample evidence that Sunday became the primary day of Christian worship by the end of the first century. Postapostolic witness affirms it, and by the third century its meaning was well established. Writing from Rome, Justin Martyr described an early service, as did Pliny in his famous letter to Emperor Trajan in which he explained how Christians met on a fixed day to sing a hymn and recite a form of words.

The Old Testament commandment to observe the Sabbath (Exod. 16:29; 20:8; 31:15; Lev. 23:3) was not repeated in the New Testament. As Willy Rordorf stated, the Sabbath commandment was "surpassed in the reality of Christ, in the liberty of the children of God."[10]

Sunday was observed strictly by the Puritans as the new Sabbath, and to some extent this is retained by those of Reformed tradition. However, Sunday as a day of rest has virtually disappeared in American society.

Following the Edict of Milan, Emperor Constantine elevated Sunday to the statutory day of rest in the Roman Empire. Luther and the Reformers accepted the Lord's Day as the Christian Sabbath, but Luther felt that every day and every hour were suitable for hearing God's Word. The Lord's Supper, however, was invariably observed on Sunday.

Some with missionary fervor view the Sunday morning service as not for worship but for outreach. The uniqueness of a common gathering is thus diminished or relegated to another day. Pressure also comes from Christians whose work demands of the week leave them questing a day of recreation, not worship. Furthermore the emergence of what has been called the "megachurch" in American culture reflects the use of multiple services, beyond the use of Sunday, to fit the particular tastes and wishes of the congregation.

Whether the church will manage to preserve Sunday as the Lord's Day is problematic. Appeals to Christian liberty and to sociological realities need the healthy correctives of a theology that is solidly biblical. Blurring distinctions between believers and unbelievers, worship and mission, and obedience to God and our narcissistic impulses has indeed created confusion. Individualism, personalism, pragmatism, and narcissism sit in judgment before a lofty God who seeks worshipers. Consumerism, ruled by personal preference and tastes, must not be allowed to capture the soul of the Christian church. Ascribing worth to God, not acquiescing to preference and taste, is the only focus for the church if it is to bring honor to God.[11]

The people of God are deserving of a richer share in the service of worship than that of being passive auditors. Worship is not to be limited to the "ministers," nor is it to be a mere human program for undisciplined self-expression. It is a corporate act of sacrifice to God for the sole purpose of honoring God the Father, God the Son, and God the Holy Spirit.

9
The Church and the Gospel

To speak of an "evangelizing" Church is to indulge in a tautology, for if there is no mission to the world, there is no Church.

—Jacques Ellul

Our task is to make the faith intelligible but not credible or palatable, for the Spirit does that: Our aim is to clarify the gospel, to set forth its scandal without ambiguity mitigating this scandal.

—Donald B. Bloesch

IN SEVERAL SMALL COMMUNITIES in Brittany, France, there are some unusual architectural oddities. These intricate stone monuments are usually built in prominent places near the entrance to the parish church. Often Gothic in design, they are graphic reminders of the story of the gospel. While sketching one of these monuments near the coastal village of Concerneau, I asked a local citizen what it was. He told me that it was a "gospel." Apparently communities in the region would vie to see which village could erect the most elaborate artifacts. While the designs varied by size and intricacy, each depicted the gospel story from the annunciation of the birth of Jesus to His ascension. "You see," my new French friend explained, "the people were ignorant and poor, in most cases illiterate. The local priest would gather the villagers together around the visual display and explain the gospel story." Long before the flannelgraph, videos, picture books, and *Jesus* films, the gospel story was being visually and verbally passed along, told and retold to generations of villagers by the use of these "gospels."

The gospel is the pivotal content of God's revelation. What the inner core is to a tree, the gospel is to the church. It is the heartwood of the faith.

In 1521 Martin Luther wrote to his fellow Augustinian brothers at Wittenberg about the abuse of the Mass. In his letter he said, "What is the Gospel? No better answer can be given than these words of the New Testament: when 'Christ gave His body and shed His blood for us for the forgiveness of sins.'"[1] Luther was correct in understanding the gospel as the crux of the faith. The gospel is the "good news" that Jesus came to announce, that the apostles were set apart to preach, and what Philip told the first African convert. What was passed along by revelation to the early church we must pass along to the world in gospel witness.

The Essential Gospel

The English word *gospel* comes from the Old English word *godspel* (*god*, "good," and *spel*, "recital"), "good news." In the New Testament the *angelos* ("messenger") proclaimed or announced the gospel as good news. The four Gospels record the good news of salvation through Christ. The apostles' preaching rehearsed the key events of the Gospel narratives— the life, death, and resurrection of Jesus of Nazareth.

Our Lord calls members of His church to be living epistles or letters, "known and read by everybody" (2 Cor. 3:2). The spiritual house or church that Jesus came to build, according to Peter, is to be made up of "living stones" (1 Pet. 2:5). Unlike those quaint stone oddities eroding away in French villages, the gospel is alive and well. Its essential message can save sinners and bring healing to the nations.

Early Christians boldly adopted the word *gospel* from secular usage to express their conviction that the carpenter's son from Nazareth brought salvation through His death and resurrection.

The Gospel—Biblical Foundations

Mark began his account of the life of Jesus with these words: "The beginning of the gospel about Jesus Christ, the Son of God" (Mark 1:1). Mark seemed to be the only Gospel writer to use the word *euangelion* ("gospel") as a technical term. Of all the New Testament authors Paul was foremost in explaining the term.

We do know from the Gospel records that Jesus used the term to describe His mission. When John the Baptist sent messengers from prison to inquire of Jesus and to confirm His messianic identity, Jesus gave this reply: "Go back and report to John what you hear and see: The blind receive sight, the lame walk, those who have leprosy are cured, the deaf hear, the dead are raised, and the good news is preached to the poor" (Matt. 11:4–5). "Good news is preached" translates a verbal form of the noun *euangelion.*

In Pauline writings the word *gospel* became associated with the *kerygma* (preaching) of the church. However, in the Gospels and the Epistles the *gospel* was also associated with the *didachē*, or teaching of the church. The few references to the gospel in Hebrews (Heb. 4:2, 6), Peter's writings (1 Pet. 1:12, 25; 3:19; 4:6), and the Revelation (Rev. 14:6) stand apart.

The Gospel—Its Christocentric Message

In his famous summary of the gospel the apostle Paul referred to the gospel as a Christ-centered message that was received from God: "Now, brothers, I want to remind you of the gospel I preached to you, which you received and on which you have taken your stand. By this gospel you are saved, if you hold firmly to the Word I preached to you. Otherwise, you have believed in vain. For what I received I passed on to you as of first importance: that Christ died for our sins according to the Scriptures, that he was buried, that he was raised on the third day according to the Scriptures, and that he appeared to Peter, and then to the Twelve. After that, he appeared to more than five hundred of the brothers at the same time, most of whom are still living, though some have fallen asleep (1 Cor. 15:6, NIV). Then he appeared to James, then to all the apostles, and last of all he appeared to me also, as to one abnormally born" (1 Cor. 15:1–8).

Paul's entire missionary activity was summed up in his call to preach the gospel (1:17). He identified himself so completely with its message that he called the gospel "my gospel" (Rom. 2:16; 16:25) and "our gospel" (2 Cor. 4:3; 1 Thess. 4:5). Also he called it the gospel of Christ (2 Cor. 2:12).

He was not ashamed of it (Rom. 1:16), for it was the gospel of salvation (1 Cor. 15:2), peace (Eph. 6:15), and glory (2 Cor. 4:4). By the content of the gospel, believers' lives are to be ordered (Phil. 1:27). Those who do not obey the gospel will face eternal punishment (2 Thess. 1:8–9).

So compelling was the message of Christ that Paul was willing to "put up with anything" rather than hinder the gospel of Christ (1 Cor. 9:12). In its context this verse implies that he was willing to go without compensation, although the ideal was that those who preach the gospel should receive their living from the gospel (9:14).

It is no wonder that John Mark, Paul's missionary companion, would later add the word *gospel* to his account of the Great Commission: "Go into all the world and preach the good news [*euangelion*] to all creation" (Mark 16:15).

The Gospel—Treasure of the Church

The church is to proclaim "the gospel of God" (Rom. 15:16; 1 Thess. 2:8). In performing this duty, the entire theological spectrum of salvation history and salvation witness is on display. It was this profound truth—that God was in Christ reconciling the world to Himself—that Timothy was to guard (1 Tim. 6:20; 2 Tim. 1:14). The "good deposit" Paul referred in 2 Timothy 1:14 was something he openly labeled a "treasure" possessed in jars of clay (2 Cor. 4:7). Here "gospel" was equated with "ministry" (4:1) and "light" (4:4–6).

Martin Luther, in his objection to the abuse of money and the veneration of the saints in the Roman Church, wrote and spoke of the true treasure of the church, the community of saints. The "holy people" did not consist of a special order, but of all the people of God redeemed by the blood of Christ. The lives of the saints, he believed, are a treasury of the church, not because of merit but because of Christ's suffering on their behalf. Luther's understanding of the gospel shattered the idea that the merits of the saints comprise a treasury in heaven. Medieval theology distorted the gospel, focusing on the merits of saints rather than the merit of Christ. But Christ's work on the cross is good news to sinners, who are saved when they place their faith in Christ. No one is saved by good works

(Eph 2:8–9; Titus 3:5), but every believer should carry out good works as a result of salvation.

This gospel treasure presupposes the Law and its limitations. By the Law, death was *pronounced,* but by the gospel, life is *announced.* One introduces us to sin; the other overwhelms us with grace. The cross of Christ both makes us guilty and rescues us. In this regard the gospel is both bad news and good news. It is good news that we have a Savior, but it is also bad news that we are sinners in need of the saving grace of God.

PRESERVING THE PURITY OF THE GOSPEL

Evangelicals tend to idealize the "perfect" church of antiquity. However, it comes as no surprise to serious readers of the New Testament that the apostolic church of the first century was far from pure. It was factious, legalistic, and arrogant in its use of spiritual gifts, prone to defection, and susceptible to heresy. These were all precursors to problems in our churches today. Nevertheless the apostles urged purity of faith and doctrine in their times.

This was especially true when it came to the central truths of the gospel. These foundational truths of Jesus Christ were being corrupted by leaders who peddled the Word of God for profit (2 Cor. 2:17) and who preached another gospel (Gal. 1:6–7).

Defection from the gospel was no isolated problem. References to churches in trouble beyond Galatia reveal corruption at the core of the Corinthian church ("a Jesus other than the Jesus we preached," 2 Cor. 11:4). A false gospel was also being taught in the churches at Philippi, Colossae, Ephesus, and Thessalonica. Paul's references to deceiving spirits and false teachers (1 Tim. 4:2–5) and even to certain named individuals deceiving the churches (Hymenaeus and Philetus, 2 Tim. 2:17) bear witness to the slow erosion of faith in the earliest days of church expansion. The fact that the gospel had been preached throughout the known world by midcentury (Col. 1:6) was no guarantee of a pure faith in the churches.

Apocryphal Gospels began to be circulated after the first century, leading to widespread confusion among Christians. Only four—Matthew, Mark, Luke, and John—were deemed canonical. The first three are called

Synoptic, because to a considerable degree they share the same accounts of the life and teaching of Jesus and in much the same order. Together they gave what the two Greek words *syn* ("together") and *opsis* ("view") conveyed—a common view of the gospel story.

But this was not the case with the apocryphal Gospels. These so-called hidden Gospels bear little resemblance to the first four books of the New Testament. Origen, third-century scholar from Alexandria, noted the existence of the true and false Gospels. "The Church possesses four Gospels," he wrote, "heresy a great many."[2]

Over twenty years ago a Russian artist living in Carmel-by-the-Sea, California, asked me if I knew about the Gospel of Thomas. She told me that if she could find a community like the one described in that book, she would sell everything she had and go there to live. Her spiritual search gave me opportunity to present the true gospel of the saving grace of Jesus Christ, a gospel that commands the very dedication she was willing to give to a false gospel. New Age devotees tend to like the Gospel of Thomas, which was probably the most Gnostic of all the pseudo-Gospels.

The apostle Paul said he was entrusted with the gospel (1 Thess. 2:4). This high calling was not accompanied by comfort and success in the usual sense of the words. At least in Thessalonica this calling brought suffering, insult, and opposition (2:2). Yet the gospel also brought radical changes to people. Those who accepted the gospel turned from idols to serve the true and living God (1:9). They had been rescued from the coming wrath (1:10). There in Gentile territory churches became imitators of the Judean churches (2:14). These Gentile converts were willing to place themselves in harm's way in the tradition of Jesus and the prophets. They were targets of abuse by those who attempted to keep Christians from proclaiming the gospel, the message of salvation.

In an effort to put the gospel in terms the world would understand, Walter Rauschenbusch and other theological liberals emphasized the social nature of the gospel—to the exclusion of the spiritual or "soulish" nature of the gospel. To him gospelizing the world meant "Christianizing" the social order.[3] However, the gospel announces divine forgiveness, not to an already universally redeemed humanity, but in response to personal faith. What Isaiah the prophet announced in Isaiah 53:4–6, we, too, must proclaim:

"Surely he took up our infirmities and carried our sorrows, yet we considered him stricken by God, smitten by him, and afflicted. But he was pierced for our transgressions, he was crushed for our iniquities; the punishment that brought us peace was upon him, and by his wounds we are healed. We all, like sheep, have gone astray, each of us has turned to his own way, and the LORD has laid on him the iniquity of us all."

The gospel offers forgiveness of sins, rescues from eternal punishment, and promises eternal life and the certainty of full and complete redemption in glory.

A NEW KIND OF "SUCCESS GOSPEL"

At the turn of the twentieth century a doctrine of human progress swept America, a teaching that said it was wrong for Christians to be poor. This same "success gospel" survives today in some circles but has largely been labeled as bogus Christianity. However, a new "prosperity theology" is emerging. Its message is, "Come to Jesus and you will get rich."

Priests of material prosperity have a phony ring to their message. The gospel according to Kenneth Copeland and Robert Tilton is that you can have both Jesus and a generous bank balance.[4] Arguing that the Bible promises financial, physical, and spiritual prosperity, these salesmen of success are convinced that Jesus promised a hundredfold return on your money for accepting personal salvation (Mark 10:29–30).

When television evangelists Jim Bakker and Jimmy Swaggart fell morally, the prosperity gospel suffered, yet the idea is still alive. What is of deeper concern is an emerging gospel compatible with American consumerism and New Age thinking. The older success model made the gospel seem like a bottled elixir. The new gospel hedges a bit on the wealth promises, but hypes self-fulfillment and happiness. In this model, consumerism is king.[5] However, a marketing approach to the gospel is flawed theologically. "To give the whole store away to match what this year's market says the unchurched want," exclaimed Martin Marty, "is to have the people who know least about faith determine most about its expression."[6]

Every generation has had to minister the gospel in differing cultural settings. But what must be guarded is the treasure of the gospel with its corpus of truth centered on Christ and the Cross. To offer a new success model of a gospel geared to self-fulfillment, personal esteem, and happiness is to miss the mark. Jesus' words are clear: "It is not the healthy who need a doctor, but the sick. I have not come to call the righteous, but sinners to repentance" (Luke 5:31–32).

THE MISSION AND MANDATE OF THE GOSPEL

The church is not to keep the gospel a secret, jealously guarded as a keep-sake of the faith. It must be given away. The gospel carries with it a mandate, a command stated in the Great Commission of our Lord (Matt. 28:19–20; Mark 16:15; Luke 24:47). The apostles and the early church responded eagerly to the early mandate (Acts 1:8; 14:21). The Lord who calls dis-ciples also commissions Christians to disciple others. Jesus' followers are to witness to the world (John 17:18).

At the heart of our mission is the compassionate love of God (2 Cor. 5:14), which compels us to be "ambassadors" for Christ (5:20). The "gathered community" of the saints needs to be the "scattered community" of mission-aries, sowing the gospel and reaping its fruits in the harvest fields of the world.

The church's concern must never be the preservation of its own institu-tional structure. Rather, it must concern itself with the gospel, which, by its very nature, thrusts the church outward in evangelism and missions.

The Great Commission

What is it that Jesus commanded His church to do? While Matthew's ac-count of the Great Commission is the most familiar, each Gospel writer emphasized the energy of Jesus' words. Matthew prefaced the command-ment by a great claim, "All authority in heaven and on earth has been given to me" (Matt. 28:18). Thus His mission is couched in the power-fully regal splendors of heavenly sovereignty: "Therefore go and make disciples of all nations, baptizing them in the name of the Father and of the Son and of the Holy Spirit, and teaching them to obey everything I have commanded you" (28:19–20).

Glimpses of Jesus' unlimited power are seen in the Gospel records of

His ministry (8:1–4; 9:27–34; 11:27; 26:53). Power that was once veiled in human flesh was unveiled in the words of the Great Commission.

The "go" of the gospel contrasts with Christ's invitation to "come" (11:28). From the Incarnation onward it is clear that the evangelism of the world is in view. The mission Jesus gave His church is to propagate the gospel throughout the entire world.

Other Gospel writers give accounts similar to that of Matthew, emphasizing aggressive involvement in evangelism: "Go into all the world and preach the good news to all creation" (Mark 16:15); "Repentance and forgiveness of sins will be preached in his name to all nations, beginning at Jerusalem" (Luke 24:47); "As you [the Father] sent me into the world, I have sent them into the world" (John 17:18;); "As the father has sent me, I am sending you" (20:21).

Christ's ministry sets the pattern for the church's mission. Jesus the Sovereign came to serve (Matt 20:28). The style of church mission is thus set firmly in a servant mold. A servant church is in contrast to a church obsessed with its own power. Following the explicit words of our Lord, the church is to be a preaching, witnessing, caring, discipling church. There is no avoiding it: Evangelism is the mission of the church.

Sinners are not commanded to go to church; the church is commanded to go to sinners.

In the 1974 Lausanne Conference declaration on the nature of evangelism, the church's mission was defined in the form of a covenant:

> To evangelize is to spread the good news that Jesus Christ died for our sins and was raised from the dead according to the Scriptures, and that as reigning Lord he now offers the forgiveness of sins and the liberating gift of the Spirit to all who repent and believe. Our Christian presence in the world is indispensable to evangelism, and so is that kind of dialogue whose purpose is to listen sensitively in order to understand. But evangelism itself is the proclamation of the historical, biblical Christ as Saviour and Lord, with a view to persuading people to come to him personally and so be reconciled to God. In issuing the gospel invitation we have no liberty to conceal the cost of discipleship. Jesus still calls all who would follow him to deny themselves, take up their cross, and identify themselves with his new

community. The results of evangelism include obedience to Christ, incorporation into his church and responsible service in the world.[7]

Missiological Adaptation for the Sake of the Gospel

The New Testament gives evidence of a driving force to be obedient to God's call to mission. In its response to be "witnesses in Jerusalem, and in all Judea and Samaria, and to the ends of the earth" (Acts 1:8), the church in effect contextualized the gospel. Paul articulated this process of contextualization to the Corinthian church: "Though I am free and belong to no man, I make myself a slave to everyone, to win as many as possible. To the Jews I became like a Jew to win the Jews. To those under the law I became like one under the law (though I myself am not under the law), so as to win those under the law. To those not having the law I became like one not having the law (though I am not free from God's law but am under Christ's law), so as to win those not having the law. To the weak I became weak, to win the weak. I have became all things to all men so that by all possible means I might save some. I do all this for the sake of the gospel, that I may share in its blessings" (1 Cor. 9:19–23).

Missiologists have long felt that many of the ways of the Western church are not synonymous with the gospel. From indigenous attempts at gospel work to the more modern transcultural missionary work, believers have attempted to follow Paul's example. However, clear distinction must be made between the church ministering the gospel in cultural contexts and the church shaping itself to the culture. The first was inevitable as the gospel spread through all the world. The second is a trap to avoid. Theologian James Packer warned of accommodating the gospel to culture: "The content of the gospel message must always control its communication."[8]

A biblical theology of missions must include the following five pillars. Beyond these, there is ample room for methodological adaptation.

1. God has spoken in history by the prophets and supremely and finally by Jesus Christ. This is the starting point of mission. It is God who creates, who initiates love, forgiveness, and redemption, and who has spoken eloquently and completely in Jesus Christ (John 1:1–14; Heb. 1:1–2).

2. All of God's creative order, while termed "good" by God Himself, has suffered from the Fall. Sin taints all humanity, its relationships and its corruption of nature itself, thus necessitating redemption. Sin is universal, its consequences eternal, and its judgment final. The Good News is the offer of eternal life to all who believe in Jesus Christ and who accept His offer of forgiveness for sin. Those who declare that there is hope apart from the gospel are false teachers. Justification does not rest on human merit, but is by grace alone through faith alone.

3. Christ, God's only Son, is the center of the gospel. Salvation is accomplished by the mediatorial work of Christ alone. As the Cambridge Declaration affirmed, "We deny that the gospel is preached if Christ's substitutionary work is not declared and faith in Christ and his work is not solicited."[9]

4. The Scriptures alone rule the church's life and work, and the work of the Holy Spirit cannot be disengaged from Scripture. The Bible alone teaches all that is necessary for salvation. Syncretism, the mixing of religious elements from many "faiths," is the enemy of biblical mission. While general revelation may reveal truths about God's nature and being, only the special revelation of Christ through the infallible written Word announces the gospel of saving truth.

5. The mission of the church involves sending God's people into the world. This outward movement of the church is in response to Christ's call to witness to the gospel and to serve humanity. Ultimately the eternal gospel will be proclaimed to people in "every nation, tribe, language and people" (Rev. 14:6).

The church must humbly search its soul and examine its methods so as not to corrupt the essential gospel. The Cross is still an offense (1 Cor. 1:18), but what it represents brings healing, that is, spiritual health to those who believe.

The term *missions* carries the unfortunate baggage of paternalism and Western dominance. Yet we cannot always be revising words and rewriting history to fit what is currently in vogue. The plain truth is that the world needs Jesus, whom the Bible declares to be the only Savior of the world.

Jesus told the story of the narrow way that leads to life everlasting and the broad way that leads to destruction (Matt. 7:13–14). Syncretism, with its many ways, and universalism, with its wide-open ways, both ignore the fact that salvation is only through Jesus Christ (Acts 4:12). The contemporary church, in all its innovations and cultural sensitivity, must never forget Jesus' words, "Enter through the narrow gate" (Matt. 7:13).

Evangelism and Church Growth

In the 1950s, Donald McGavran, a missionary to India, coined the phrase "church growth." Disillusioned by the output of evangelism, he reasoned that when people believed, they were added to the church. Since McGavran, the term *church growth* has come to replace *evangelism* as an adequate term for describing the principle of gospel expansion. Church-growth principles focus on five key elements: the importance of numerical growth, a focus on receptive peoples, people movements in response to gospel witness, science as a valid tool for measuring growth, and application of right methods to guarantee large response to the gospel.[10]

Critics of the church-growth approach accuse it of reducing faith to principles and methods. They point to its false confidence in human ability and methodology, in sociology divorced from a sound theology, and in marketing. These critics say that emphasis on institutional expansion seems to supplant the inward work of the Holy Spirit in the person to whom the gospel is being witnessed.

Undoubtedly abuses arise out of imbalance, failure to understand the efforts of fellow Christians, quickness to judge motives, and lack of goodwill and grace toward those who differ in ministry style. The Bible offers an example of openness toward those who differ in methodology. While the corollaries and parallels may not be the same in our day, a principle remains from the example of Paul's attitude toward others who differed from him: "What does it matter? The important thing is that in every way, whether from false motives or true, Christ is preached" (Phil. 1:18).

DEVELOPING A GLOBAL STRATEGY
IN WORLD MISSIONS

The first Christians were intentional about outreach. To minimize the mission of the Christian church is to trivialize the gospel. One evangelical leader put it succinctly: "Missions is not the partial task of part of the church; it is the total task of the total church." I have these words inscribed in my Bible.

Former congressman Walter Judd of Minnesota was known to have had a profound respect for the worldwide expansion of Christian witness. He once described his childhood and how he grew up in a home where prayer and Bible reading were common. He told how his parents had placed a map of the world on a wall near the kitchen table. "I grew up," he said, "looking at the world." That is exactly the perspective evangelical Christians need to have.

While traveling in England, I once visited the farthest reaches of Cornwall, not far from the famous but tiny village of Land's End. Just to the north along the windblown coast lies St. Just. The quaint little church in that town contains a description of its long history. In the sixth century, Saint Just had been sent by Augustine, the first archbishop of Canterbury, to convert the Saxons. In those days the farthest point of land to the west must have seemed like a world away from Canterbury in Kent. It profoundly impressed me that a Christian had made an intentional decision to reach out to the pagan successors of the ancient Celts and to travel a great distance to share the gospel.

This kind of story has been repeated in myriad ways. Gospel witness has been both spontaneous and planned, local and global. God has had His witness in remote parts of our globe. While the successes of the gospel are obvious, much is yet to be done.

A biblical strategy for world evangelization should include the following items.

1. Evangelism is the natural outgrowth of a healthy church that understands the nature of the gospel.

2. Evangelism, to be successful, must be intentional.

3. Evangelism involves the entire church wherever it is found on earth.

4. Special designation of evangelists and missionaries is essential, involving full-time expressions of spiritual gifts.

5. A foundational theology and the affirmation of doctrinal purity are essential for all mission work.

6. Prayer and unity assure a spiritually attuned approach to gospel content, culture, recipients of the witness, and the development of support systems for world outreach.

7. Accountability to the church is assumed with ample room for innovation and experimentation within the boundaries of biblical principles.

8. Conversion accompanied by growth and maturity in the church form the focus of all mission efforts.

9. Compassionate ministries along with evangelism must constantly be developed and guarded, lest a division arise between "gospel work" and social responsibility.

10. Communication theory, technological skill, and sociological understanding will of necessity be subservient to the gospel and the law of love. The love of Christ serves as the primary motivation in reaching others with the gospel.

11. While it is recognized that God has spoken of Himself through general revelation, mission is sharing the news of God's special grace through Christ. The principles of sowing the seed, planting, watering, and harvesting are applied in recognition of God's effective call to everyone to believe in Christ.

12. People are to be viewed not only as recipients of gospel witness but also as potential disciples who in turn will disciple others. Gospel witness is not merely addition; it is multiplication, and this comes by the power of the Holy Spirit. Such expansion may defy definition and human quantification. Mission is the work of God; the church is only a partner in the gospel.

13. Recognition of God's sovereignty shapes the conscience and perspective of those in mission outreach.

14. World culture shapes expressions of faith and work wherever the gospel takes root. In Christ there is no East or West. Cultural arrogance has no place in mission strategy; in fact, it is detrimental to the gospel.

15. All mission strategy recognizes the world's religious pluralism. Without compromise, the church must learn to witness in love and with tolerance toward others who differ. God, who has created us all in His divine image, extends the offer for people to accept or reject the gospel. Compassion for souls must be accompanied by equal compassion for the wholeness (though incompleteness) of humanity.

Martin Luther, in his Smalcald Articles, expressed his firm conviction about the gospel: "The gospel shall without ceasing sound and resound through the mouths of all Christians; therefore we should joyfully accept every possibility of hearing it, lift up our hands and thank God, because we can hear it everywhere."[11]

The Necessity of Evangelism

In the Baptist Church of historic Bedford, England, there is a striking piece of stained-glass artistry. Positioned on the west wall of the simple sanctuary so as to catch the lingering light of day, the beautiful window depicts a scene from *Pilgrim's Progress*. Bedford was the home of John Bunyan, the seventeenth-century dissenter who was imprisoned for twelve years for refusing to stop preaching the gospel. While behind bars he wrote the all-time classic of Christian allegory.

The window depicts Evangelist pointing the way to Traveler, worn out by a heavy burden of sin. In *Pilgrim's Progress*, Bunyan paints the scene in the quaint language of an old classic: "Then said *Evangelist*, pointing with his finger over a very wide field. . . . Do you see yonder Shining Light? He said, I think I do. Then said *Evangelist*, Keep that Light in your eye."[12] As I looked at the window and the powerful arm pointing the way, I wondered if today's generation understands anything about pointing *the* way to anything. The "you choose your own way" dogma was foreign to Bunyan, as well as to Jesus' words "I am the way" (John 14:6).

Bunyan, like his apostolic ancestors and generations of faithful disciples of Christ, did not yield to the idea that heaven can be reached by any number of roads. In his preaching and witness he pointed the way to the Cross—and so must we.

Evangelicalism must unequivocally stand its ground, insisting on the necessity of the Cross and evangelism. Though offensive to the modern mind, evangelism flows from the heart of God who loved us enough to send His Son into the world to save us from our sins. This is the very heart of missions.

In his preface to *The Young Church in Action*, J. B. Phillips wrote that Christians talk about difficult days as though we should wait for better ones to come and more favorable world conditions before witnessing to the gospel. It is heartening to know that the gospel took root in conditions highly unfavorable to faith. Phillips wrote, "It is a matter of sober historical fact that never before has any small body of ordinary people so moved the world that their enemies could say, with tears of rage in their eyes, that these men 'have turned the world upside down!'"[13] In his preface to *Letters to Young Churches* Phillips continued his description of the priority early believers placed on witnessing: "These early Christians were on fire with the conviction that they had become, through Christ, literally sons of God; they were pioneers of a new humanity, founders of a new Kingdom. They still speak to us across the centuries." This innovative paraphraser of Scripture concluded with this pointed remark: "Perhaps if we believed what they believed, we might achieve what they achieved."[14]

The New Syncretism

Within the rise of neopaganism, the popularity of New Age thought, and the threat of Islam, Christianity faces a crisis of identity. The exclusivity of the gospel is in conflict with religious pluralism. The question, "Is Jesus the only way to God?" becomes important in world missions.

Efforts over the centuries to reconcile Christian faith with opposing beliefs have led to "syncretism," a word that means a mixture of thought. Nineteenth-century liberalism attempted to harmonize Christianity with non-Christian thought. Various syncretistic controversies within Christianity arose over the question of whether Protestant and Catholic views could be united and over the question of whether various denominations and interpretations will be merged. Currently, however, syncretism is looked on as an enemy of the pure gospel. It carries a negative nuance of an inadmissible mixture of belief and unbelief.

The new syncretism in evangelicalism is subtle. It is fairly easy to define Buddhism in contrast to Christianity, but the particular practice of meditation, for example, may evoke the admiration of believers whose understanding of true Christian worship is partial or defective. Believers are also baffled by the fanaticism of Islamic "fundamentalists." Terms have become "noses of wax," bent and twisted in a confusing array of usage. Unfortunately many Christians know little of what they profess to believe and thus are easily seduced into accepting false teaching and unbiblical practices.

Postmodernism, with its existentialism and denial of fixed absolutes, has seduced some into believing that it really doesn't matter what a person believes, so long as he or she is sincere and accepting. Loss of objectivity in belief and the elevation of a feeling-faith have produced a weakened church. The very foundations of a theology of mission are being eroded by messages that counter Christian truth. In efforts to find unity the church dare not give ground to theological syncretism. Loss of theological certainty is an enemy of evangelism.

On the other hand, it is important for Christians to find common ground—where such exists—for purposes of witness. A new interest in spirituality in America provides openers for the gospel. Evangelical witness has always included both the defense of the gospel and a dialogical approach to witness. Both are amply illustrated in the record of the gospel's early expansion.

Other enemies of evangelical witness are too numerous to expound. The important task of the church is to know the faith and to witness faithfully to that hope held out in the gospel.

Ultimately, what brings people to salvation is not human attempts to syncretize beliefs, but the supernatural convicting and regenerating work of the Holy Spirit.

Some early church fathers, including Clement of Alexandria, Origen, and Gregory of Nyssa, believed that all free moral creatures (even angels and devils) will share the grace of salvation. And universalism, the belief that all will ultimately be saved, is still prevalent. Fed by Protestant liberalism and dabbled in by a few who call themselves "evangelical," universalism is a belief that makes evangelism unnecessary. Why call people to trust in Christ if everyone will be saved anyway? Merely announcing to people that they are already saved is a far cry from the message of the gospel.

Christian mission, carried out in the current milieu of pluralism, must be theologically astute, yet compassionately sensitive. It must be daringly bold, yet humbly trusting. Credible, intelligent witness must not become an anomaly of our times; it must be normative.

Spin the dial in nearly any direction and century, and you will find deviant witness to the gospel. Gnosticism at the end of the first century, Nestorian missionaries in ancient China, Manichaean heresy in Africa, or New Age thought in the late twentieth century[15] —all these heresies call for carefully guarding the gospel.

We do not have the luxury of making up our own gospel. The Christian experience is not like a class in which faith is crafted to fit each generation. Jude, the brother of James and servant of Jesus Christ, understood this very well. Compelled to write about the salvation we all share, he urged his readers "to contend for the faith that was once for all entrusted to the saints" (Jude 3). The gospel is the message of a reconciling God seeking to bring people to Himself through faith in Christ. Our task is to share that message of reconciliation. As Paul wrote, "All this is from God, who reconciled us to himself through Christ and gave us the ministry of reconciliation: that God was reconciling the world to himself in Christ, not counting men's sins against them. And he has committed to us the message of reconciliation. We are therefore Christ's ambassadors, as though God were making his appeal through us. We implore you on Christ's behalf: Be reconciled to God. God made him who had no sin to be sin for us, so that in him we might become the righteousness of God" (2 Cor. 5:18–21).

10
The Church and the World

Can Christianity retain its authentic identity and demonstrate its relevance at the same time, or must one be sacrificed to the other? Are we obliged to choose between retreating into the past and making a fetish of the present, between reciting old truths which are stale and inventing new notions which are spurious? Perhaps the greater of these two dangers is that the church will attempt to recast the faith in such a way as to undermine its integrity and render it unrecognizable to its original heralds.

—John Stott

THE CHURCH IS TO BE A MODEL of grace and love in the world. Its transformational stance is to be one of salt and light, of involvement rather than withdrawal. The Christian call to faith, while radically countercultural, stands in contrast to two extremes: an "over-against-the-world" posture and one that blesses the present order of the world.

Authentic disciples refuse to indulge in either a flight from culture or the secularizing of the church under the ruse of reaching that culture. "World" and "Word" are inherently in conflict. If we accommodate the Word in our efforts to reach the world, we water down our message. On the other hand, if we fail to engage the world, we remain in isolation. Christianity, we must remind ourselves, is not an isolationist movement. The church must penetrate its culture in order to display the love of God and the saving grace of our Lord Jesus Christ.

This penetration of the world is not to be a power ploy for institutional or personal aggrandizement. It is to be a genuine demonstration of humility. Any display of power other than that of the Holy Spirit is an abomination to the gospel of grace. Like fertile seed planted in soil, the church must die before it manifests life. If the gospel is to be heard and believed, it must be lived for all to see. Our practice of faith needs to match our profession of faith.

From earliest times the church's stance on the world has evidenced a variety of approaches. From fourth-century monasticism to twentieth-century modernism, a plurality of postures has produced a confusing collage of institutional expression. We do well to examine again the roots of transformational faith in the context of world culture.

THE COUNTERCULTURAL NATURE OF THE GOSPEL

While it may be difficult to divorce one's own world-view while affirming the truth of Scripture, it is nevertheless essential to affirm biblical truth in straightforward fashion. We have an unchanging core of truth that refuses to be twisted by context, philosophical presuppositions, and experiential subjectivism. If Christianity did not radically transform its first followers, how then can we account for "aliens and strangers" (1 Pet. 2:11) being made one in Christ? This "oneness" was more than theological. It transcended national, ethnic, racial, and gender boundaries (Gal. 3:28). To walk in newness of life meant to treat despised slaves as human beings, Gentiles as fellow citizens, women as equals, to render to Caesar what was his due, to manifest the fragrance of Christ in an uncivil society, and to become a mediating force in a world unfriendly to faith.

Our belief in Christ should affect what we do; it should transform our character and our actions. Paul, the champion of grace, wrote often of the need to link *knowing* and *doing.* To the Ephesians, he affirmed that believers are the workmanship of God, "created in Christ Jesus to do good works" (Eph. 2:10). And to Titus he wrote, "Those who have trusted in God [must] be careful to devote themselves to doing what is good" (Titus 3:8). Furthermore, there is no contradiction between Paul and James, as some have claimed. From the evidence of the New Testament, both could have written the same truths: "What good is it, my brothers, if a man claims to have faith but has no deeds? Can such faith save him?" (James 2:14). They both could conclude, "Faith without deeds is dead" (2:26). Radical faith has intellectual, moral, social, political, and global dimensions.

"The cross that is planted at the heart of the history of the world," wrote Jacques Ellul, "cannot be uprooted."[1] It may be corrupted, but it cannot be stamped out. Its enemies may empty it of meaning, but it still represents Christ's substitution in our place, and grace and pardon to sinners. It represents what God did for us, not what we can do for our own salvation. It represents foolishness to the world, but to those whom God has called, the Cross represents the power and wisdom of God (1 Cor. 1:24–25).

The Two Worlds of the Church

How is the church to be separate from the world and yet involved in it? Jesus prayed to the Father for His disciples "whom you gave me out of the world" (John 17:6). In particular, verses 13–19 express the tension between the "in-the-world" and the "not-of-the-world" dimensions of Christian reality: "I am coming to you now, but I say these things while I am still in the world, so that they may have the full measure of my joy within them. I have given them your word and the world has hated them, for they are not of the world any more than I am of the world. My prayer is not that you take them out of the world but that you protect them from the evil one. They are not of the world, even as I am not of it. Sanctify them by the truth; your word is truth. As you sent me into the world, I have sent them into the world. For them I sanctify myself, that they too may be truly sanctified."

The world, from the vantage point of the New Testament, expresses the organized life of all of God's creation. The Greek word *kosmos* expresses not simply the created universe, but also human society that stands opposed to God. First John 2:15 contains a warning not to love the world, that is, the sinfulness of human society. Christians are not to be attracted to "the cravings of sinful man, the lust of his eyes and the boasting of what he has and does" (2:16). These, John concluded, come from the world and not from God the Father. That *kosmos* and its evil desires will pass away, but believers who do the will of God live forever (2:17).

The tensions then between the transient and the permanent, the temporal and the eternal, describe the two world spheres of the church.

Augustine, like Abraham, longed for a city of God not built by human hands. Because of these polarities, Christians have interpreted the *kosmos* as evil, despite the positive commendation by Paul of all that is good in the world and worthy of Christian attention (Phil. 4:8).

"Christianity is not world-denying," wrote New Testament scholar I. Howard Marshall in a paper delivered to the Lausanne Committee for World Evangelization.[2] The world remains God's world. Legitimate love for the world—the people of the world and the created yet fallen order—should lead the church to bridge the two worlds in which it lives, one heavenly and the other worldly, without giving in to evil.

History records the church's approaches to living in the world. The earliest and most continuous form of escapism or withdrawal came through monasticism. Viewing the world as essentially evil, monastics were motivated by asceticism and other forms of self-deprivation. Taking root by the fourth century, monasticism basically was made up of two strains of thought and life. One elevated the hermit life and the other the common life. Both were monastic, forgoing marriage, taking vows of poverty, and focusing on contemplation and prayer. Monasticism continues today to some extent in Roman Catholicism, Anglicanism, and Eastern Orthodoxy. Its tenets, however, have largely been rejected by most Protestants, although the literature of the mystics and monastics has influenced pietists and some evangelicals.

Saint Augustine's prayer book includes the following prayer, in which its line about despising the world reveals the prevalent monastic view of that day:

> Remember Christian soul
> that thou hast this day and every day of life
>> God to glorify
>> Jesus to imitate
>> A soul to save
>> A body to mortify
>> Sins to repent of
>> Virtues to acquire
>> Hell to avoid

> Heaven to gain
>
> Eternity to prepare for
>
> Time to profit by
>
> Neighbors to edify
>
> The world to despise
>
> Devils to combat
>
> Passions to subdue
>
> Death perhaps to suffer
>
> Judgment to undergo.[3]

Another stance toward the world was exhibited by the Anabaptists in sixteenth-century Europe. Their enemies called them Anabaptists ("rebaptizers") because of their opposition to infant baptism and their practice of rebaptizing as adults those who had been sprinkled as infants. Emerging in Switzerland, the Anabaptists spawned the Mennonites, Hutterites, and Moravians. English Baptists adopted Anabaptist teachings in their attempts to purify the church. Anabaptist views on social equality, congregational autonomy, and a church of believers separate from the state led some to take antigovernment stances.

Over the years various forms of pacifism, quietism, and pietism have emerged, reflecting Christian attempts to deal with the world. Pacifism, the view that warfare is evil, is espoused by Anabaptists and Quakers. Quietism, minimizing all human effort, views perfection as the goal of the spiritual life. Abuses of quietism have led to its demise as a way of living in the world. Pietism, on the other hand, still attracts followers. Believers who held this view in the late seventeenth and eighteenth centuries believed that a retreat to the inner life of devotion was commendable. Acts of philanthropy and benevolence under Count von Zinzendorf, Philipp Jacob Spener, and others balanced this view. Its views influenced the Wesleys in England and continues to influence contemporary evangelicals who seek to recover the cultivation of the inner life of devotion.

While it is impossible to "withdraw" completely from the world, separatist ideas still persist. Heartfelt faith is still attractive to Christians who honestly believe that the church must be purified from within, avoiding all appearance of evil.

A more recent and damaging stance reflecting the church's attitude toward the world emerged in the late nineteenth and early twentieth centuries. Modernism, with roots both in German rationalism and European existentialism, approached the world with a radically different posture than that of the separatists. Seeing no possibility of reconciling supernaturalism with prevalent scientific naturalism, modernists denied fundamental tenets of the faith, such as the virgin birth of Jesus, substitutionary atonement for sins, the authority of the Scriptures, and eternal punishment. This abandonment of the historic Christian faith was based on the belief that there was no possibility of mediating the New Testament Jesus to our modern times.

Others followed with radical notions, including the death of the idea of God in the world. God, they presumed, was no longer a useful construct to explain how humankind was to order life, meaning, and destiny. Thomas Altizer, to name only one of its proponents, actually believed that "to cling to these traditional images of Jesus is to pose an insuperable barrier to the appearance of Jesus in our flesh."[4] This world-view denies the historicity of Jesus, the historic Christian faith, and the church as the divinely revealed agent of proclaiming the gospel to the world. It renders the church powerless in addressing the *kosmos*, which lies under the influence of satanic power. Devoid of an objective basis for truth of any kind, the church from this vantage point becomes only one more human institution in a vast sea of purposelessness.

This loss of mission is tragic. Modernism and its successor, postmodernism, abandon all hope of bringing meaning and even hope itself to our world. Left only to a directionless subjectivism and moral relativism, society is ultimately threatened by nihilism, the death of all ideas.

One of the severest critiques of the accommodationists' approach to the world came from twentieth-century fundamentalism. The reaction of Christians to uncritical cultural adaptation produced a rising tide of revolt that eventuated in the publication in 1905 of *The Fundamentals*, a restatement of the major tenets of orthodox Christian faith. One might also claim that the lost mission of mainline Protestant denominations, which were held hostage to destructive modernist beliefs, led to the inevitable resurgence of evangelism by midcentury. Also rising voices within a corrupted Protestantism and a declining Catholicism became more and more strident. From the window on Rome came the voices and writings of Hans Küng and Karl Rahner. In a number of instances, in their call for reforms they "out-Luthered" Luther.

Furthermore, a voice from French Protestantism could not be silenced. Prolific author Jacques Ellul leveled blistering charges against a corrupt Protestantism. A descendant of the sixteenth-century French Huguenot movement, Ellul wrote as an informed Christian and academician. His works include more than twenty-one books in which he criticizes culture and the church's weakened message to present-day culture. Having lived all his life in a thoroughly secularized culture, this World War II resistance fighter addressed the strange perversion of ecclesiology by the accomodationists. In his book *The Subversion of Christianity*, he addressed the faulty attempt to keep up with modern times. "Christianity imbibes cultures like a sponge," he wrote. In a longer critique, Ellul leveled a withering barrage of words like a prophet of older times.

> Each generation thinks it has finally discovered the truth, the key, the essential nub of Christianity by veneering itself with the dominant influence or modeling itself on it. Christianity becomes an empty bottle that the successive cultures fill with all kinds of things. It is not because we are now discovering socialism or Islam that we are in some way more authentic before God than were our predecessors, so full of kindly feelings toward the poor savages that we have to bring them out of their misery, ignorance, sin, etc. Christianity has always been as elastic with cultures as with political regimes. I have said it a hundred times: monarchist under a monarchy, republican under a republic, socialist under communism. Everything goes. In this regard, too, Christianity is the opposite of what we are shown by the revelation of God in Jesus Christ.[5]

When the church adopted the world, kings gained approval, and colonialists and crooked capitalists were supposedly blessed, since their riches were assumed as a sign of divine benevolence. A happy announcement that all is well with the world brought temporary euphoria and the sanction of human values over God's values. Removal of guilt, the consummate goal of a therapeutic society, became the work of therapists, not the priestly work of Jesus Christ.

Quite obviously, this attempt to value human achievement and worldly advance is contrary to the biblical doctrine of justification by faith in Christ's atoning work on the cross. Again, the gospel is the norm by which the world is judged, unless it becomes the gospel shaped by each faddish thought in the name of relevancy. Erasing distinctions between the Scriptures and the world is always destructive to the church.

The Christian's Threefold Conversion

I believe it was Oscar Cullmann who first posed the idea that Christians need three conversions: one from the world to Christ in repentance, the second to the church in commitment, and the third to the world in witness. There is a lot of truth in this observation.

Evangelicals have been quite effective at announcing a "born-again" gospel. They have been less certain about what the conversion to the church is all about, preferring to personalize faith and to ignore the corporate dimensions of faith. As long as the church can be accepted in individual terms, believers are happy to join the circle. Doctrine is subsumed, minimized, or even ignored.

When the bishop of Woolwich, J. A. T. Robinson, startled the world with his paperback, *Honest to God,* Christians were shocked to read that a clergyman could actually accept the death-of-God idea. In reality, God has been dead in many churches for years, and the born-again converts to an evangelical faith know it. Many resist church for church's sake, preferring to cluster in bands of homogenous groupings that reinforce their own views of culture.

Christ calls us to Himself, and thus to His church. He calls us to oneness, even with those who differ socially from us. Paul declared that he was debtor "both to Greeks and non-Greeks, both to the wise and the foolish" (Rom. 1:14). To preach the gospel to these outsiders was one thing, but to fellowship with converts from differing social classes was quite another. That was and still is a radical idea.

The church should model its mission by its willingness to assimilate people of differing backgrounds. Our attraction to the church should be on the basis of our relationship to the Head of the church, not primarily to the social class of its adherents. Conversion to the church is a theological act, not a social joining. The dividing walls of hostility and enmity are shattered by the work of Jesus Christ, who brings people near to each other through His blood (Eph. 2:13).

Conversion to the world, the third "conversion" of Christians, is a controversial idea, unless it is conversion to the world for the sake of mission. In no way does this mean adaptation to *worldliness.*

The Bible tells us we are to be involved in the world, giving testimony to God's saving grace. If there is no mission to the world, there is no sense in calling any fellowship a church.

If God loved the world, so must we. But we must be clear as to what this means. As agents of reconciliation we are to accept the biblical truth that the world must be reconciled to God—not the church to the world. Unregenerate people are enslaved in sin, without hope, and without God in the world (2:12). The church is thus in the world to announce freedom in Christ to people in bondage to all forms of addiction—materialism, drugs, sexual perversion, selfism, gluttony, and political and economic power. To those who say they do not need God, Christ, or the church, we are to point the way to the Cross. To those who ask, "Is there anyone who cares?" we are to demonstrate concern that reflects the love of Christ

The Christian who has experienced God's love and grace, who clings tenaciously to the fellowship of a church, and who understands the call of Christ to serve in the world, is irrelevant, in a sense, by the world's standards. Jesus told His followers that they would be unpopular and persecuted, yet they would know His peace (John 16:33). In defense of his ministry, Paul answered a charge that he lived by the standards of this world: "For though we live in the world, we do not wage war as the world does. The weapons we fight with are not the weapons of the world" (2 Cor. 10:3–4).

The church does not have to show its relevance by a preoccupation with current events, being "up" with the times, or in tandem with current fads. The church is relevant in the true sense because the gospel that it proclaims holds answers to people's doubts, concerns, and suffering. The insertion of the eternal into the temporal is always relevant. Reliance on divine power marks the Christian presence in the world.

A creative writer once captured the dimensions of a relevant faith in a bit of free verse entitled "Hallowed Be Thy Name."

> In industry, God be in my hands and in my making.
> In the arts, God be in my senses and in my creating.
> In the home, God be in my heart and in my loving.
> In commerce, God be at my desk and in my trading.
> In healing, God be in my skill and in my touching.
> In government, God be in my plans and in my deciding.
> In education, God be in my mind and in my growing.
> In recreation, God be in my limbs and in my leisure.[6]

Christian Separation Revisited

American evangelicalism is still reeling from the modernist-fundamentalist controversy of the twentieth century. Its battles, like those of the two great world wars of this century, are not entirely forgotten, nor should they be. To a younger generation, raised neither on war or on a settled peace, the divisiveness, suspicion, character assassination, and outright hostility of Christians toward one another, which often characterized the controversy, seem remote and irrelevant. An important distinction needs to be made between cultural fundamentalism and doctrinal fundamentalism. The first is an aberration, the second is vital to understanding biblical truth. Truth battles have kept the church on edge since early times. Various formulations, creedal battles, lifestyles, and cultural mores have divided Christians. Aren't Christians to do battle with the devil rather than one another? we ask.

Dissent, disunity, and division result from our fallen sinful nature. James understood this when he asked the question, "What causes fights and quarrels among you?" (James 4:1).

Despite the abuses of Christians fighting each other, is there a legitimate place for the biblical teaching about separation from the world? Did not Paul command, "Do not be yoked together with unbelievers. . . . Therefore come out from them and be separate" (2 Cor. 6:14, 17)? What about Demas, who deserted Paul and thus was criticized because he loved this world (2 Tim. 4:10)? And did not John issue the command, "Do not love the world or anything in the world" (1 John 2:15)? And Timothy was warned to flee youthful lusts (2 Tim. 2:22), to turn away from godless chatter (1 Tim. 6:20), and to avoid a host of other wrong actions and attitudes. Believers are warned to have nothing to do with false teachers, and Christians are urged to abstain from the very appearance of evil (1 Thess. 5:22), and are even to hate what is evil (Rom. 12:9). And did not Jesus say, "My kingdom is not of this world" (John 18:36)?

The answer to this issue is simple yet complex. It is simple in that light and darkness do not mix. Believers are to separate from all forms of evil. The world, that is, the *kosmos* described in 1 John 2:15–17, is at enmity with God. This is the fallen race Noah condemned (Heb. 11:7). This is the world that was not worthy of martyrs (11:38). This is the world that Jesus said was not worth gaining (Matt. 16:26). This "world" is passing away (1 John 2:17), and, as such, was contrasted by Paul with the "Lord's affairs" in 1 Corinthians 7:31–33.

James defined pure Christian piety, or godliness, as keeping oneself from being polluted by the world (James 1:27), and Peter wrote of escaping "the corruption in the world caused by evil desires" (2 Pet. 1:4). Peter also referred to knowing the Lord and Savior as an escape from the corruption of the world (2:20). By revelation and by experience, Paul understood the corrosive effects of sin on the human race and wrote about them in detail (Rom. 1:18–32). As a follower of the risen Christ, he labeled the wisdom of this world "foolishness in God's sight" (1 Cor. 3:19).

Some have charged that Christian separation comes from a pessimism toward the world, similar to the prevailing attitude of some ancient Greek philosophers. Such, however, was not the case with John, Paul, Peter, or James. They were realists, describing things exactly as they saw them. Contrasted with the holiness of God, all that is worldly is exposed as fallen, flawed, and ripe for judgment.

The issue of Christian separation is also complex, as seen by a study of related Greek terms for *world*. For instance, the Greek word *aiōn*, "age," is used 122 times in the New Testament, but only 4 times does the New

International Version translate it "world." Jesus said that people of this "world" are more shrewd than are people of the light, that is, believers (Luke 16:8). In the parable Jesus commended this kind of shrewdness. Yet the other three uses of the word for "world" reflect either a neutral meaning or a condemnatory one. Those rich in this "world" are not to be arrogant (1 Tim. 6:17), and Demas, who loved this present "world," was not presented in a good light (2 Tim. 4:10). Paul used the word *aion* rather than *kosmos* in Romans 12:2, in which he warned believers not to be conformed to the pattern of this world.

How do we typify our own age? The cultural battles being waged are as real today as they have been at any time in the history of the church. John gave new meaning to "truth in labeling" when he wrote, "We know that we are children of God, and that the whole world is under the control of the evil one" (1 John 5:19). With this condemnation how are believers supposed to thread their way through the minefields of our world? Paul gave us a clear and comprehensive answer in Titus 2:11–12, in which he instructed Titus in the grace of our Lord. This grace that appeared in history, bringing salvation, is also a grace that teaches. Its pedagogical dimension extends to specific directives: saying no to ungodliness and worldly passions, and yes to self-controlled, upright, and godly living in this present age.

The words of Martin Luther can help us understand the issue of personal separation from sin. His direct, bold, and down-to-earth manner guided his congregation in his age and may likewise help us in our own:

> For we are not made for fleeing human company but for living in society and sharing good and evil. As human beings, we must help one another to bear all kinds of human misfortune and the curse that has come upon us. We must be ready to live among wicked people, and there everyone must be ready to prove his holiness instead of becoming impatient and running away. On earth we have to live amid thorns and thistles (Gen. 3:18), in a situation full of temptation, hostility, and misfortune. Hence it does not help you at all to run away from other people; for within you are still carrying the same old scoundrel, the lust and evil appetite that clings to your flesh and blood. Even if you are all alone, with the door locked, you still cannot deny your

father and mother; nor can you discard your flesh and blood and leave them on the ground. You have no call to pick up your feet and run away, but to stay put, to stand and battle against every kind of temptation like a knight, and with patience to see it through and to triumph.[7]

The church is in the world, just as the Spirit is in the world, restraining evil, tempering passions, making peace, and rebuking wrongdoing. While it is true that complete isolation from the world is impossible and counterproductive, the pulpits of our churches need to sound warnings about worldliness. Failure to do so is wrong, for silence on sin is itself a sin. A generation raised never to feel guilty about anything needs to know that guilt has passed on all humankind in that all have sinned and fallen short of God's glory (Rom. 3:23). They also need to know that Christianity is the only faith that gives an adequate answer to the problem of guilt. The announcement that there is no condemnation for those in Christ Jesus is indeed good news (8:1).

Saints of the past encourage us to reject the world's ways. Moses refused to be called the son of Pharaoh's daughter, identifying rather with suffering people. Joseph refused to succumb to temptation. Daniel stood his ground and suffered for it. The list is long, but the faith to overcome is strong, as these and other biblical examples show us. The same overcoming faith is ours today. To be in the world but not of it is difficult, but with God's presence and help it is not an impossibility.

We live in a real world, and God is far from dead. Christian theology takes seriously the task of understanding the context into which our Savior came and into which the church is to go in mission. While tensions remain between world and Word, between walking in the Spirit and not according to the flesh, Christians need not adopt a gnostic dualism to explain the world. "This is my Father's world," affirms the first line of a hymn written by Maltbie Babcock. God is still Ruler; the battle is not done.

God's world is the sphere of divine activity despite the evil of the present age. The whole creation, as Paul declared, "has been groaning as in the pains of childbirth" (8:22). This earth, this age, and this world were the arena of the Incarnation. It continues as the stage for the will of God ("Your will be done on earth as it is in heaven," Matt. 6:10). Christ, the Hope of the world, calls us to wait patiently until hope is fully realized. Meanwhile, we are to occupy planet earth until He comes. To this profound truth, early Christians would reply, "Maranatha" (Aramaic for "Come, O Lord," 1 Cor. 16:22).

BIBLICAL METAPHORS OF
THE CHRISTIAN WITNESS IN THE WORLD

The Bible portrays the church in the world as salt and light. Through this rich imagery, divine truth is pictured in graphic everyday terms. What could be more common and necessary to human experience than something as humble as salt and as sustaining as light?

Salt

Jesus' followers, He said, are like salt (Matt. 5:13). In Roman times salt was an extremely valued commodity, even to the extent that it was taxed. That is difficult for us to understand, since salt saturates the modern diet and is a cheap item on grocery store shelves. For years, one enterprising company that markets salt has had as its motto, "When it rains, it pours." Christian witness, like salt pouring from a salt shaker, needs to permeate our world.

In Old Testament times salt was considered a purifier (Exod. 30:35). Its curative and preservative properties were obvious. Yet salt can be destructive to plant life, as the German Army discovered when they broke the dikes of Holland during World War II, flooding fields with salt water. Abimelech, a conquering ruler in the Old Testament, salted the fields of the enemy to assure the ruination of crops (Judg. 9:45). But despite the destructive impact of salt on soil, it is generally portrayed in the Bible as a positive metaphor. Elisha added salt to purify bad water (2 Kings 2:19–22). A godly life, like salt, influences the world for good and for God.

Out of these and other contexts of Old Testament truth, the New Testament usage of salt as a metaphor is almost always positive. The only exception may be Jesus' reference to judgment in Mark 9:49: "Everyone will be salted with fire."

Salt is linked to grace in Colossians 4:6. Believers are urged to let their conversations be "always full of grace, seasoned with salt." Such a gracious manner toward others ought to accompany the proclamation of the gospel to "outsiders," that is, unbelievers (4:5). Being salt of the earth is the happy privilege of every believer, and corporately the church can influence culture. Just as the world cannot exist without salt, so the world needs the influence of the gospel.

Jesus' warning about salt losing its saltiness should be heeded. Who wants to bear the label, "No longer good for anything" (Matt. 5:13)?

Has the church lost its salting influence in our world? Not so long as it remains in the world offering the message of saving grace. The powerful metaphor of salt is useful for describing the beneficial presence of the church in the world.

Light

The church I attended as a young boy had a model of an actual lighthouse sitting out front. It was built by the father of evangelist Cliff Barrows of the Billy Graham evangelistic team. It stood for years as a symbol of the church, pointing people to the Savior.

Light has always symbolized the presence of God, who is light (1 John 1:5). Jesus used the metaphor of light to identify believers in the world. From a Galilean mountainside He said, "You are the light of the world" (Matt. 5:14). God has shed His light in the world both in creation and in the new creation. There is no more pervasive metaphor for portraying salvation than that of light. Light is linked to God's presence and blessing in His world (Ps. 44:3), in salvation (Ps. 27:1), and to His Son (John 1:9).

John the Baptist was called to bear witness to the Light (John 1:15), linking the eternal Word to our Lord as John the Evangelist faithfully wrote. Just as light dispels darkness, so when the true Light came into the world, darkness could not extinguish it.

At the Feast of Dedication, also known as the Feast of Lights, when people celebrated by carrying torches and lighting their houses, Jesus said, "I am the light of the world. Whoever follows me will never walk in darkness, but will have the light of life" (John 8:12).

Speaking of Himself as light, Jesus invited followers to become "sons of light" (12:36). This seems to be the pattern for all Christian witness in the world. To be lights in the world means to call people to the Light. Paul understood this to mean that converts from darkness were "light in the Lord" and thus were to "live as children of light" (Eph. 5:8). Explaining the metaphor, Paul said the fruit of light is "goodness, righteousness and truth" (5:9).

By contrast, light exposes the darkness of the human condition of sin. For this reason, Jesus warned that light must be fully displayed, not hidden by a bowl. The humble Near-Eastern clay lamp containing olive oil and a flax wick was ineffective if hidden (Matt. 5:14–16).

Has the church lost its light? Not if its witness to the light of the gospel is open, available to all, and unhindered. People "darkened in their understanding and separated from the life of God" (Eph. 4:18) need the bright light of God's truth. The Word, which the psalmist epitomized as "light" (Ps. 119:105), is to be open to all.

Christians are to be luminaries, shedding the gospel light in a sin-darkened world. Our Christian churches become houses of light only when the Word is taught and lived.

Another biblical metaphor has sometimes been used to describe Christian influence in the world. Just as light and salt influence everything they touch, so a little lump of leaven or yeast influences its surroundings. Leaven has usually been viewed as a corrosive element. At the Passover, for instance, only unleavened bread was to be used. Jesus warned His listeners about false teachers: "Be on your guard against the yeast of the Pharisees and Sadducees" (Matt. 16:11). When Paul noted that "a little yeast works through the whole batch of dough" (Gal. 5:9), he was referring to invasive legalism in the Galatian church.

How then could leaven have any redeeming property? In one of the parables of the kingdom in Matthew 13, yeast was used to describe the good influence of Christ's kingdom rule (13:33). This rare use of leaven in a positive image cannot be used as a driving metaphor of church influence in the world. Major Bible doctrines cannot be fully developed from metaphors of speech. However, God's present spiritual rule is indeed an invading force, and to that extent the use of the metaphor of leaven may relate to the role of the church in the world.

THE CHRISTIAN EXPERIENCE IN CULTURAL CONTEXT

Living the Christian life is not a private matter; it is a public issue. If we deny the escapist approach and adopt one of purposeful engagement, every Christian virtue becomes subject to scrutiny by the world. Christians are to be living advertisements for the faith.

In his letter to the Ephesians Paul wrote of the distinct role of the church in affirming the wisdom of God. "His [God's] intent was that now, through the church, the manifold wisdom of God should be made known to the rulers and authorities in the heavenly realms, according to his eternal purpose which he accomplished in Christ Jesus our Lord" (Eph. 3:10–11).

The unique role of the church is highlighted, but individual responsibility is taught as well. Paul urged Timothy to set an example for believers "in speech, in life, in love, in faith and in purity" (1 Tim. 4:12). In particular, the command that followed revealed both the inner and outer dimensions of the believer's life. "Watch your life and doctrine closely," Paul wrote. "Persevere in them, because if you do, you will save both yourself and your hearers" (4:16).

The Bible has no ambiguity on how believers are to conduct themselves in the world. The admonition, "Be very careful, then, how you live" (Eph. 5:15), is direct enough so none may miss its message. "Conduct yourselves in a manner worthy of the gospel of Christ" was the word for the Philippian Christians (Phil. 1:27). "You must no longer live as the Gentiles do," Paul wrote to believers living in the shadow of the immoral cult of Diana (Eph. 4:17).

Appeals for godly living in the New Testament were couched in a context of awareness that piety was on display—not in the Pharisaical manner of calling attention to oneself, but in an awareness of the impact on unbelievers. Peter pointedly wrote, "Live such good lives among the pagans that, though they accuse you of doing wrong, they may see your good deeds and glorify God on the day he visits us" (1 Pet. 2:12). This moral appeal extended to the intimacy of marriage as well as the public arena. The tantalizing possibility of their mates being won by example rather than talk is noted in 1 Peter 3:1–3, where Peter urged wives of unbelieving husbands to be submissive. Quoting from Psalm 34:12–16, Peter concluded his instructions to wives and husbands with a convincing summary of how to live in the world as a Christian: "Whoever would love life and see good days must keep his tongue from evil and his lips from deceitful speech. He must turn from evil and do good; he must seek peace and pursue it. For the eyes of the Lord are on the righteous and his ears are attentive to their prayer, but the face of the Lord is against those who do evil" (1 Pet. 3:10–12).

Specific New Testament teachings about moral virtue make particular reference to the context of a watching world. The following qualities form the basis of a life-view for contemporary evangelicals interested in making an impact on the world.

1. Blamelessness and purity (Phil. 2:14–16). Here the appeal is to shine like stars in the universe. No inner-directed piety is addressed here; rather, it is a penetrating image of witness in a "crooked and depraved generation."

2. Good works (1 Pet. 2:12). Doing good puts the lie to charges of wrongdoing. Peter's eschatological perspective (e.g., "glorify God on the day he visits us") formed the basis of moral appeal. It also gives a hint of evangelistic purpose in the world. Paul urged believers to "do good to all people, especially to those who belong to the family of believers" (Gal. 6:10).

3. Unspiteful living (1 Thess. 5:15). Retaliation of any kind is forbidden. Evil generates evil. Believers, by God's help, are to break the cycle by not paying back wrong for wrong. Paul was aware of the much larger context of society in urging kindness toward wrongdoing by the use of the words "and to everyone else." The "each other" grouping refers to the church, while "everyone else" refers to outsiders.

4. Reputation (1 Tim. 3:7). Here the appeal is directed to leaders in the church. The use of the word "outsiders" places unusual emphasis on avoidance of public disgrace and entrapment by the devil.

5. Humility (Titus 3:2). Humility is an outward virtue to be shown to all, not just to the inside cluster of the faithful.

6. Love. While believers are to show love within the circle of the church body, the great thrust is outward. This "royal law," as James called it, was simply "Love your neighbor as yourself" (James 2:8). Combined with the many verses that urge love of one another and even of enemies, this all-encompassing command speaks to a Christian ethic that transcends a narrow application. Believers are to be recognized by their love (John 13:35).

7. Mercy. Again, this universal virtue of mercy is to be applied in a broad cultural context. From the prophets to Jesus to the apostles, mercy is one of those virtues that, when applied, demonstrates the very essence of God. "Be merciful," Jesus said, "just as your Father is merciful" (Luke 6:36). James declared that mercy triumphs over judgment (James 2:13). Mercy ought to be the distinguishing feature of the church since it claims to be the recipient of God's mercy.

8. Peacemaking. The psalmist's dictum, "Seek peace and pursue it" (Ps. 34:14), is repeated twice in the New Testament (2 Tim. 2:22; 1 Pet. 3:11). Jesus gave special blessing to peacemakers (Matt. 5:9). Peace, as a virtue, was prominent in salutations, benedictions, and exhortations. We are called to live in peace (1 Cor. 7:15), for living at peace with everyone is to be a distinguishing mark of the church (Rom. 12:18; Heb. 12:14). As a fruit of the Spirit peace must accompany witness to the gospel of peace. Peace is both a bonding element within the body of Christ (Eph. 4:3) and a beneficial reproducer of the righteous life. "Peacemakers who sow in peace," James wrote, "raise a harvest of righteousness" (James 3:18). Without doubt, peacemaking in Jesus' name helps wins converts to Christ.

9. Unity. The unity of believers is perhaps the most powerful witness to the world of the saving grace of our Lord. This unity, explicitly related to the world, was a central petition of our Lord's prayer for His own. "May they also be in us so that the world may believe that you have sent me. . . . May they be brought to complete unity to let the world know that you sent me and have loved them even as

you have loved me" (John 17:21, 23). A unified church in the world is more than an ideal; it is a compelling and attractive necessity.

TODAY'S WORLD—CHALLENGE OR THREAT?

This question is not unique. It is as ancient as the church. Everywhere in our world there are social patterns destructive to humans, oppressions of every kind, crushing poverty, and evil of unlimited proportions. The challenge to the church is immense. Suffering, experienced little in American Christianity, and all forms of injustice cry out for solutions. Honest religion—the kind mentioned in James 1:27—carried with it the double-edged sword of effectiveness. The dimension of keeping oneself from being polluted by the world must never override the first concern, symbolized by acts of compassion shown to widows and orphans.

Evangelicalism is at a crossroads. But it has been there before. Our times are not necessarily unique. A spiritual battle is being waged between the forces of darkness and light. If the church goes where the pain is greatest and demonstrates that God can remove the pain, then Christian credentials are seen as good and the message may be accepted. Christian love exposes the forces of evil in our world that produce the pain. Only a spiritual solution will heal. Yet an essential part of the spiritual solution is to apply those many virtues of the Christlike life to the hurts of humanity. Faith that takes to the streets, that works in the marketplace, that engages the secular mind, when combined with love and hope, becomes a triumphant triad. Faith, hope, and love (1 Corinthians 13) —those enduring qualities extolled in the great love chapter of the Bible— are to shape all the church does in the world.

The Epistle to Diognetus, written in the second century A.D., reveals that Christianity had by that time reached all segments of society. This anonymous letter, though not part of Scripture, is the earliest surviving apologetic for the Christian faith. Its writer understood quite well the biblical teaching about the church's presence in the world.

> The distinction between Christians and other people lies not in country or language or customs. Christians do not dwell in special houses or

districts of cities, nor do they use a peculiar dialect, nor do they have any extraordinary customs. Their teaching has not been discovered by the intellect or thought of clever men, nor do they advocate any human doctrine. Wherever they live they follow local customs, eating food that local people eat, living in ordinary houses, and wearing clothes indistinguishable from those of their neighbors. It is in their attitudes that they are distinctive. They live in the lands where they were born, but see themselves not as owners of that land, but as sojourners; they are strangers on this earth. To them, every foreign land is like their fatherland, and every fatherland like a foreign land. They behave as perfect and upright citizens, according to the laws of the state they inhabit; but they see themselves as citizens of another state, the kingdom of God.[8]

11
The Church and Suffering

This is the course I have adopted in the case of those brought before me as Christians. I ask them if they are Christians. If they admit it I repeat the question a second and a third time, threatening capital punishment; if they persist I sentence them to death.

—Pliny the Younger

INEVITABLY THE CHURCH WILL EXPERIENCE SUFFERING and tribulation. Jesus predicted it, the apostles and early believers experienced it, and the long history of the church gives agonizing testimony to this reality. Like a buzz saw that hits the heartwood of a log, Christian witness cuts to the core of a corrupted society, and that results in the world's dislike and disdain of the church.

The passion of Christ set for all time the example of suffering for the early church. The scandal of the Cross formed the heart of apostolic preaching, and predictably, it provoked persecution. And it was through the historic reality of Christ's triumphant resurrection that perseverance and tenacious hope has characterized common believers and martyrs alike.

A New Testament theology of the church ought to include a theology of suffering. The New Testament writers wrote about it so that congregations of faithful believers would be better prepared to face all kinds of trials.

The apostle Peter gave extensive attention to it. Had he been like so many evangelical populists today, hungry to sell a book, he might have titled his first epistle *Ten Easy Steps on How to Suffer for Jesus.* Then again, today's generation might consider the topic irrelevant. Quite fortunately for us, Peter considered it relevant. His words grace the text of Scriptures with balance and divine insight:

> Dear friends, do not be surprised at the painful trial you are suffering, as though something strange were happening to you. But rejoice that you participate in the sufferings of Christ, so that you may be overjoyed when his glory is revealed. If you are insulted because of the name of Christ, you are blessed, for the Spirit of glory and of God rests on you. If you suffer, it should not be as a murderer or thief or any other kind of criminal, or even as a meddler. However, if you suffer as a Christian, do not be ashamed, but praise God that you bear that name. For it is time for judgment to begin with the family of God; and if it begins with us, what will the outcome be for those who do not obey the gospel of God? And, "If it is hard for the righteous to be saved, what will become of the ungodly and the sinner?" So then, those who suffer according to God's will should commit themselves to their faithful Creator and continue to do good. (1 Pet. 4:12–19)

WHAT IS NORMATIVE CHRISTIANITY?

This question has occupied my mind throughout my nearly six decades of following Christ. Peddlers of cheap grace offer a painless, bland brand of faith. Ascetics, on the other hand, want to make it more painful than it should be. Legalists institutionalize faith, like a system calling for conformity to human rules. But missing from all these is the voice of reality.

The Bible provides that reality, that wise and sensible word that lays out life as it really is, with all its agony and ecstasy. For Christians, suffering is more normative than we care to admit. Jesus was not the casual victim of random violence; He suffered for a cause. Christians, in similar fashion, have been called to suffer in Jesus' name. Our suffering, when and if it comes, links us to our Lord. As He bore His suffering and learned obedience through it, as Hebrews 5:8 attests, so may we bear our suffering and learn from it. In this respect, Christian suffering is lifted from the purely physiological aspect of any given trial, test, or torture. When done in Jesus' name, it bears the mark of the Cross.

The case for suffering being normative rests on three biblical truths. *First, all of creation suffers while awaiting the consummation of the age.* Everything this side of glory is imperfect, tainted by sin and human depravity, and involves suffering. Redemption, while obtained through faith in Christ's death on the cross, awaits the final transformation of our bodies (Phil. 3:21).

The apostle Paul placed the reality of present sufferings alongside a description of creation waiting in eager expectation for the sons of God to be revealed. Now subjected to frustration, yet hopeful of liberation from its bondage to decay, creation looks ahead to the glory yet to be revealed (Rom. 8:18–27). Present sufferings, Paul affirmed, do not compare "with the glory that will be revealed in us" (8:18).

Paul compared our suffering and that of all creation to the pains of childbirth, thus portraying suffering as a natural phenomenon in our fallen world. In all of this, however, we are not left helpless. The Holy Spirit helps us and intercedes for us, along with all the saints, in accord with God's will (8:26–27).

Second, suffering is normative for believers, as seen in verses on the theme, many of them spoken by Jesus Himself.

> Blessed are you when people insult you, persecute you and falsely say all kinds of evil against you because of me. Rejoice and be glad, because great is your reward in heaven, for in the same way they persecuted the prophets who were before you. (Matt. 5:11–12)

> All men will hate you because of me, but he who stands firm to the end will be saved. (Mark 13:13)

> If the world hates you, keep in mind that it hated me first. (John 15:18)

> Remember the words I spoke to you: "No servant is greater than his master." If they persecuted me, they will persecute you also. (15:20)

> "In this world you will have trouble. (John 16:33)

Third, suffering is part of the believer's identification with Christ. It is no isolated theme; it permeates the Bible. Nowhere is this more clear than in 1 Peter 2:21: "To this you were called, because Christ suffered for you, leaving you an example, that you should follow his steps."

Suffering, even persecution, follows as a result of this imitation of Christ. Paul made this clear to Timothy by preparing him for the reality of suffering: "In fact, everyone who wants to live a godly life in Christ Jesus will be persecuted, while evil men and impostors will go from bad to worse, deceiving and being deceived" (2 Tim. 3:12–13). Normal Christianity, then, includes suffering.

Is there a relationship between the sufferings of Christ and the sufferings of the church? Is there any sense in "making sense" of suffering? The Scriptures point to a bond that unites all sufferers with Christ. This does not mean that the suffering of the saints is the same as that of our Lord. Rather it is an interlocking of association. No witness to the truth of the gospel can ever be far from the Cross or from suffering.

F. F. Bruce placed the cross of Christ and continuing Christian witness in perspective. "Jesus," he wrote, "who began to act and teach on earth in the years immediately preceding A.D. 30, has continued to act and teach since that year by His Spirit in His servants; and the history of Christianity ought to be the history of what He has been doing and teaching in this way down to our own times—a continuous *Acts of the Apostles*."[1] He likened the history of the church to that of a great river, narrowing at times, flooding at other times, even going underground. While not exclusively such, church history has largely been a history of suffering.

From the vantage point of the first act of a continuous drama, Paul wrote of a purposive dimension to suffering and the church: "Now I rejoice in what was suffered for you, and I fill up in my flesh what is still lacking in regard to Christ's afflictions, for the sake of his body, which is the church" (Col. 1:24). Does this mean apostolic suffering was redemptive in some way? Was something lacking in the atoning value of Christ's sufferings? Must we add to the merits of our Lord by enduring suffering?

No, rather, Paul was continually participating in his identification with Christ by suffering. Testimony that the "sufferings of Christ flow over into our lives" (2 Cor. 1:5) demonstrated the "filling up" aspect of His suffering.

Paul desired during his trials that Jesus' life be revealed in his suffering body (4:10). Paul identified with Christ by showing calm endurance.

The afflictions of Christ for the sake of the church mentioned in Colossians 1:24 refer to His actual sufferings on the Cross. Paul's suffering was not to redeem, but rather to contribute to the ongoing spread of the good news of the gospel.[2]

There is no special merit in suffering, but there is great reward. All suffering in Jesus' name fulfills the high purpose of knowing Christ and the power of His resurrection and the fellowship of His sufferings. Suffering carries the weight of glory, allowing the Christian to become "like him in his death" (Phil. 3:10).

THE BIBLICAL MEANING OF SUFFERING

The word *passion* comes from the Greek word *paschō*, "to suffer" or "to endure." For the Greeks suffering was a path to knowledge, and as seen in Greek tragedies, suffering was to be accepted as fate.

The Bible counters this by focusing on the purpose of suffering, as in the case of Joseph's being sold into slavery (Gen. 50:20), which eventually resulted in blessing for the nation Israel. God directs all things for good. This potent idea, that God directs all things for good, is clearly evident Jesus crucifixion. The Cross countered Greek stoicism and all forms of fatalism. Suffering that improves character, a Wisdom Literature idea (Prov. 12:1; 13:1), was superseded by the vicarious element of messianic suffering in Isaiah 53. The Suffering Servant, the Davidic Messiah, was seen as bearing punishment for others. Christ's suffering on our behalf, as recorded in the Synoptic Gospels, fired the zeal of the church.

The salvation aspects of Christ's suffering form the basis of understanding all suffering. The Cross was no accident of history or act of random violence; it was divinely purposed.

The Author of our salvation (Heb. 12:2) is also the model for all suffering. In giving His life for sinners, the Sinless One tasted death for everyone (2:9). This mystery of the passion revealed One who bore the sins of many in obedience to the Father (Phil. 2:8; Heb. 5:8). His suffering was atoning (Rom. 3:25; Heb. 9:15; 1 John 2:2; 4:10), but ours is exemplary.

217

Out of the foundational truth that suffering has purpose and meaning, the church can confidently and triumphantly face its own suffering. All evil is short-lived (Rom. 8:18; 1 Pet. 1:6). Whatever is lost in life, even life itself, is like nothing in comparison to what one attains in Christ. Christians therefore endure suffering patiently.

Christian suffering is normative and unavoidable. It is to be viewed as for the gospel (2 Tim. 1:8), and suffering for Christ is nothing to be ashamed of (1:12). Christians are encouraged to face suffering with genuine joy (Matt. 5:12; James 1:2; 1 Pet. 1:6). Reactions to suffering are to be tempered by the Cross. Thus nonretaliation and love are extolled as virtues in the face of suffering. Believers are to imitate Christ in response to all acts of cruelty (Matt. 20:22; 1 Cor. 4:10–16; 1 Thess. 1:6). When cursed, we are to bless; when slandered, we are to act kindly.

In a sense all suffering is missionary in character,[3] for it serves to identify the true servants of Christ and His church. We are to suffer as Christians (1 Pet. 4:16), that is, in the name of Jesus (Acts 9:16; Phil. 1:29) and for the gospel (2 Tim. 1:8).

Suffering in this sense is eschatological. Its end is perfection (Heb. 2:10). Hope of eternal glory shrinks the "little while" phrase of 1 Peter 1:6 and 5:10 and amplifies the glory aspect.

Polycarp, an early martyr who refused to recant or to deny his Lord, was reported to have told his tormentors, "You threaten me with fire that burns for a few minutes and is then quenched."[4]

This eternal perspective has often led those who suffer to face trials with perseverance. "Do not look for status or glory on this earth," wrote Ignatius of Antioch, who hailed from the very city in which believers were first called Christians. "Desire God alone, that he may desire you, and so guide you into his eternal kingdom." These were words of a believer on his way to death. They reflect the temporal nature of suffering in the light of eternity.

Jesus' suffering was physical, emotional, and spiritual. In solidarity with all people, believer and unbeliever, Jesus suffered from hunger, weariness, scourging and, finally, crucifixion. He was tested on all points, like all humans, yet He was without sin. He taught His followers that all who would follow Him would suffer and be humbled enough to go the way of

the Cross (Matt. 20:22; Mark 13:9; Luke 9:23). In His suffering, He identified Himself with the poor and the outcast (Matt. 25:35–40).

Jesus also taught that all who share His suffering will share in His
kingdom. "I am among you as one who serves. You are those who have
stood by me in my trials. And I confer on you a kingdom, just as my
Father conferred one on me, so that you may eat and drink at my table in
my kingdom and sit on thrones, judging the twelve tribes of Israel" (Luke
22:27–30). While these remarks were directed to His disciples, the concept of a shared kingdom extends to all the faithful. To the church at
Smyrna, the angel of the church spoke a shocking yet reassuring truth: "I
know your afflictions and your poverty—yet you are rich! I know the
slander of those who say they are Jews and are not, but are a synagogue of
Satan. Do not be afraid of what you are about to suffer. I tell you, the devil
will put some of you in prison to test you, and you will suffer persecution
for ten days. Be faithful, even to the point of death, and I will give you the
crown of life" (Rev. 2:9–10).

John, whose own suffering on the Island of Patmos led to his death,
wrote of the certainty of great reward and final victory in the new heavens and the new earth: "He will wipe away every tear from their eyes.
There will be no more death or mourning or crying or pain, for the old
order of things has passed away" (Rev. 21:4).

THE PATH OF MARTYRDOM

Evangelicals have generally resisted the idea of Jesus being called a martyr,[5] preferring quite properly to use the biblical designation, "Savior of
the world." It was John Foxe, an Englishman born in 1517 at Boston,
Lincolnshire, who referred to Jesus as the first martyr and popularized
martyrdom by writing a lengthy history of martyrs.

"The first Martyr to our holy religion," Foxe wrote in his *Christian
Martyrs of the World*, "was Jesus Christ himself."[6] Without detracting from
his redemptive work, the word *martyr* may well describe the One who
first gave a good confession (1 Tim. 6:13). However, theological liberals
have wrested the term and made it void of redemptive meaning when
applied to our Lord.

219

The blood of martyrs has been called "the seed of the church," a phrase reportedly coined by the church father Tertullian. Luther once preached that it is impossible for the church to exist without shedding blood. Persecution, in other words, was viewed as the path of church growth.

In the early 1520s, two Christians were martyred at the hand of Rome for preaching the gospel in the Netherlands. Luther commemorated their heroism in a poem:

> Flung to the heedless winds,
> Or on the waters cast,
> The martyrs' ashes, watched,
> Shall gathered be at last;
> And from that scattered dust,
> Around us and abroad,
> Shall spring a plenteous seed
> Of witnesses for God.[7]

Luther himself was willing to die for the gospel. As early as 1520 he had anticipated martyrdom, when John Eck came to Germany fresh from Rome with the pope's announcement that Luther was to be excommunicated from the church. Luther considered martyrdom not only an honor to the victim, but also an asset to the church.

Oddly enough, the church itself has engaged in persecution of heretics and others. From its long history can be drawn many examples of Catholic and Protestant persecution of dissidents. Luther, however, repeatedly preached against returning evil with evil. He felt that the false church of Rome had taken to fire and force to protect itself from Scripture. But this gave no license to kill. When and if persecution would come, Luther urged believers not to resist, but to endure. All was in God's hands, he said. Referring to his enemies and to God's protection of his life, he gave glory to God. Luther once cited his own stance in the face of evil: "I did nothing; the Word did everything." He thus counseled believers at Wittenberg to quiet the radical image-breakers who were using violence in their efforts to reform the church.

The Meaning of the Word Martyr

It should not surprise us that the English word for martyr comes from a word meaning "witness." The Greek noun *martyria* comes from the verb *martyreō*, to "bear witness, or to testify." The word and its various forms appear most frequently in Acts and the Johannine literature. "You will be my witnesses," Jesus said on the eve of His ascension to the Father (Acts 1:8). Jesus witnessed to Pilate about His kingly role: "You are right in saying I am a king. In fact, for this reason I was born, and for this I came into the world, to testify [*martyreō*, 'give witness'] to the truth" (John 18:37).

Paul testified (*martyreō*) to the zeal of Jews (Rom. 10:2), to the generosity of the Macedonian churches (2 Cor. 8:3–5), and to the care of the church by Epaphras ("I vouch for him," Col. 4:13). Paul also witnessed to the gospel, testifying that God raised Christ from the dead (1 Cor. 15:15). His preaching was the proclamation of the testimony of God (2:1). In each case a witness was given.

In Acts the term *witness* was extended to Stephen. The New International Version translates the word *martyria* in Acts 22:20 as "martyr," thus identifying Stephen as the faithful witness and first martyr of the Christian church. The Revised Standard Version, on the other hand, translates this word *martyria* as "witness." Revelation 2:13 refers to Antipas as a "faithful witness who was put to death" for Jesus' sake. In the Tribulation many believers will be martyred for their "testimony to Jesus" (17:6).

Christian witness, then, refers to Jesus' testimony about Jesus Himself, the believer's testimony to the gospel of God's grace, and the proclamation of truth. A powerful summary of apostolic action and persistence occurs in Luke's account of John and Peter's response to the rulers, elders, and teachers of the law in Jerusalem: "We cannot help speaking about what we have seen and heard" (Acts 4:20).

Witness for Christ encompasses a vast arena. Nowhere is this more evident than in the "faith" chapter of Hebrews 11. All the signs of martyrdom are evident throughout the list of those who suffered for Jesus. They are given a lofty accolade by the writer to the Hebrews who called them "a great cloud of witnesses" (12:1).

Forms of Persecution

The New Testament bears witness to various forms of persecution and in some instances to the methods used to torture Christians. This is not meant to be an exhaustive list but may prove helpful in understanding the way faithful witness was rewarded with persecution.

First, there is reference to the Roman arena. Condemnation to the arena was reserved for the worst offenders against Roman law. Under the Roman emperor Caligula (A.D. 37–41), Christians may have been forced to face starved beasts, even lions, in the arena. He had erected a gilded statue of himself inside the temple, forcing compliance to his severe rule. The text of 1 Corinthians 4:9 probably refers both to a victory march of a conquering emperor and death in the arena: "For it seems to me that God has put us apostles on display at the end of the procession, like men condemned to die in the arena. We have been made a spectacle to the whole universe, to angels as well as to men."

Josephus, the early Jewish historian (around 37–100), wrote about these Roman arenas, which were similar to our own stadiums. The center arena with its sand or dirt surface, was the scene of contests of all kinds, including the sport of gladiators. Condemnation to the arena, however, did not always mean death. According to Josephus, Herod Agrippa was reported to have made over one thousand criminals fight in his amphitheater at Berytus (modern-day Beirut). Not all died in the arena. Paul's reference to fighting wild beasts in 1 Corinthians 15:32 may be a figurative expression of the ignominy and humiliation of being made a spectacle before the world.

Another form of persecution in New Testament times was stoning. This was a form of execution reserved under Jewish law for blasphemers or those caught in adultery. Usually, stoning was more a phenomenon of mob violence than the result of legal sentencing. The stoning of Stephen (Acts 7:57–60) and of Paul (14:19) are examples of this method used either to intimidate Christians or to hold back the inevitable advance of the church.

Crucifixion was a common Roman form of execution for criminals. To Christians, the Cross, a despised symbol of torture, became the focal point not of criminal guilt but of redemption. Ample evidence comes from historians and writers of early centuries of the church that many early Christians, both Jews and Gentiles, died by this method. Deuteronomy 21:22–23 and Galatians 3:13 give insight into the despised nature of death by crucifixion. Death by hanging on a tree may have been a Jewish method of execution and became linked to the uniquely Roman method of constructing a cross of wooden beams.

Another technique of torture was the use of fire. Death by burning became legal in the Greek and Roman cultures. Burning was known in the Old Testament (Gen. 38:24; Lev. 20:14; Josh. 7:25–28). Under Nero, Christians were burned at the stake, possibly serving as convenient scapegoats for his own crime of burning Rome in A.D. 64. The quenching of "the fury of the flames," mentioned in Hebrews 11:34, probably referred to this method of execution. The eighteenth-century hymn "How Firm a Foundation" poetically illustrates death by burning fire. The third stanza portrays persecution, God's protection, and its spiritual meaning for the good of the church. Its words recall the words of the prophet Isaiah in Isaiah 43:2.[8]

> When through fiery trials
> thy pathway shall lie,
> My grace, all sufficient,
> shall be thy supply:
> The flame shall not hurt thee;
> I only design
> Thy dross to consume
> And thy gold to refine.

Imprisonment, another form of punishment, was used extensively to persecute Christians. An old method of restraint, it became legal after the Exile. In Christian times, incarceration was commonly used to detain prisoners until a trial. Flogging, scourging, and other means of torture were often used along with imprisonment (Deut. 25:2–3; Acts 5:40; 16:37; 22:25; 2 Cor. 11:24). Paul reminded the Corinthian church that he had been beaten five times with thirty-nine lashes. On one occasion when he was about to be flogged, Paul appealed for mercy based on his Roman citizenship (Acts 22:25).

Later Christian witnesses invited flagellation (flogging) of the body to purify the soul. There is also evidence that the *stigmata*, the driving of an actual spike into the hands of a devout believer, served to identify the Christian with the stigma of the cross of Christ. These simulated aberrations of real persecution never became widespread in monastic times, but they illustrate how elevated persecution had become as a means of purifying the church.

Martyrdom for the faith intensified until the time of Constantine, when Christianity gained imperial favor. It is to this unfinished story of the church that we now turn.

Persecution and Martyrdom in Church History

It has been estimated that twenty-two million Christians now live in pockets of persecution.[8] Totalitarianism, intolerant Islamic fundamentalism, tribalism, nationalism, and ugly hatred all have played a part in persecutions of the church. The story will never be fully chronicled, but God, the righteous Judge, will bring retribution in His time.

The church was first tolerated as a legitimate form of Judaism. However, as opposition from Jewish leaders escalated, the Roman government began to persecute Christians. These persecutions grew out of misunderstandings over the secrecy of Christian worship and rites, particularly the Lord's Supper. This led to charges of cannibalism, incest, and promiscuity. Early Christian apologists defended Christianity against these and other false charges. Enforcement of the Roman law banning religions not approved by the government was probably mixed, depending on local situations. The deification of Caesar, "Caesar is God," flew in the face of believers who affirmed the earliest creed, "Jesus is Lord."

Generally speaking, early Christians followed the advice of the apostles, such as that in Romans 13:1–6, warning believers not to resist government or to become seditious. The tension between free exercise of faith and oppression of faith was epitomized by the words of Peter, "We must obey God rather than men!" (Acts 5:29), in contrast to Paul's dictum, "obey civil magistrates" (Rom. 13:1, KJV).

The age of Diocletian has been called the bloodiest period of martyrdom in the history of the church. In 284 Gaius Aurelius Valerius Diocletianus ascended to power as the Roman emperor. On February 23, 303, his Edict of Nicomedia called for burning of churches and Christian books. His fury toward Christians left a trail of blood, even a baptism of blood predicted by our Lord (Mark 13:9–13). Intense persecution ended with Constantine's defeat of Maxentius, a Roman emperor, in 312. The Edict of Milan (313) extended freedom of worship and Christians were given back their confiscated property.

The elevation of martyrs grew over time. They were highly esteemed, as Hebrews 11 attests. Eventually they were venerated and even elevated to sainthood. Until 1969 the Roman Church required that relics of martyrs had to be contained in every consecrated altar. This is still a law in the Eastern Orthodox Church.

Some people wrongly view martyrs as intercessors. Special celebration of martyr days, the presence of paintings and images of selected suffering saints, and other forms of veneration are still in vogue. While the martyrs' examples of faithful witness assist us in our own faith, martyrs in no way become advocates or intercessors on our behalf. That role is reserved for the Holy Spirit and our Lord.

Martyrdom was the fate of nearly every apostle, except John, who died in prison. Stephen died a martyr, as did James. Acts 8 reveals an outbreak of persecution against the church at Jerusalem. Believers were scattered throughout the Roman world, but the apostles remained in Jerusalem. Saul of Tarsus was among the tormentors. Later, he himself would die as a martyr. Under Herod, James the brother of John died by the sword. But despite the prevalence of suffering in the New Testament, there are no instances in the Bible of the veneration of saints, martyrs, or even Mary.

The first martyrology, or story of Christian martyrs, that survives is in the form of a letter from the church at Smyrna in 155. At a festival for the ruling Caesar, a number of Christians were thrown to wild beasts. The letter tells of the astonishment of the crowd by the conduct of the "God-beloved and God-fearing race of Christians." Yet the crowd cried out, "Away with the atheists." This was a common epithet applied to Christians because they refused to worship heathen idols and had no images of their own. In this unusual document, the martyrdom of Polycarp, one of the most celebrated Christians, is described in detail from his arrest to his final death. When his captors came to get him, he said, "Let the will of God be done," and then he proceeded to offer food and drink to the soldiers.

"Swear by the genius of Caesar," they told him. "You need only say, 'Away with the atheists,' and your life will be saved."

Turning to the crowd of pagans, Polycarp said, "Away with atheists." This spurred both the crowd and the proconsul to anger. Again they commanded, "Take the oath and revile Christ." Polycarp replied, "For eighty-six years I have been his servant, and he has done me no wrong. How can I blaspheme my King who saved me?"

The old man was then led to the stake, refusing to be tied or restrained, offering himself willingly to the flames.[9]

It is erroneous to assume that every witness for Christ is a martyr. Even in the New Testament, some distinction was made between a mere witness and a martyr. Our various translations indicate the different uses of the term and the care given in selectively reserving the word *martyr* for those who suffered death for their witness. A confessor who was faithful to death, as in Jesus' case (1 Tim. 6:13), may bear the title with distinction. Thus from Eusebius onward, a martyr denoted a believer who voluntarily died for his or her confession of faith.[10]

Martyrdom for the faith has increased over the centuries. There are uncounted numbers of believers whose witness for Christ and subsequent deaths qualify them as martyrs. To use a phrase from Isaiah the prophet, the grave "enlarges its appetite" (Isa. 5:14). Beginning with the drowning of Anabaptist leader Felix Manz in January 1527 in the Limmat River in Zurich, church and state opposition to the Anabaptist movement persisted for almost two hundred years.[11]

Many Anabaptists suffered severely at the hands of church leaders, who wanted to wipe out what they considered a troublesome sect. Anabaptists were drowned, burned at the stake, and beheaded. Many were banned from their homeland and their property confiscated.

History records divisions in the church from early times over what to do with Christians who lapsed in faith or recanted in the face of martyrdom. In 249–50 Novation led a rigorous party that refused to make any concessions to those who recanted. Even if they later repented, they were barred from church membership and the sacraments. In the same manner the Melitian and Donatist schisms in the African church were due in part to the view that Christians who renounced their faith were not welcome in the church. The Donatists even went so far as to separate from other Christians who defended restorative efforts to renew fellowship with those who had recanted.

Evidence of the same attitudes in the Ukrainian and Romanian churches today indicates a problem for Christian unity. In these cases, which I have personally witnessed, Christian ministers who suffered under communism have difficulty identifying with younger leaders, who were never called on to suffer imprisonment or death. Reportedly a new legalism is emerging that elevates sacrifice over nonsacrifice, suffering over nonsuffering. While sympathetic with an older generation that paid dearly for their confession of faith, younger leaders want to get on with the future witness of the church and not carry the burden placed on them by those who remained true to the gospel under communism.[12]

RESULTS OF PERSECUTION, SUFFERING, AND MARTYRDOM

The evangelical church now enjoys a vantage point of history unknown in earlier times. Technology and communication have made a smaller world. A global village now exists in which news of genocide and Christian suffering comes almost instantaneously to us. The American church has become somewhat insular, immune to much persecution for the faith on domestic soil. However, the general suffering of poverty and injustice in our nation and world are never far from the knowledge of Christians, if not in their conscience.

There are several obvious results of suffering that potentially benefit the church. *First, suffering can help us better understand others who suffer.* If we were to grant the reality of suffering as normative in the church, we would be more understanding of others who are called on to suffer. Compassion must extend to believer and unbeliever alike, whose lot in life is not like our own. It would indeed be tragic if the contemporary church would stoop to class distinctions, smugly viewing the suffering of others as evidence of God's judgment and the absence of such as God's blessing. Arrogance and pride, which often accompany privilege, are foreign to true faith in Christ.

Solidarity with all who suffer ought to mark contemporary evangelicals. Without succumbing to a theology of liberation shaped by defining faith as action, the church must, nevertheless, encourage causes that are consistent with a biblical view of God's justice. Our solidarity is with all who are victims of injustice and prejudice. Especially is our solidarity to be with the persecuted church worldwide (1 Cor. 12:26). We are to pray for one another, share our resources, exercise our rights as citizens in enacting just laws, and reach out in genuine compassion to those who suffer.

Second, suffering can lead to the purification of the church. When Christianity became fashionable after the fourth century, the church became corrupt with power. Persecution in the church, an extreme form of human suffering, purged the church of nominalism, a curse of our times as well as then. Persecution discouraged people from joining churches. People whose supposed "faith" was not genuine fell away. Sincerity of commitment proved strong enough to withstand the onslaught of abuse. It toughened the church so it could recognize and deal with heresy. It built a church whose apologists could define true Christian faith in the face of false Christianity.

A South Korean woman, whose radiant faith transcended language and cultural barriers, once remarked to me that the church in North Korea was healthiest under persecution from communism. Commenting on the deprivation and suffering brought on by the Korean War, she said, "We were strongest when we had nothing but our Lord."

Third, suffering can result in a display of God's provision and power to overcome evil. Survival of the church under persecution is eloquent testimony to God's overcoming power. Successive waves of trial and tribulation, even those that appear now to be intensifying on all continents, have been met by overwhelming evidence of God's sovereignty turning evil for good.

Fourth, suffering can lead to a new appreciation of divine reward. An affluent church trusting in its power and materialism to bring further prosperity is in danger of developing a warped view of divine reward.

Prosperity tends to feed on itself, commending its own successes as evidence of divine favor. We need only read the eulogy of sufferers in the Bible to gain an eternal perspective on reward.

> And what more shall I say? I do not have time to tell about Gideon, Barak, Samson, Jephthah, David, Samuel and the prophets, who through faith conquered kingdoms, administered justice, and gained what was promised; who shut the mouths of lions, quenched the fury of the flames, and escaped the edge of the sword; whose weakness was turned to strength; and who became powerful in battle and routed foreign armies. Women received back their dead, raised to life again. Others were tortured and refused to be released, so that they might gain a better resurrection. Some faced jeers and flogging, while still others were chained and put in prison. They were stoned; they were sawed in two; they were put to death by the sword.... The world was not worthy of them. They wandered in deserts and mountains, and in caves and holes in the ground. These were all commended for their faith, yet none of them received what had been promised. God had planned something better for us so that only together with us would they be made perfect. (Heb. 11:32–40)

Reward does not come only in this life. Perfection is the eternal prize for anonymous sufferers. The weight of eternal glory tips the scales, thereby giving us perceptions we would not otherwise enjoy. The pedagogy of suffering is tuition-free and priceless.

It is fitting to ask why the church should develop a theology of suffering. For one thing, it will keep the church close to Christ, the "faithful and true witness" (Rev. 3:14). A church constantly reminded of our Lord's "good confession" before Pilate will not easily stray from its Master.

The factual content of Christian witness that is true to the gospel will be seen as far superior to an emotional, experiential faith. In an age of increasing religious pluralism, twenty-first century apologists need a well-informed faith to do battle with ideas unfriendly to faith. A thin, antiintellectual activism may produce church growth of a kind, but it will not withstand persecution.

There is much at stake today. We may be living in a time when the most politically incorrect thing to do is to be a witnessing Christian. Facing this increasing unpopularity, the church has a choice. It may accommodate its message to the times or hold true to Christ. The church must choose the latter, aware that just as Paul declared four times, God is my witness" (Rom. 1:9; 2 Cor. 1:23; Phil. 1:8; 1 Thess. 2:5), so the Lord is aware of our suffering as well.

Also a theology of suffering will help us see the need for perseverance. As Paul wrote, "Suffering produces perseverance" (Rom. 5:3). The end results are character and hope, two commodities in short supply today. Perseverance, James taught, is the by-product of testing (James 1:3). Peter linked it to self-control and godliness (2 Pet. 1:6), and Paul commended the saints to God's love and Christ's perseverance (2 Thess. 3:5). James, echoing the blessing of Jesus, gave his own beatitudes to suffering (James 1:12; 5:11). Perseverance, according to the author of Hebrews, is merely the God-given tenacity of one who does the will of God (Heb. 10:36).

The path of perseverance is rough, but its end is rewarding. Just as love perseveres (1 Cor. 13:7), so faith must press on. As the emperors of Rome could not quench the prison-bound witness of the apostle John at the end of the first century, so no human government may completely stifle the witness of persevering believers. Perseverance may land believers in jail, but it will overcome. Neither Domitian (81–96), or Vespasian (69–79) could stamp out the spreading flame of Christianity.

In all this discussion about the suffering church, consolation comes from Paul's word to the Thessalonian believers: "For God did not appoint us to suffer wrath but to receive salvation through our Lord Jesus Christ" (1 Thess. 5:9). The hope of the church is the return of Christ, not His wrath.

Among the vast literature on the theme of suffering, there has emerged a classic, *The Suffering Savior*, by F. W. Krummacher. Originally printed in 1854, it was written for the encouragement of Christians. Facing the inevitability of pain, tribulation, and suffering, as well as future reward, this godly German scholar wrote comforting words. Though flowery and stilted by today's standards, his words convey a marvelous perspective: "Let us then tune our harps, and hold our festive garlands in readiness, while awaiting the right moment that shall put an eternal end to all the sadness and anxiety of the human heart."[13]

12
The Church and Its Hope

> A fairer Paradise is founded now
> For Adam and his chosen sons, whom thou
> A Saviour art come down to re-install;
> Where they shall dwell secure, when time shall be,
> Of tempter and temptation without fear.

—John Milton

SHAKESPEARE ONCE WROTE that people who are miserable have no other medicine but hope. Today our self-made society has lost its reason for hope. A false sense of immortality has dulled the senses of moderns. To the self-satisfied, there is no need of hope. Only when crisis comes do people cry out for help and hope.

Because the Bible portrays a bright future for the redeemed, believers are encouraged to face the future with confidence and hope. Christian hope serves as fuel for living and guards us from fear of the enemy called death. As a virtue, it endures along with faith and love. Anchor of the soul and purifier of life, hope offers a golden route to glory.

Hope, like the famous diamond of the same name, contains many facets reflecting the light of God's truth. Our hope resides in God, who has given us hope through the gospel. It is not mere anticipation and wishful thinking; rather, it springs from vital faith in the resurrected Christ. Hope is virtually synonymous with trust in God.

In view of our Christian hope we are to lead sober, upright, and godly lives. We cherish the blessed hope of Christ's appearance and the hope of eternal life. New Testament hope, according to Ernst Hoffmann, "is a patient, disciplined, confident waiting and expectation of the Lord as our Saviour."[1] It is hope centered only on Christ, who is our hope (1 Tim. 1:1; Col. 1:27). Christ alone, and the future He has made certain, is the hope of the church in life and in death.

HOPE—JEWEL OF THE FAITH

A Christian woman who had been sexually abused by her abductor once stated, "I understand God less but trust Him more." Hope rises in the human heart from a clear faith in God, not as a result of a crystal-clear understanding of all that the future holds. It sprouts from the fertile soil of confidence in God. In the shifting and treacherous tides of daily living, we all need an anchor. Hope, like a precious diamond formed by pressure and heat, emerges from faith under trial. Faith produces hope.

Christian hope refuses to bow to despair or cynicism. Bertrand Russell, the agnostic twentieth-century philosopher, wrote of his own hopeless life: "The life of man is a long march through the night, surrounded by invisible foes, tortured by weariness and pain, toward a goal that few can hope to reach, and where none may tarry long. One by one, as they march, our comrades vanish from our sight, seized by the silent orders of omnipotent death."[2]

Our hope as Christians comes not from human optimism, but from the divine act of salvation accomplished by Christ, our salvation that is both present and future. Paul wrote of both of these dimensions. "But by faith we eagerly await through the Spirit the righteousness for which we hope" (Gal. 5:5). And anticipating our final adoption as sons, he wrote, "in this hope we were saved" (Rom. 8:24).

The Bible clearly indicates the hopeless condition of unrepentant sinners. In the New Testament, the hopeless are described as having cast off all feeling (Eph. 4:19). Christians in Ephesus were reminded by Paul that at one time they were without hope and without God in the world (Eph. 2:12). And he instructed Thessalonian believers not to grieve like the rest of the human race, who have no hope (1 Thess. 4:13).

Hope is the product of the gospel (Col. 1:23). God holds out hope to all who respond to the free offer of salvation in Jesus Christ. Salvation, gospel, and hope all go together. Eternal encouragement and "good hope" are the fruit of salvation. There can be no gospel apart from God's salvation and no hope apart from the gospel.

Because of salvation our hope is "in Christ" (Eph. 1:12). And while salvation has many benefits, it has only one focus, according to Ephesians 4:4—one hope.

Those who place their faith in Christ are born again "into a living hope," that is, a genuine, active hope, not a false, dead one. This is possible because of Jesus' resurrection from the dead (1 Pet. 1:3). This hope is stored up in heaven like a deposit in a reliable bank (Col. 1:5). Paul's testimony to the Corinthian church was direct and simple: "He has delivered us . . . and he will deliver us" (2 Cor. 1:10). In this one sentence all bases are covered for the believer. Therefore we have good reason for hope.

Christian hope is dependent on trusting God, a fact that helps believers live supernaturally. "Hope that is seen," Paul wrote the Roman believers, "is no hope at all" (Rom. 8:24). In the great definition of faith in Hebrews, "faith is being sure of what we hope for" (Heb. 11:1).

Christian hope is not merely a restless waiting. It is a joyful and peace-giving attitude of living. In Paul's benediction in Romans 15:13, he expressed the whole point of hope as being joy and peace, not merely an endurance contest to the end. This kind of hope may rightly be labeled "overflowing" hope.

Christian hope does not rest on possessions, but on the assurance that God will keep His Word. Thus Paul could write to Corinthian believers that they were to be pitied if their hope was only in this life and its worldly possessions (1 Cor. 15:19). True hope does not disappoint us. Its possession is more than a passing thing of this life. It endures all the way to glory. Hope is a virtue that endures (13:13).

Few Christians live to see all their service come to fruition. Yet others like the apostle Paul can point to people won to Christ and pointed toward heaven: "For what is our hope, our joy, or the crown in which we will glory in the presence of our Lord Jesus when he comes? Is it not you?

Indeed, you are our glory and joy" (1 Thess. 2:19–20). Life then for the serious Christian is one of sowing seeds of hope for an eternal harvest.

Christian hope is centered in Christ. It has substance only in faith in a resurrected Christ. Ancient Job asked, "If a man dies, will he live again?" (Job 14:14). The New Testament revelation of the reality of resurrection answers his question and forms the heart of the message of the primitive church. Oscar Cullman, writing on the earliest Christian confessions, believed that the center of the faith of primitive Christianity was the lordship of Christ, inaugurated by His resurrection and exaltation at the right hand of God.

Without doubt, the resurrection of Christ formed the basis of the preaching of the gospel ("He was raised on the third day according to the Scriptures," 1 Cor. 15:4). His resurrection is central to the gospel (Rom. 4:25; 8:11; 10:9; 2 Cor. 4:14-15; Gal. 1:1; Eph. 1:20; Col. 2:12; 1 Pet. 1:21).

Christian hope is not in reincarnation but in resurrection. The classic passage dealing with immortality and resurrection is 1 Corinthians 15:17–18. Resurrection deals with the immortal body, not another mortal one. It is a one-time event, not a repeated phenomenon in successive lives. Immortality through resurrection is the ultimate state of redemption. It involves a state of a perfected body, not one in the process of perfection through a series of lifetimes. Since believers have been raised with Christ and will someday be translated or resurrected from this earthly life, we are to set our hearts on things above. Christian hope is setting our minds on things that are heavenly (Col. 3:1–10). The new life, of which Paul wrote in Romans 6:4, is to be lived as a result of Christ's being raised from the dead to the glory of the Father.

Immortality without resurrection would be a monstrous thing. What would survival after death mean if it did not include fellowship with our Lord? But hope of future resurrection does not dull joy in this life. It lights up the darkness of death.

John Milton (1603–1674) once described despair in his classic poem, *Paradise Lost*. This book has fascinated its readers for generations. But who remembers reading his other classic, *Paradise Regained*? In two succinct passages, Milton described both despair and Christian hope.[3]

A Dungeon horrible, on all sides round
As one great Furnace flam'd, yet from those flames
No light, but rather darkness visible
Serv'd only to discover sights of woe,
Regions of sorrow, doleful shades, where peace
And rest can never dwell, hope never comes
That comes to all; but torture without end
Still urges, and a fiery Deluge fed
With ever-burning sulfure unconsumed. . . .

—*Paradise Lost* 1:60

At the end of *Paradise Lost*, Milton gave a glimpse of *Paradise Regained*.

Some natural tears they dropped, but wiped them soon;
The world was all before them, where to choose
Their place of rest, and Providence their guide:
They hand in hand with wandering steps and slow
Through Eden took their solitary way.

—*Paradise Lost* 12:645

The Bible contrasts despair and hope in much clearer, if less poetic, fashion than Milton, who gained his inspiration from the Bible. "Then death and Hades were thrown into the lake of fire. The lake of fire is the second death. If anyone's name was not found written in the book of life, he was thrown into the lake of fire" (Rev. 20:14–15). "He will wipe every tear from their eyes. There will be no more death or mourning or crying or pain, for the old order of things has passed away" (21:4).

A word needs to be said about the certainty of Christian hope. Our certainty or assurance of what we hope for (Heb. 11:1) must be based on the God of hope (Rom. 15:13). Three times in Hebrews the Greek word *hypostasis* occurs, and it is variously translated "assurance," "substance," "confidence" (Heb. 3:14), "being sure" (11:1), and in Hebrews 1:3 it carries the meaning of invisible, transcendent reality. In 1:3 Jesus is revealed as the essence and exact likeness of the Father. Early scholars translated the word in Latin as *substantia*, from which we get our word "substance." While the word seems to be linked primarily to faith, it is linked to hope in Hebrews 11:1. Melanchthon advised Luther to translate *hypostasis* as "sure confidence." Faith in this light is a personal, subjective conviction, a departure from the objective use of the term in 1:3. We usually think that the subjective dimension is transient and thus tenuous. Yet when linked to the objective fact that Jesus is the reality, or "demonstration," of our sovereign God, the word *substance* or *certainty* moves beyond subjective experience. Hope rests on certainty or substance, not on mere transient feelings. The statement, "We have come to share in Christ if we hold firmly till the end the confidence we had at first" (3:14) is a fundamental admonition of Hebrews. It summons hope to cling to established faith.

The hymn writers understood both the subjective and objective elements of our faith and hope. Isaac Watts (1674–1748) confidently addressed God in the hymn, "O God, Our Help in Ages Past." God was to him "our hope for years to come." A century later Edward Mote (1797–1874) wrote, "My hope is built on nothing less than Jesus' blood and righteousness." Charles Wesley's lyrics combine both:

> In hope against all human hope
> Self desperate, I believe;
> Faith, mighty faith the promise sees,
> And looks to that alone;
> Laughs at impossibilities,
> And cries: It shall be done.[4]

The cheering hope we long for is an abiding reality of the Christian experience. "Because God has promised," wrote David Hubbard," we can hope with full confidence. All that he has foretold will take place. Because God has promised, even what we hope for will be filled with surprise; the surprise that comes from seeing him, from being with him, from watching him make all things new—even us!"[5]

THE CHURCH AS AN ESCHATOLOGICAL COMMUNITY

Traditionally the doctrine of the last things has centered around the end of the age, the second coming of Christ, the resurrection of the dead, the last judgment, and the new heavens and new earth. This chapter, which concerns itself specifically with the hope aspect of the church, is not meant to provide a full eschatology (Greek, *eschatos*, "last"; *logos*, "word"). Our focus is on the church as a community of people of hope.

Christ's call to Himself is far more than to a temporal life enhanced by His presence. It is a call offering eternal life that touches the present and future.

Peter, who has been called the apostle of hope, understood this. "But in your hearts," he wrote to scattered believers whose existence was far from hopeful, "set apart Christ as Lord. Always be prepared to give an answer to everyone who asks you to give the reason for the hope that you have" (1 Pet. 3:15). The ultimate apologetic for the faith is the hopeful life. Peter added that such an answer was to be given with gentleness and respect, backed up by a clear conscience. Hope in this dimension is to be the continuous state of the redeemed. When secular society asks, "Where is there any hope in this world?" Christians can be ready with the answer.

We give the name "hope" to hospitals, charitable organizations, and churches. This is only proper and even biblical in the broadest sense. In an even more significant way, churches should be havens for the hopeless, offering hope through the gospel (Col. 1:23).

By faith we began our Christian life, with hope we continue it, and by faith we look ahead to glory. Without faith, hope is merely presumption. Our hope rests on God's mercy and not our merits.

Paul referred to "the hope of salvation as a helmet" (1 Thess. 5:8). Believers are to put on this helmet in the same manner as they are to put on faith and love as a breastplate. Life for the church is a pilgrimage during which it is preserved by hope.

As a community of hope, we are to wait on the Lord (Heb. 2:13). Luther said the two words *expectabo Dominum* ("I will wait for the Lord") in the Vulgate translation of this verse are the summary of Christian doctrine.[6] The New International Version translates these words in this verse, "I will put my trust in him." Hope is like a guiding star to a ship on a vast sea. What oxygen is for the lungs, hope is for the Christian.

The truth of the return of the Lord is the hope of the church. For those who do not believe in the existence of God, hope, however, is an absurdity. But to the faithful body of believers, hope rests on the promises of God. For the church this is not mere speculative conjecture. The future is as real as the promises of God. And His promises are as real and reliable as He is. All this is a matter of faith and hope in God Himself.

The fulfillment of human destiny cannot be found in any political order. This false substitute for the kingdom or rule of God is the result of corrosive secularism that has eaten away at the very foundations of the faith. Secularity knows no transcendent realities. In the secular world hope is merely the enhancement of human capabilities.

For the church, however, hopeful living moves toward the climax and culmination of God's divine program of redemption. It longs for a city not made by human hands. Its pilgrimage marches confidently toward the day when God will be all in all. Destiny is wrapped up in the reality of God's creative endeavor manifest in creation, the new creation, and in His ultimate rule. This lordship of God will be total and final when all the saints—past, present, and future—gather around His throne and offer praises to God the Father, God the Son, and God the Holy Spirit.

Meanwhile we struggle to find the meaning and significance of the promises of God about the end times. Yet in our study of what the Bible says about the future we must keep our eyes on Christ, our Alpha and Omega, the First and the Last (Rev. 1:8). The content of our Christian hope includes expectation of the return of Christ for His church that has been purchased with His blood. It includes the expectation of bodily resurrection of the dead in Christ and the translation of living saints with resurrected bodies. This hope focuses on our complete sanctification or perfection in Christ, and our future reward. Christian hope also looks forward to eternal fellowship in heaven.

John F. Walvoord, whose writings have helped countless Christians understand this hope, once wrote a very useful word of caution: "The prophetic hope of the world," he wrote, "was never intended by God to be an arena of theological debate, but rather a magnetic goal, attracting the pilgrim saint as he struggles, stumbles, and yet climbs upward."[7] Scholars have indeed differed, even within evangelicalism. These differences have touched nearly every aspect of eschatology, except the single overarching doctrine of the personal return of Jesus Christ. On that we can all agree.

Avowedly premillennial in stance and accepting two aspects to Christ's second coming—one for His own and the other for the establishment of His kingdom—I am drawn to the teaching of an imminent return of Jesus Christ. This was the hope of first-century saints, as it is ours today. Of course the ways and purposes of God are complex. Only when faith turns to sight and hope is rewarded in the fulfillment of prophecy will believers know as they are known (1 Cor. 13:12). In this life, our knowledge is only partial. Thus positions held on various doctrinal themes, especially the last times, should be held with humility and with love toward those believers who differ. Obviously vigorous debate is helpful and there can be no mixing of belief and unbelief when it comes to the vital truths revealed in Scripture. We part company with those who believe that there is no second coming of our Lord, for this makes the very words of Jesus a falsehood. Paul made the profound statement, "If only for this life we have hope in Christ, we are to be pitied more than all men" (1 Cor. 15:19).

A word must be given here about the ethical implications of Christian hope to be developed later. Lewis Sperry Chafer once wrote, "Knowledge of Biblical prophecy qualifies all Christian life and service."[8] The Scriptures often focus on living holy and godly lives in light of our Lord's return.[9]

A student of Martin Luther once asked what he would do if he knew the Lord was returning the next day. Luther replied that he would continue doing what he was doing, only he would do it better. Living the hope-filled life better is the whole point of Christian hope.

Helmut Thielicke believed that eschatology opens the horizon of Christian ethics, writing that the "one day gives us standards for 'today.'"[10] This is the perspective of church hope that I believe can unite believers and purify the church.

The Church and the Kingdom

Jesus preached that His followers should first seek His kingdom (Matt. 6:33). His early pronouncement, "Repent, for the kingdom of heaven is near" (Matt. 4:17; see also Mark 1:15), raised the kingdom question, which persisted in the Synoptics and was raised at the trial scene before Pilate (John 18:33). What did Jesus mean by a kingdom?

Christians have held radically differing views on the meaning or meanings of the word *kingdom*. Disciples in Jesus' day were themselves confused. Jewish zealots envisioned an earthly kingdom that would match, if not overcome, imperial Rome. Augustine's *City of God*, written in the fifth century, inspired the medieval church to develop a theology that equated the church with the kingdom of God.

Christians still sing the lines of Timothy Dwight's eighteenth-century hymn, "I Love Thy Kingdom, Lord, the House of Thine Abode." What do we mean by this?

In the Bible the use of the word *kingdom* is based on the fact of God's sovereign rule of the universe (1 Chron. 29:11; Ps. 145:13) as King. The earliest example in which Yahweh is called "King" is in Isaiah 6:5: "My eyes have seen the King, the LORD Almighty." Even before the prophet Isaiah, the concept of God's rule was recognized: "The LORD will rule over you" (Judg. 8:23). The royal psalms (Pss. 2, 45, and 110) celebrate the rule of God. God's kingdom is "over all the earth" (47:2). As King He eternally "reigns over the nations" and over "the kings of the earth" (47:8–9). "His throne [is] in heaven, and his kingdom rules over all" (103:19). Daniel 7:13–14 speaks of the kingdom of the son of man, a prophetic reference to the Messiah's reign.

In the New Testament the Greek word for kingdom, *basileia*, is used of divine, satanic, and earthly kingdoms. As a key word *kingdom* is always defined or qualified by its context. In the Synoptic Gospels "the kingdom of God" and "the kingdom of heaven" seem to refer to the same thing. In 2 Timothy 4:1 Paul referred to Christ's kingdom, that is, His future millennial rule. When Philip "preached the good news of the kingdom of God" to Samaritans (Acts 8:12) and when Paul preached the kingdom of God in Rome (28:31), they were affirming that those who place their faith in Christ will participate in Christ's future millennial kingdom on earth. The parables of the kingdom in Matthew 13 give additional truths about the intervening age between Israel's rejection of the King and the future acceptance of Him when He returns. These parables are "mysteries" or divine "secrets" because they give facts not given in the Old Testament. These kingdom parables "reveal that an entire Age [the church age] would intervene between Israel's rejection of the king and her later acceptance of him."[11]

The concept of the kingdom of God is heavily linked to an explicit Christology. A serious student of the Bible will want to trace the various uses of the word *kingdom* in 1 Corinthians 15:24–28; Ephesians 5:5; Revelation 5:10; 11:15; and 22:3–5.

God's "kingdom" exists in various stages: His past rule over Israel, His present rule over the church until the end of the age, and His final rule in Christ's millennial reign on earth.[12]

The kingdom is far different from the church. The Greek words *ekklēsia* ("church") and *basileia* ("kingdom") each carries a different meaning and therefore are not to be equated. In the Gospels, the church was viewed as future ("I *will* build my church," Matt. 16:18), whereas the kingdom was at hand in the sense that the King was present and was offering His kingdom (4:17). Jesus never said "I will build My kingdom." Kingdom truth is dominant in the Gospels, while gospel truth and the existence of the church is prevalent in Acts.

History reveals the abuse of power that occurs when the church views itself as the kingdom. From Constantine's time until the Reformation, power coalesced in the Roman Church, bringing arrogance as well as failure of mission and servanthood in the world. Only redeemed sinners, who constitute the church, are called on to be ambassadors (2 Cor. 5:20) of the King. Believers are citizens of the kingdom and are to recognize only Jesus as King. The church's mission in the world implies preparing people for the future kingdom. Believers are, furthermore, heirs of the kingdom (Heb. 12:28) and "co-heirs with Christ" (Rom. 8:17). As the bride of Christ, believers will reign with Him (2 Tim. 2:12; Rev. 1:6; 5:10; 20:6). Properly, Christians pray that the Lord's kingdom, the Millennium, will come (Matt. 6:10).

Related to the kingdom is truth about "glory." *Glory* is a word that has been eclipsed in our day. Charles Gabriel's gospel song, "O That Will Be Glory for Me," has a quaint sound to it as we enter the twenty-first century. A culture bent on living it up with little or no thought of heaven does not share turf with the notion of glory by and by. It is no longer stylish to sing about glory. But this is what the kingdom is all about.

When this "glory song" was introduced in 1900, it became an instant success. Charles Gabriel had long hoped to write a song that would become famous. He got his wish. Inspired by a rescue-mission superintendent in St. Louis, Missouri, who would often break out with the word *glory* while preaching, the hymn writer articulated what every believer will someday experience.

At the Mount Hermon Calif. Conference Center, the "glory song"[13] was a favorite of Samuel Sutherland, president of Biola Bible College, later to become Biola University. He reveled in leading the conferees in singing it. Despite this song's decline in popularity, the concept of glory is solidly biblical.

The believer's participation in glory, as in the church and in the kingdom of Christ, is both present and future. The present aspect of it is evident in three ways: (1) God's work in the believer. Romans 8:30 addresses this: "And those he predestined, he also called; those he called, he also justified; those he justified, he also glorified." This is a present reality, even though future glory is ahead. (2) The unfading ministry of the Spirit. Paul referred to the Mosaic Law that "came with glory . . . fading though it was" (2 Cor. 3:7). His reasoning was that if that ministry under Moses condemned people and yet was called glorious, how much more glorious is the ministry of grace that brings righteousness. The church now shares in the glory of God's grace through the Holy Spirit. (3) The believer's transformation. New life in Christ includes increasingly more visible signs of the glory of Christ. "And we, who with unveiled faces all reflect the Lord's glory, are being transformed into his likeness with ever-increasing glory, which comes from the Lord, who is the Spirit" (3:18).

Though glory is an object of hope, yet in a sense we participate in it now. This is not to say, however, that glory and kingdom are equated. They are not identical, but the relationship is coterminous. That is, the final consummation of the age will eventuate in glory.

The future realization of this glory is evident from Scripture. When Christ appears, we "will appear with Him in glory" (Col. 3:4). This has reference to the glorious appearing of our Lord to establish His kingdom. Our appearance with Him presupposes our being with Him when He comes.

The renewal of our physical bodies is also promised. We will be made like Jesus (1 Cor 15:42–44, 53; Phil. 3:20–21; 1 John 3:2). The bliss of eternity will include unfading glory, as described in Revelation 22:3–5. This will come when the Chief Shepherd appears (1 Pet. 5:4).

The kingdom of God, then, operates over the church. The church cannot, so to speak, bring in the kingdom. That is the sovereign work of the King. Meanwhile, we are to spread the gospel while awaiting the future Millennium.

To participate in the future millennial kingdom of God, people must accept it now as little children (Mark 10:15). That is, they must turn to God in humble trust. Preparation for the kingdom included Christ's death on the cross and the promise of the New Covenant. The Lamb of God slain before the creation of the world (Rev. 13:8) is the only One qualified to open the book of destiny and bring history to its culmination in the kingdom of God.

The most natural understanding of the millennial reign of Christ (Rev. 20) is that it will follow Christ's second coming (19:11).[14] Then when this thousand-year reign ends, God will usher in eternity to come.

The important truth about the future of the church is that its hope is the return of Jesus Christ for His own.

THE CHURCH AND ISRAEL

Bible scholars differ over the subject of the church and Israel. Is there continuity or discontinuity between the Old and New Testaments? Old Testament hope was centered chiefly around the nation Israel and its future in the land. During the present church age Israel is in unbelief, having rejected Jesus as its national Messiah (Matt. 27:22–25). Nevertheless Israel has not been entirely set aside, as Paul argued in Romans 9–11.

It is important to establish some boundaries between the terms *church* and *Israel*. Some theologians point to the church as the new Israel, which inherits in a spiritual way all the promises given to the nation Israel. Is there, then, any future for Israel apart from the church that now includes Gentiles and Jews? Indeed there is. There will be salvation for the Jews (11:25–28).

Are Israel and the church identical? If not, how do they differ? If they are similar, what do they have in common?

First, it is important to note that God has a united plan for Israel and the church. Believing Israel and the church are one people of God. Yet a distinct earthly future for Israel as a nation is assured.[15] Demarest and Lewis view the church and Israel as both spiritual and institutional in nature.[16] Both Israel and the church find acceptance with God through divine grace. There are not two ways to salvation, one of law and the other of grace. All who are saved by grace through faith form one spiritual people. The basis of this salvation, as Charles Ryrie has written, is always the death of Christ.[17] Oneness, therefore, is certain (Gal. 3:28–29).

Israel as a nation is related to the older Mosaic Covenant; the church is related to the New Covenant. Israel occupied land; the church has no country but is like a wandering pilgrim. God gave legislation to Israel to regulate its social and political structure; the church disciples and teaches its members. Neither Israel nor the church is to be confused with the kingdom of God. Both are the outworking of God's plan. Robert Saucy summed up the matter this way: "The broad outline portrayed in Scripture suggests there is no basis for a reductionist interpretation which levels Israel and the church in a total continuity. Rather, the picture is one of basic unity of the people of God, yet with functional distinction in the historical outworking of salvation of God's kingdom."[18] Israel was established as a nation in Moses' day (Exod. 19:1–8), but the church began on the Day of Pentecost (Acts 1:8; 2:4; 11:15).

While Israel was to serve as a witness ("light") to the Gentiles (Isa. 42:6), the church's task is to present the gospel to all peoples, to Jews and Gentiles alike (Rom. 1:16). Paul's prayer for Israel that they may be saved (10:1) should be the prayer of the church. Our grafting into the branch (Paul's figure in Romans 11) means simply that we partake of life from the root, which is Christ. In the present church age believing Jews and Gentiles are "heirs together . . . members of one body" (Eph. 3:6), the church.

It must be noted that none of the *physical* blessings given to Israel appear in the New Testament passages that speak of the New Covenant (see Jer. 31:31–40; Ezek. 36:24–58; 2 Cor. 3:6–7; Heb. 8:8–13). This is extremely significant, for it means that promises for Israel and the church differ. Promises for Israel include physical and spiritual blessings, but the church receives spiritual blessings and no physical blessings. The church is never promised a land with specific boundaries like those specified for Israel in the Abrahamic Covenant, recorded in Genesis 15:18–21.

Both the church and Israel are exhorted to be watchful because the Lord is at hand. The final stage, redemption, is drawing near (Luke 21:28). The Lord's coming is indeed near (James 5:8); He may come at any moment.

Reigning with Christ

Few of us can imagine the inexpressible joy of being in the presence of our victorious Lord. The coming judgment seat of Christ, when believers will receive or not receive rewards in no way dims the prospect of our being in heaven with Christ. As the assembly of undeserving sinners, the church has a bright future. Temporarily the church lives in the present age, yet spiritually it belongs to the age to come (Matt. 12:32; Mark 10:30). The believer's citizenship is in heaven, not on earth (Phil. 3:20; Eph 1:3; 2:6).

When the millennial kingdom comes, all church-age saints, as stated earlier, will reign with Christ (2 Tim. 2:12; Rev. 1:6; 5:10; 20:6). Apparently part of this rule or reign will involve serving in the role of judge. "The saints will judge the world," Paul taught the Corinthians, warning them to settle disputes in the church without going to the courts of unbelieving judges (1 Cor. 6:2).

What does it mean to reign with Christ? In what some scholars believe to be an early Christian hymn, 2 Timothy 2:11–13 is a remarkable revelation of the future of the church. The text is prefaced with the words "Here is a trustworthy saying" (2:11), which can literally be rendered "faithful [is] the word." This is reminiscent of how Jesus often prefaced His teachings with the words, "I tell you the truth" (for example, Matt. 5:18; John 3:3; 5:19).

Great theological truth often emerges from verses whose primary intent is to reveal another doctrinal theme. In 2 Timothy 2:11–13 Paul wrote of suffering and glory and the virtue of endurance. Using typical Hebrew parallelism, Paul introduced four "if" clauses: "If we died with him, we will also live with him; if we endure, we will also reign with him. If we disown him, he will also disown us; if we are faithless, he will remain faithful, for he cannot disown himself."

In this passage Paul moved easily from the church's present life to its future life. This illustrates how believers are to have one foot on earth and the other in heaven. Christians live, die, and then will reign with Christ on the earth. Paul elsewhere linked the "now" and "then" in the great resurrection chapter, 1 Corinthians 15. Life, death, and resurrection for the believer move in a straight line into the future. Absence from the body means presence with the Lord (2 Cor. 5:8).

While our comprehension is limited and the Bible does not state exactly what our reigning with Christ will entail, we know we will participate in what the psalmist called "the glory of all his saints" (Ps. 149:9). Reigning will carry an awesome responsibility and privilege for the saints.

Meanwhile the church is to serve the Lord in humility and steadfast watchfulness. The incident of two disciples clamoring for prominence in the kingdom and Jesus' rebuke give ample warning to Christians about not seeking honor of their own (Matt. 20:20–28). Greatness in the kingdom—even reigning with Christ—carries with it the upside-down teaching of Jesus: The first shall be last, servant of all.

Anyone who has ever listened to the singing of Handel's *Messiah* cannot miss the grandeur of God, the accolades due Him alone, taken straight from the text of Scripture: "Amen! Praise and glory and wisdom and thanks and honor and power and strength be to our God for ever and ever. Amen!" (Rev. 7:12). From Patmos, John by revelation piled word upon word to impress his readers with the glory of the reigning Christ. From the first public rendition of the *Messiah* in 1792 in Dublin, Ireland, audiences have been lifted to the heights of ecstasy while listening to this musical tribute to the Lamb on the throne. Handel did not honor *our* reign with Christ, but only the reign of our Savior, Lord, and King. Yet the saints will share in the kingly reign and rule with Christ.

Our preaching and teaching on the subject of the saints' role in reigning should be done in great humility. There is no human triumphalism in these truths. All honor and glory must be reserved for God, who through Christ has provided our salvation.

The Church Triumphant

As noted in earlier chapters the term *the church triumphant* refers to the dead in Christ, believers who have entered their heavenly rest. The church, the community of the saints, includes all in this present age who live and die as believers in Christ. Older theologians spoke of the church militant as well as the church triumphant. The first refers to the church on earth, the second to the church in heaven.[19] Roman Catholics, in time, added a third category of the church—the suffering church. This is in reference to those who, according to the Catholic belief in an intermediary state of purgatory, are not yet purified of their remaining sins. There is no biblical evidence, however, for this teaching.

The church triumphant—all believers in heaven—has exchanged the Cross for the crown, suffering for victory, battle for triumph. The hymn, "For All the Saints," by Bishop William W. How (1823–1897) captures the meaning of the church triumphant:

> For all the saints who from their labors rest,
> Who Thee by faith before the world confessed,
> Thy name, O Jesus, be forever blest:
> Alleluia! Alleluia.
> O may Thy soldiers, faithful, true, and bold,
> Fight as the saints who nobly fought of old,
> And win with them the victor's crown of gold:
> Alleluia! Alleluia.[20]

HOPE AND HOLINESS

Early Christians were criticized for their belief in the fiery dissolution of the current world order. During the reign of Nero, historians and politicians warned the Roman government that Christians were given to a "novel and baneful superstition." The Roman historian Tacitus (around A.D. 56–120) described these early Christians as notorious for their depravity.[21] Undoubtedly this opinion was due to misunderstanding. Christian eschatology did look for the fiery dissolution of this world: "The present heavens and earth are reserved for fire," Peter wrote, "being kept for the day of judgment and destruction of ungodly men" (2 Pet. 3:7). The heavens, Peter taught, will disappear with a roar. The elements will be destroyed by fire and the earth and everything in it will be laid bare (3:10).

Disliked by ordinary Romans, believers remained aloof, as did the Jews of the times. They wanted no part in the idolatry and immorality of Rome.

When Rome caught fire, the Christians were charged with arson. After all, did not these despised Christians look for the city of God, a new kingdom of the saints erected on the ruins? Only after sanity returned did the people realize that Christians were scapegoats for Nero's imperial savagery.

What were the early beliefs of Christians about the future? What was their hope? New Testament Christians expected an immediate end to the present world order, the return of the Lord, and judgment on the nations. As centuries passed, however, without Christ's return, other interpretations of the end times prevailed.

The expectancy and hope of the saints fired the zeal of the first churches. It was fuel for appeals to godliness, but unfortunately it was also fodder for false teaching and deception. Apostolic instructions were noble efforts to set the record straight about the future and to correct apostasy.

Without any questions, the focus of apostolic expectation was the imminent return of Christ. Yet it was not based on an exact timetable. Certainly the teachings of Jesus, Peter, Paul, and the others could never lend credence to date-setting for the Lord's return. The church's hope was the literal return of Jesus, His *parousia* ("appearing or coming"). Because Christ in His resurrection is the "firstfruits" of those who will be raised (1 Cor. 15:23), believers are next in line for the blessings of the kingdom. This in its broadest meaning was the hope of the church. In the *parousia*, they anticipated the imminent return of the triumphant Saviour. The first advent focused on the suffering Savior; the second focuses on the triumphant Redeemer.

The Rapture of the church involves a rescue from coming wrath (1 Thess. 1:10; 5:9). While exact teaching in Scripture on the Rapture of the church is limited, it is nevertheless compelling. Paul's teaching about being caught up in the clouds to meet the Lord in the air (4:17) seems to fit best a Rapture before the time of God's wrath, the Tribulation.[22] Tribulation for the church is a certainty in the world (John 16:33), but what is called the Great Tribulation, based on an interpretation of Daniel's seventieth week (Dan. 9:24–27), is quite another matter. Paul instructed believers to encourage one another with words of hope about the imminent Rapture (1 Thess. 4:18).

Two strains of teaching affirm hope for the church—immediacy or imminence of Christ's return and the "caught up" nature of the event. Arguments made for differing views and convictions need not divide believers. All must affirm their hope in the Lord's return. Their hope is not escapism. Nor is it a denial of perseverance needed by all believers. This hope, confirmed by the witness of the Holy Spirit (Rom. 15:13), is called the blessed hope (Titus 2:13).

The central issue of His coming is its purifying effect on the church. This motif is desperately needed in our churches. Defense of truth is one thing, but undue speculation is another. What good is it if our doctrine is correct and our character weak?

This is no appeal to a thin, experience-oriented piety in our churches. Nor is it an appeal to avoid the difficult questions of eschatology. It is, however, where the rubber meets the road in that the believer's hope has a purifying effect.

There is no doubt that even within the life of the apostolic church, belief in Christ's return wavered. Yet Paul affirmed its strength among Philippian believers (Phil. 3:20), and Peter asserted that Jesus' coming is imminent (1 Pet. 1:13; 4:13; 5:4). James wrote of the nearness of the Lord's coming (James 5:8). The writer to the Hebrews wrote that "in just a very little while, He who is coming will come" (Heb. 10:37). John did not speculate *if* Jesus would come again. He confidently wrote about *when* He comes (1 John 2:28).

Each of these writers, inspired by the Holy Spirit, based his appeal for godliness and purity of life on the reality of Christ's return.

The case for a morality based on eschatology is persuasive. The Bible demonstrates a moral intent to teachings about the Rapture and the second coming of Christ to the earth. The proof of being a Christian is not merely orthodoxy of belief, but "orthopraxy" of conduct as well. Right conduct must match righteous standing before God.

Hope is a truth that transforms character. John wrote of confidence or boldness and being unashamed at Christ's coming (2:28). This implies a pure heart and conscience. John then repeated the certainty of Christ's return, speaking of "when he appears" (3:2). This hope, he concluded, purifies believers (3:3). He linked this purity to the virtues of the coming

King: "even as he is pure." The believers who hope in Christ will purify themselves, not ceremonially, but morally. The Greek word for purify means free from moral stain (see 2 Cor. 11:2 in reference to a "chaste" virgin, and also Phil. 4:1).

Where is this truth being taught in our Christian churches? Why the growing absence of teaching on the Lord's return? Excesses of the past are no excuse for avoidance of the moral demands of God based on Christ's spotless character and the certainty of His return. The warning given wavering believers in the first century is also warning for today: "Let us hold unswervingly to the hope we profess, for he who promised is faithful" (Heb. 10:23).

All that is written in the Scriptures brings hope to the church (Rom. 15:4). This hope ought to galvanize us for the spiritual battle and unify us with all others who hope in Christ.

As stated earlier, the biblical teaching of the destruction of the present heavens and earth and the coming of a new city of God so alarmed Roman leaders and citizens that they persecuted the early Christian church. Yet even this profound truth, which Peter taught in 2 Peter 3:11–14, was intended to prompt hope and purity. "Make every effort," he wrote, "to be found spotless, blameless and at peace with him" (3:14). Make no mistake: The hope of the church is the imminent return of Christ.[23]

13
The Church and Renewal

*The greatest risk is a polarization among evangelicals. Into one camp will
cluster the modern monastics—those holding to truth and tradition but
isolated from society. In the other camp will cluster the modern post-Christian
secularists—the sociologically relevant who are no longer truly Christian.*
—Leith Anderson

*Today the church is in a Babylonian captivity. . . . Not that it is in the
clutches of a pagan emperor or a corrupted religious hierarchy, but rather in its
easy acquiescence to the values of a thoroughly secularized culture.*
—Charles Colson

THE CHURCH is perpetually in need of renewal. Encouraged by hope,
purified by trial, and strengthened with love, the church is moving
toward the day when it will be presented to Christ "without stain or
wrinkle" (Eph. 5:27).

Christians are pilgrims living in the expectation of a heavenly home,
but they are not yet in that home. Someday the church will be perfected
as a radiant church, holy and blameless. But we are not there yet, for there
is no perfect church this side of heaven.

The New Testament places emphasis on spiritual renewal. Paul wrote
of the church's need for cleansing: "Christ loved the church and gave himself up for her to make her holy, cleansing her by the washing with water
through the word" (Eph. 5:25–26). And this cleansing or renewal comes
as believers obey God's Word. "The Bible is the preacher for preachers,"
wrote P. T. Forsythe in 1907.[1] In the same manner the Bible is the infallible guide for the church.

Christ's rule and kingdom are not of this world; that is, they are not to
take the shape of what the world may call successful. To base renewal on

the management model rather than on truth glorifies consumerism and threatens to corrupt the community of faith at its core.

The symbol of the Cross with all its rough-hewn crudeness and humiliation ought to exemplify the living church. The image-shapers of our world can never eliminate the offense of the Cross. Faith-substitutes—whether theologies of revolution, feminist theologies, scientism, or religious syncretism—do not qualify as replacements for the timeless truths of the reality of sin, salvation, and reconciliation by means of the Cross. The pursuit of ways to make the Cross palatable to moderns detracts from the humiliation of Christ and the demands of His call to repentance.

Lesslie Newbigen pointed out that a faith shaped by secularity offers little hope to our world. "A secular society in which the traditional authority of social forms is broken needs more and not less of the prophetic spirit which knows the voice of the living God."[2] In the renewal of the church there are no shortcuts. Just as an architect keeps a picture of the finished building in mind, believers are to keep a vision of a faithful, perfected church in view, in light of the coming of Christ.

A CRITIQUE OF CONTEMPORARY EVANGELICALISM

Christianity does not suffer from a lack of critics. Its antagonists have chipped away at the church for centuries. Thus to attempt a critique of contemporary evangelicalism has some inherent traps. One extreme is to tear down the church, while the other is to engage in a kind of triumphalism. Neither the wrecking-ball approach nor trumpeted hype will help the church. Hopefully the following assessments will help lay the groundwork for a broad-based approach to renewal.

De-emphasis on the Word in a Therapeutic Society

Self-absorption in the modern psyche is replacing confidence in faith. How evangelicals define their mission and implement their witness as they enter the twenty-first century may well determine their continuing vitality. If evangelicals become entrapped in the current national psyche that is turned inward and that rejects any ruling authority other than the "self," their days are limited. They will be like a growing segment of our society that has adopted relativism, privatism, and a "feel-good" faith.

An evangelical is obviously one who believes in the Evangel Jesus Christ, the only begotten Son of God, and the only Savior of the world. Some have defined evangelicalism in both theological and sociological terms. Martyn Lloyd-Jones, for instance, listed five distinct characteristics of an evangelical.[3] An evangelical, he wrote, is one who (1) is subservient to the Scriptures, (2) distrusts human reason alone, (3) rejects sacramentalism, (4) emphasizes personal regeneration from sin, and (5) elevates the primacy of preaching and evangelism. As John Stott argued in his rebuttal to liberal scholar David J. Edwards in *Evangelical Essentials*, "submission to Scripture is for us Evangelicals a sign of submission to Christ."[4]

The term *evangelical*, however, has become ambiguous. It has become an umbrella term to describe people of disparate strands of denominational or nondenominational loyalty. Scholars Nathan Hatch and Michael Hamilton speak of a serious issue of evangelical survival. "Over the last 50 years, evangelicals and their institutions have been highly successful. They have attained the good life and become very comfortable with American culture. The crucial question now is whether their acceptance of suburban mores has diluted the gospel to the point that it no longer has the power to convict and convert."[5]

Before looking at further evidence and warnings about diminished evangelical confidence in the Scriptures, a definition of the ruling ethos called the "therapeutic community" may prove helpful. The term itself describes a habit of mind wherein the power of psychological therapy is placed in contrast to the historic Christian confidence in the power of gospel preaching to cure the soul and shape how people live. Such a polarity between therapy and truth is unfortunate, but it serves to accentuate a problem of authority in the church. In the twentieth century we have witnessed a dramatic rise in the social sciences. These "soft sciences," as they have sometimes been called, have helped explain human behavior, interpersonal relationships, social groupings, economics, cultural and political issues. Currently psychology tends to dominate. It is safe to say that this particular field offers valuable explanations to people who are in need of direction and help. At the heart of the current ruling ethos, however, there seems to be a preoccupation with getting in touch with oneself, rather than with God. Earlier generations, of course, faced similar maladies of the soul, but they tended to find personal fulfillment within the social framework of family, church, and society. What has changed is the disintegration of these traditional structures. What has also changed is a perception of human individualism creating a felt need for self-fulfillment rather than seeking God's help.

The displacement of theology as a means of establishing values in society has been gradual. Scientism—the reliance on science to establish meaning—has become the god of our age. Psychology, one of the sciences, is now the new determinant of human behavior and meaning.

Christopher Lasch first described the ruling ethos of the therapeutic community that is affecting contemporary evangelicalism. "The contemporary climate is therapeutic, not religious. People today hunger not for personal salvation, let alone for the restoration of an earlier golden age, but for the feeling, the momentary illusion, of personal well-being, health, and psychic security."[6]

One may view the current rise of Christian therapists and counseling centers as a mixed blessing. Some may see this as an extension of traditional pastoral care at a more professional level. Others see this phenomenon as a threat to truth issues best handled by a knowledgeable theological basis for faith and life.

Time will resolve this apparent conflict in the church, yet one is suspicious that with the de-emphasis on theological understanding, the church may be left with little objectivity in judging values, working for maturity of the faith, and building an understandably powerful and biblical approach to ministry.

Which way will evangelicalism go? Will its churches become archaic defenders of an obscure orthodoxy, or will they become therapy centers offering dubious cures, which build a dependency on therapists? Renewal in the church will mean a continuing debate over the integration of the social sciences and revealed faith. Perhaps a practical starting point is David Bebbington's description of the essentials of evangelical faith. Implied in this list is a platform for renewal: "Biblicism (a reliance upon the Bible as ultimate authority), conversionism (stress upon the new birth), activism (an activistic, individualistic approach to religious duties and social involvement), and 'crucicentrism' (a focus upon Christ's redemptive work as essential to Christianity)."[7]

The Word of God, rightly understood, rightly taught, and rightly lived, builds healthy congregations. Evangelicalism, which claims to represent the historic faith that springs from a cross and an empty tomb, provides a witness to the power of God's grace and a defense against deviants from the true gospel.[8]

When the confessional element of evangelicalism is weakened or disappears, the voice of the church will be weakened. Older fundamentalism saw clearly that sin and compromise were enemies of truth. Some evangelicals, in their attempts to broaden the scope of the community of faith and to be open to the prevailing culture, tend to reject narrowness of any kind. Today there seems to be less sharpness, less boldness, and a blurring of theological vision.[9]

The time has come when people will no longer endure sound doctrine. The Bible teaches that this will accelerate in the end times (2 Tim. 3:1–5). Theology is dying in our churches. The synthetic substitutes of a therapeutic society offer no lasting cure for the human soul.

Misplaced Trust in Human Organization and Power

American preoccupation with technology and organizational structure has influenced the church. Pragmatism drives many evangelicals. Witness the rise of seminars sponsored by large churches for the purpose of learning organizational science. Functionalism is ultimately the enemy of faith if the life of a church can be defined purely in secular terms.

Leadership is being defined more in terms of our management culture than by the principles laid down in Scripture. Charles Colson decried the disturbing signs of the institutional church—its shallowness, its sellout to marketing, and its departure from its mission.[10]

The church needs theological leadership that is trained in true discernment of the times and not merely in functional efficiency. This requires more than intellectual training. Spiritual formation should be first and foremost. An articulate faith in God's power and presence is essential.

Managerial science, like all the social sciences, must inform but not set the agenda. Our current "Babylonian Captivity" of the church is to the sciences, which are often treated as ends and not as means.

The new orthodoxy is one of style, fashion, and method. A success syndrome rules. The older orthodoxy made no claims for progress and success. In fact, it invited struggle, trials, testing, and even persecution; yet it conquered Western civilization.

Conflicting views of the Christian community tend to confuse Christians, dividing congregations and often leading to disillusionment. In an article in *Leadership* seven evangelical leaders sketched out their answers.[11] Leonard Sweet stated that our challenge is to help people believe the right thing. He wrote, "I'm an indigenous missionary to this culture, which means I live and look and act as part of this culture, though it's not my home. I'm not going to anchor in this culture, I'm going to anchor in God's Spirit and in God's word."[12]

Another respected leader in the same symposium was quoted as saying that we are not supposed to be dealing with the culture. "We're supposed to be dealing with God." A pastor of a megachurch proposed that in the 1990s the church must be on a "niche hunt." Another pastor urged that Christians be involved in the Great Commission (Matt. 28:19–20) and the cultural mandate (Gen. 1:28). Another urged churches to proclaim the gospel and not to protest the culture, while still another pointed to compassion and care as central to church effectiveness.

James Montgomery Boice held out for Bible exposition as central to church life. "The heart is good theology, explaining right belief in God," he wrote. "The church has to rediscover who God is, come to know him, and fellowship with him. The avenue for that has always been Bible exposition and teaching. There's no shortcut."[13]

A sound theology will serve as a corrective to both a thin experientialism and a rampant pragmatism. While all answers to the question of what the world needs now may prove valuable to some extent, the theological substance of a Bible-based ministry must form the core. History demonstrates that the Word has power for renewal.

Paul argued, "Be strong in the Lord and in his mighty power" (Eph. 6:10). Facing the challenges of our generation, we are prompted to ask the same question the apostle asked: "Who is equal to such a task?" (2 Cor. 2:16). Our adequacy, he responded, is from God (3:5).

Loss of Unity

The church is to be viewed as the community of saints. Whoever belongs to the church is a member of a body and thus is to share with others in that same group. In the third century Cyprian of Carthage spoke of the unity of the church, using the analogies of the sun, a tree, and a stream. Having many rays, the sun is one light. A tree with one trunk has many branches. From one source of water flow many streams. "So also the Church," he wrote, "extends her rays over all the globe: yet it is one light which is diffused everywhere and the unity of the body is not broken up."[14] Early creeds asserted the oneness of the church.

Sadly, the unity of the church today is broken up and is in need of renewal. The prayer of our Lord "that they may be one" (John 17:11) has never been fully answered. As Christ's emissaries, we are instructed in the Scriptures, "Make every effort to keep the unity of the Spirit through the bond of peace" (Eph. 4:3). The basis of Jesus' prayer was the unity of the Trinity, and Paul's appeal was based on the unassailable truth that "there is one body and one Spirit" (4:4).

Christian unity is not a luxury or an elective of the faith. It is a necessity, the capstone of Christian truth and the mark of a true church. At the heart of the Protestant Reformation was the emphasis on the church's oneness. Luther's *Little Prayer Book* of 1522 affirmed the Reformer's view of Christian unity. While Rome accused him of dividing the church, Luther believed in "one holy common Christian church on earth throughout the whole world." That belief is the belief of evangelicalism.

The task of evangelicals is to demonstrate these centrally held beliefs and not be party to a divisive spirit. Division and strife dishonor the price Christ paid for our redemption.

There are two levels of unity, one local and one universal, or global. Within each congregation the bonds of unity are to be strengthened. Beyond the congregation, the church at large and the church scattered are to be considered one. Some Christians find it easy to be one with the "invisible" church, but difficult within their own local body. The Scriptures give us no luxury for living a divided life—holding true Christian unity with the one communion of saints, while living in disunity at the local-church level.

Our evangelical entrepreneurs and individualists lead us astray from the unity mandated by Scripture. Developing a comprehensive unity with all believers in every place who call on the name of our Lord Jesus Christ (1 Cor. 1:2) should be every believer's agenda. By living at peace with one another, Christians preserve the oneness that the Spirit gives to all who are baptized into the body of Christ (12:13).

Union elevates the importance of being part of one organization, while *unity* emphasizes the essential bond in Jesus Christ that in turn builds what a hymn writer called "mystic sweet communion." Evangelicals have avoided linkage with ecumenical bodies, yet have formed their own in two groups. The World Evangelical Fellowship and the National Association of Evangelicals seek to elicit participation, fellowship, and common service without creating a hierarchy. Such evangelical ecumenism is laudable and exemplary of shared life and service in Christ. Beyond these visible inter-church organizations are parachurch groups that rally the faithful around a common mission. Much progress is still needed within communities to assure that Christian unity is fleshed out in relationships between local churches. The current trend to remove denominational labels from congregational names does not seem to fulfill the biblical teaching on Christian unity. Supposedly the purpose is to remove barriers in the minds of the unchurched, but eventually the very message and manner of corporate life of these congregations will denominate them. Meanwhile believers do well to accentuate their oneness rather than their differences.

It has been commonly held that theology divides, whereas Christ unites. This clever turn of words, however, should not be used to deny the importance of sound theology, which helps the church separate truth from error. Christ indeed unites, but not at the expense of truth.

Weakened Message and Apologetic

The breakdown of rational thought and the crisis of truth have spawned serious social problems. Many evangelicals are deeply worried about

America's spiritual moral decline. Society at large is at the mercy of a new culture of information shaped by popular music, the media, home videos, Hollywood films, and tabloids.

In 1994 Michael Novak, in accepting the Templeton Prize for Progress in Religion, challenged his audience by stating, "We owe ourselves a reckoning." Vulgar relativism, he said, was undermining the culture of liberty. "In this dark night of a century, a first fundamental lesson was drawn from the bowels of nihilism itself: *Truth matters.* Even for those unsure whether there is a God, a truth is different from a lie. Torturers can twist your mind, even reduce you to a vegetable, but as long as you retain the ability to say 'Yes' or 'No' as truth alone commands, they cannot own you."[15]

In our commitment to biblical faith we must be concerned about any diluting of these essentials and any appearance of false teaching. Evangelicals have given altogether too little attention to the intellectual life. Mark Noll notes that "modern evangelicals have not pursued comprehensive thinking under God or sought a mind shaped to its furthest reaches by Christian perspectives."[16]

In the early centuries of Christianity, the great academies played a vital role in defining and defending faith. I fear that a weakened message will not withstand the insidious attacks from New Age thought, religious pluralism, and universalism.

Treating the gospel as merely a product to be marketed invariably dilutes the faith. Apologist Douglas Groothuis once cautioned us about cultural adaptation of the Christian message: "Some church growth pundits champion the 'marketing of the gospel.' This notion often goes uncriticized, since advertising permeates every square inch of our culture. If marketing other things works well, why not market the gospel? Marketing attempts to meet an audience's existing desires or create new desires for the purpose of selling a product. Marketing typically appeals to selfishness, covetousness, vanity, and fear. It is the science of psychological manipulation for economic ends."[17]

We must be fully biblical in our cultural adaptations to reach people with the gospel.

The postmodern world abandons truth as a reality. The temptation is always there to weaken an absolute truth so as to make it palatable to the modern mind. Vernon Grounds clearly stated exactly what our task should be in contemporary witness and apologetics:

> Polemical defense of traditional orthodoxy may not be our personal responsibility, but we are grateful for the work of scholars who are called to that ministry. We realize that any such ministry, no matter how graciously it is carried on, precipitates controversy. Indeed it is inescapably controversial because it is not simply a hairsplitting discussion about academic issues. It is spiritual warfare in which inexpressibly momentous issues are being debated. Sometimes the heretical deviation may seem trifling, but ultimately in the battle between truth and error the eternal destiny of human beings, God's image-bearers, is at stake. Hence those prayerfully engaged in polemical ministry are agents of the Spirit of truth in his ceaseless struggle against the spirit of falsehood (1 John 4:1–6).[18]

A renewed church will value the reflective, vital scholarship of defenders of the faith. It will also place a high value on the education of ministers of the gospel, in order that they may be able to define and defend truth, guard the purity of confessional elements of the church, engage in critical judgment within the larger culture of society, involve believers in meaningful service to others, and advance the propagation of the gospel by engaging the heart and mind of the culture with the biblical message of the Cross.

Diminished Sense of Urgency in World Missions

One of the repercussions of the demise of theological and biblical preaching is an increasing lack of interest in world missions. Theological universalism, the belief that ultimately all will be saved, destroys the motive for global evangelism. This is an obvious fallout of wrong belief. Without minimizing the sovereign mercy of God, we nevertheless affirm the necessity of personal faith in Jesus Christ, who alone is the Savior of the world.

Missions is seeking to distribute the gospel message around the world. Currently that distribution is terribly skewed, with only a small percentage of Western missionaries doing pioneer work in unreached people groups. If the current decline in career missionaries continues, the lamplight of the gospel witness will dim. Yet at the same time we are witnessing unprecedented church growth in third-world countries. For this the church must rejoice and support the indigenous works and crosscultural mission efforts of believers around the world.

Nearly forty years ago a group of Central American leaders were challenged to think in terms of churches sending their own missionaries into all the world. The excuses for not having produced a "sending church" related mainly to economics. Today missions strategy includes a discipling approach, equipping believers to think in terms of obedience to the commission of Christ. Thus in Asian, Latin American, and African countries, where the gospel was planted by people from other nations, the impetus is outward, toward their own and other unreached people groups. These missions efforts have served as a corrective to American Christianity, which tends to focus on single-culture missions.

Innovative missions strategy now encompasses a wide range of support skills in linguistics, education, medicine, literature, and compassion.

American Christianity, while enjoying support at the polls, is turning inward in a kind of isolationism. Often confused by the burgeoning influx of immigrant groups, loss of homogeneity, and cultural shifts, some churches tend to develop a survival mentality. While American materialism makes it possible for churches to have excellent programs and attractive church buildings, it also can divert evangelical attention and finances away from addressing human needs.

Furthermore confusion over exactly what constitutes missions has separated Christians. Some evangelicals have expressed animosity toward social activists, who argue for social justice as a form of mission. This divisiveness makes churches ill-equipped for developing a biblical synthesis that incorporates proclamation and demonstration of social change.

In 1980 a group of evangelical leaders from many countries met in Hoddesdon, England, to attempt to develop an evangelical synthesis on this issue. Subsequent gatherings have incorporated the concerns expressed in that conference, and programs have been developed to address these issues. Among the statements that emerged from the Consultation on the

Theology of Development were the following: "We are deeply disturbed by the human suffering present in the agonizing realities of hunger, malnutrition, disease, unemployment, illiteracy, deprivation and starvation. We are deeply disturbed by the extent of apathy within the Christian church in the face of widespread suffering and injustice in the world."[19]

The American church has to face up to at least two realities: (a) missions and church growth are now centered in developing countries and away from America and western Europe, and consequently (b) American influence on world-missions strategy is diminishing. We should not be surprised by this work of the Spirit. Christian humility ought to override any paternalism and effort to control the new thrusts in mission work. This does not signal the twilight of American or Western influence, since our greatest contributions may be stewardship of our wealth and provision of schooling opportunities. Meanwhile an informed, energized, mature church must keep its windows always open and outward to the world, which is in dire need of God's redemptive message.

Now more than ever we need a creative stance that develops partnerships and a common dependence on God for direction and spiritual power. Such partnerships ought to reflect dignity and equality in our common fellowship in Jesus Christ.

The church should enhance its efforts to reach those whom the Bible says are "perishing" (2 Cor. 4:3). For American evangelicalism, John Wesley's famous line, "The world is my parish," describes well the scope and focus of world missions.

Trust in Competency over Character

In our present-day culture we need moral lighthouses. Evangelical churches ought to provide these, but often do not because of the moral failure of their leaders. A leading theologian once remarked that popular religion is incurably egocentric. Evangelicalism has, by and large, fit comfortably within the framework of American populism. One major flaw of populism is that the center of focus is on heroes, leaders, sports figures, and film stars. In the public eye the character of these models counts less than their popularity. Unfortunately this attitude is often transferred to the church.

Much of the attention paid to character in the church focuses on those in full-time ministry. The moral failure of leaders, however, attracts a variety of responses. Oddly enough, moral revulsion does not seem to lead the list. More often, sorrow over the loss of talent in the church overshadows the character issue.

The church is to display integrity, truthfulness, moral courage, and absolute fidelity in all relationships. For the ministry, this is particularly important because leaders set the tone of character for the congregation to follow.

Ministry is under attack. Larry Brown discusses how the clergy is currently depicted in American stage plays. The comic clergy is usually seen as hypocritical, greedy, self-serving, and preaching a gospel of paranoia, Ministers are broad-stroked with a stereotype of "baptized bigotry."[20]

The character crisis in our churches and our culture is as old as Adam and as recent as the latest scandal. It matters little if evangelicals advance church growth and build successful programs when their ethical lives leave much to be desired. The real scandal is the character scandal. This is no call for Pharisaical perfectionism. Rather, it is a word of caution as old as the Bible: "Whoever claims to live in him must walk as Jesus did" (1 John 2:6).

When evangelicals place competency over character, the moral lighthouse is in serious danger of going out with the tides.

Loss of Reverence in Worship

Search for meaning, personal pleasure, and self-fulfillment has led to numerous excesses. One such result is that people now look to churches to entertain them. But abandonment of a lofty God leaves the soul empty. The current ethos in America has shaped our attitudes toward worship. Nowhere is this reflected more than in the changing architecture of our churches.

The Reformers replaced the central altar with the pulpit. Now the centered pulpit is being abandoned for an open theatrical stage. While still not widespread, this attempt to create a stagelike worship center symbolically displaces the Word, replacing it with the actor. When churches have already replaced pastoral care with managerialism and then have adopted theatrical tactics to win converts in the church, it is not a big step toward the abandonment of preaching the revealed truth of God for experience-oriented religion.

The foundations of Christian worship were laid in the New Testament. James E. White wrote that every period of renewal has aspired to reach back to the principles and practice of the early church.[21] The exception may be the present generation which seems to base renewal of worship on secular assumptions of consumer demand. If followed to an extreme, any idol will do as long as it has appeal.

This is no call to irrelevance and boredom in worship, no elevation of stilted liturgy that has lost meaning for moderns. Rather, it is a call back to basics—a reverence for a holy God, and for a human response and expression that honors God and His Word.

Worship that ascribes worth to anything other than a lofty God, the One who is "high and exalted" (Isa. 6:1), is simply not worship. A. W. Tozer was quite right when he wrote:, "We tend by a secret law of the soul to move toward our mental image of God."[22] Only a transcendent God is worthy of worship.

Response in worship may take many diverse forms, and we are not limited in expression so long as God and His truth are honored. The great diversity of the Christian church, which spans the nations, prompts the use of a rich blend of music, word, and action. We would not expect one liturgy, one style, or one form to be accepted by all cultures. But renewal in worship at its core means a recovery of focus, not merely an adoption of new forms.

Renewal of worship, whatever form it takes, must focus on Christ and His Word, as well as human obedience and confession of Christ's lordship.

The Threat of Nominalism

Christianity is plagued by nominalism. Many people are Christians in name but not in heart. Renewal of the church must take seriously the fact that many join the church, but few are the "chosen." Faith, to many, is only a surface thing, like veneer on cheap furniture. Scratch the surface, and there is little substance beneath the veneer.

Nominalism of this kind creates a climate within the community that reduces the meaning of community itself. The uniqueness of the Christian *koinōnia* (fellowship) is its bond in Christ, whereas nominalism creates false bonds of human preference in association. Some people join a church for reasons other than obedience to Christ and His Word. This nominal "joining" leads to a weakened core of faith commitment and dullness in zeal. Churches that devise human strategies to gain adherents for the church, apart from genuine conversion, court disaster. These efforts only perpetuate nominal faith.

Making the unreal real is a tough task apart from the work of the Spirit. "Name-only Christians" are a blight to Christianity. Expansionism must never be at the expense of genuine confession of faith. Church growth that promotes nominalism is false growth.

Recovery of the Spiritual Life

The essence of the spiritual life is life in the Holy Spirit. It follows that if nominalism dulls the Spirit and diminishes the boundaries between faith and nonfaith, then only a full spiritual recovery will renew the church.

Today's quest for spirituality across our culture looks more to Native American religion, New Age thought, or to an unfocused transcendentalism and older paganism for its expression. "True spirituality is that quality of life in the child of God," wrote Lewis Sperry Chafer, "which satisfies and glorifies the Father."[23] Chafer understood the spiritual life to be the overcoming life. The Reformers said the spiritual life is vital to the community of holy people.

Of course, there is ample room in the Christian community for non-conformists. These will be individuals who reject nominalism and seek to live a kind of revolutionary Christianity without either the strictures of cultural accommodation or Pharisaical legalism. Such nonconformity aims to develop a rich, deep, and growing spirituality that does not call attention to itself. Rather, it aims to understand and to live out the biblical principles of life in the Spirit. Just as the Holy Spirit upholds Christ, so the Christian exalts Christ by a spiritual walk with Him. Such a spiritual life fulfills the prayer of Paul to the Colossians: "And we pray this in order that you may live a life worthy of the Lord and may please him in every way: bearing fruit in every good work, growing in the knowledge of God, being strengthened with all power according to his glorious might so that you may have great endurance and patience, and joyfully giving thanks to the Father, who has qualified you to share in the inheritance of the saints in the kingdom of light" (Col. 1:10–12).

Our yoke is with Christ, not with the world or the religious establishment. "The secret of the easy yoke is simple," wrote Dallas Willard. "It is the intelligent, informed, unyielding resolve to live as Jesus lived in all aspects of his life."[24]

DEVELOPING A DISCIPLING COMMUNITY

The church is more than an audience of believers. As a community of the saints it is to be a growing, serving, worshiping body. Christ's invitation to discipleship is an invitation to a life of learning and growth. This life, lived "worthy of the calling" (Eph. 4:1), is more than an ideal. It is to be the norm. Paul taught that spiritual gifts are given to the church for the purposes of diversity within a fundamental unity. This unity works itself out in the faith and in the knowledge of the Son of God so that believers "become mature, attaining to the whole measure of the fullness of Christ" (4:13).

John Calvin envisioned the church as a school of Christ. To think of the body as anything less is to do harm to the doctrine of the church. Luther's catechisms were essential to developing knowledgeable Christians. All attempts to teach converts are to be lauded. In achieving the goal of building mature saints, churches need to engage in an approach that incorporates home, church, and school.

Our current dilemma in evangelicalism is that Christian education has been weakened both by societal forces and ministerial neglect. A multioptional society places all kinds of stress on the already-fragmented American family. Sunday school is unfortunately treated like any other social organization—scouting, Little League baseball, school sports, high-school band, or Rotary International. It competes on an unfair basis, vying for time and talent among overstimulated and overcommitted individuals.

Any concerned pastor watching the steady decline of the Sunday school and the diminishing of pastoral contact with the laity must have deep thoughts about the future. New educational forms and forums offer some hope, but motivation to learn and grow must be established, regardless of the venues of learning. This area of ministry is ripe for reform.

Church and parachurch often merge over common concerns for Christian growth. Local churches have made peace with a variety of parachurch groups to reach and teach the young and old alike. Many of these structures over the years have found their comfortable and profitable place within the church. The histories of YMCA and YWCA, Christian Endeavor, the Student Christian Movement, Child Evangelism Fellowship, the Bible Club Movement, Bible Study Fellowship, Youth for Christ, Young Life, Campus Crusade for Christ, and other similar ministries reveal crossover attempts to cooperate in evangelistic and edificational efforts.

The future may be uncertain as to the survival of these independent groups, if history is any teacher at all. Yet there remain certain basic needs within the body that, if not met, will weaken church life and witness. Parachurch groups now meet many of these needs.

Another phenomenon of our time is the emergence of independently sponsored seminars, self-help groups, Christian gatherings as "events," and marketed skill-oriented conventions. These have tended to emerge out of a sense of need. A marketed niche assures their survival, at least on a temporary basis.

But what of the ongoing needs within the church body for learning and growth? Adoption of "twelve-step" counseling groups and a whole flotilla of parachurch efforts alone will not build up the local church. Some mechanism must be developed to achieve the discipleship ideal of a healthy church.

Richard Baxter, in *The Reformed Pastor,* held that no church should grow beyond the ability of pastors to know people by name. This earlier view of the church as a fairly manageable circle of saints under one leader has been surpassed by the megachurch model both in America and throughout the world. On close study of these large congregations, it becomes obvious that the people have developed growth cells composed of small groups. The many small groups make up the larger body, which is held together by strong, visionary, and often charismatic personalities.

While the megachurch model is by no means dominant, it is influential and expanding and should thus be examined carefully.

Small groups have always been a part of church life. The earliest churches met in homes and tended to be limited to the size of rooms or to homes, expanding outward as need dictated. As noted earlier, separate church buildings probably did not exist until the third century. The greatest period of church expansion may well have been in the early days, when informal groupings under separate elders were typical.

The current and rising phenomenon of multistaffed, large churches may only be a luxury of our Western affluence rather than a norm. If the underground churches of China and the former Soviet Union teach us anything, it is that we should focus on life in the Spirit rather than on organizational structure. There is ample evidence to believe that small clusters of the faithful, bonded together in love and cemented by persecution, are indeed spectacularly successful in advancing the gospel.

John Wesley effectively used small groups to advance what later came to be called "Methodism." The very method labeled these groups of nonconformists. At first, the "Holy Club" model consisted of a small group of believers meeting together for mutual encouragement, confession, and study. Later other renewal efforts borrowed these ideals and expanded the effectiveness of small groups. It is now fairly safe to say that if any church is to grow it should incorporate the small-group approach.

Will an educated laity emerge from these disparate groupings without some systematic plan? Church schooling or Christian education, whatever names are used, all have an essential place at the table of learning in the renewed church. One short sermon on the Lord's Day is not enough to equip the saints. Divided by pastoral demands on numerous fronts, busy pastors cannot hope to build a doctrinally and biblically literate congregation by themselves. The entire range of spiritual gifts exercised within the priestly work of all believers must provide the means, methods, and substance for spiritual growth under the guidance of the sovereign Spirit.

We must forestall our tendency to chase after fads without serious biblical and theological reflection. Biblical revelation, rather than the appeal of antiquity or postmodernism, must guide the church. Theologian Donald Bloesch, in a provocative chapter entitled "Pathways to Evangelical Oblivion," quoted the great London preacher Martyn Lloyd-Jones, who said, "Are we to be primarily and almost exclusively concerned with evangelistic campaigns and with the attempt to make them more efficient by new methods and techniques? Or, should we not concentrate more . . . upon praying for, and laying the basis of Christian instruction for revival as it is described in the Bible?"[25]

The two extremes of a creedal church languishing in a recited faith and of a creedless church, adrift without theological anchors, are not healthy. Only a meaningful return to responsible dogma and a well-guided spiritual approach to building up the saints will assure healthy churches.

A PLEA FOR BALANCE AND UNITY

The possibility exists that many churches will self-destruct. While the gates of hell will not prevail against the church, the body of Christ, there will be failures at local levels. Some will cease to minister because of declining membership and a failure to adapt to changing communities. Others will dwindle because of disillusionment with leaders or because of division and strife. Still others will remain as enclaves of irrelevance in a fast and shifting tide of change. The greatest danger, however, lies not in failure of leadership or nerve, but in departure from truth. When the truth base erodes, the church becomes like a house clinging perilously to the hillside, perched above a pounding coastal surf.

Truth should be our main concern. Fidelity to truth is above all else to be treasured. Yet this fidelity must be matched by love and concern for unity. Hanging onto truth at the expense of love and unity makes churches self-focused and sometimes arrogant. On the other hand, hanging onto love and the notion of unity while ignoring the erosion of truth is not wise either.

At any point in the church's long history we can find ample evidence of imbalance. Zeal without knowledge bears its own tragic fruit. Separation from the world without penetration into it for the gospel's sake leaves a trail of disillusionment. Formalism and sacramentalism apart from "heart religion" produce their own death in the pews. These and similar tendencies point the way to diminished witness.

Toward the end of a long career and fruitful life of preaching and scholarship, Francis Schaeffer penned these words: "I want to say with all my heart that as we struggle with the proper preaching of the gospel in the midst of the 20th century, the importance of observable love must come into our message. . . . The world has a right to look upon us as we, as true Christians, come to practical differences and it should be able to observe that we do love each other. Our love must have a form that the world may observe; it must be seeable."[26]

If a renewed church is to be a launching pad for meaningful change and engagement in the world, it must first be an informed church. Then it must be a loving, caring, and serving church. The entire Christian experience is a tightrope walk, fighting for balance, resisting the devil, sensitive to the fallen, restorative to the wayward. Yet all eyes must be on the goal of knowing Christ and the fellowship of His sufferings, becoming like Christ in death while anticipating the resurrection from the dead (Phil. 3:10–11).

Endnotes

INTRODUCTION

1. Jeffrey L. Sheler, "Is God Lost as Sales Rise?" *U.S. News and World Report*, 13 March 1995, 63.

2. Williston Walker, *A History of the Christian Church* (New York: Charles Scribner's Sons, 1959), 3.

3. Augustus Neander, *General History of the Christian Religion and Church*, trans. Joseph Torrey (Boston: Crocker and Brewster, 1854), 1–2.

4. Karl Rahner, "Church," in *Encyclopedia of Theology*, ed. Karl Rahner (New York: Crossroad, 1982), 205–27. Rahner, a leading Roman Catholic authority, writes, "The Fathers and the theologians of the Middle Ages never composed a treatise on the Church" (205). While early Christian creeds affirmed a doctrine of the church, no definitive work on the subject was written until after 1440. See also Juan de Torquemada, *Summa de Ecclesia* (1561). Out of necessity the Reformers gave attention to the doctrine of ecclesiology as well as soteriology.

5. Elton Trueblood, *The Incendiary Fellowship* (New York: Harper, 1967).

6. Jacques Ellul, *The Subversion of Christianity* (Grand Rapids: Eerdmans, 1988), 18.

7. "The Cambridge Declaration," *Modern Reformation* (July–August 1996): 36.

8. Origen, *Homily 16*, quoted in Everett Ferguson, ed., *Encyclopedia of Early Christianity* (New York: Garland, 1990).

9. Cyril of Jerusalem, quoted in Maurice Wiles and Mark Santer, eds., *Documents in Early Christian Thought* (Cambridge: Cambridge University Press, 1975), 168.

CHAPTER 1
THE CHURCH AND COMMUNITY OF THE REDEEMED

1. See Leon Morris, *New Testament Theology* (Grand Rapids: Zondervan, 1986), 149. "One of the things Luke is making abundantly clear is that this is not to be regarded as just another human movement. We are not to think that some garrulous Galileans managed to persuade people to throw in their lot with them" (150).

2. Charles Ryrie asserts three distinctives of the church in relationship to the words of Christ, "I will build my church": It was a future work to His earthly life, it was not the same as the kingdom, and it was distinct from the theocracy of Israel (Charles Ryrie, *Basic Theology* [Wheaton, Ill.: Victor, 1986], 397).

3. Hans Küng, *The Church* (New York: Sheed and Ward, 1967), 75.

4. L. Coenen, "Church," in *New International Dictionary of Theology*, ed. Colin Brown (Grand Rapids: Zondervan, 1967), 1:298.

5. William Hendriksen, *Exposition of the Gospel according to Matthew*, New Testament Commentary (Grand Rapids: Baker, 1973), 700.

6. Ryrie, *Basic Theology*, 394.

7. Leon Morris, "Hebrews," in *The Expositor's Bible Commentary* (Grand Rapids: Zondervan, 1981), 12:142.

8. For Calvin's complete exposition of this verse, see John Calvin, *Commentary on the Epistle of Paul the Apostle to the Hebrews* (Grand Rapids: Eerdmans, 1948), 333–35.

9. See R. B. Kuiper, *The Glorious Body of Christ* (Grand Rapids: Eerdmans, 1962), 31–35.

10. Wayne Grudem, *Systematic Theology* (Downers Grove, Ill.:

InterVarsity, 1994), 858. Grudem sees a distinction between the body metaphor of 1 Corinthians 12 and that of Ephesians 1:22–23; 4:15–16; and Colossians 2:19. In the first, Christ is seen as distinct from the body and in the second as Head of the body. Each, however, comprises the church. He warns his readers to focus on Christ as Lord reigning in heaven as well as dwelling with believers. He does not agree with the Roman Catholic view of the church as the continuing incarnation of the Son of God on earth (ibid., 859).

11. Mark L. Bailey, "A Theology of Paul's Pastoral Epistles," in *A Biblical Theology of the New Testament*, ed. Roy B. Zuck (Chicago: Moody, 1994), 354.

12. Darrell L. Bock, "A Theology of Luke–Acts," *A Biblical Theology of the New Testament*, 142.

13. John Calvin, *Commentary on a Harmony of the Evangelists, Matthew, Mark, and Luke*, trans. William Pringle (Grand Rapids: Eerdmans, 1949), 2:291.

14. Donald Hagner, *Matthew*, Word Biblical Commentary (Dallas: Word, 1995), 468.

15. John Calvin, *A Harmony of the Gospels, Matthew, Mark, and Luke*, ed. David W. Torrance and Thomas Torrance (Edinburgh: Saint Andrew, 1972), 2:186.

16. "When the church says the unrepentant person is bound in sin, the church is saying what God says about that person. When the church acknowledges that a repentant person has been loosed from that sin, God agrees" (John MacArthur, ed., *The MacArthur Study Bible* [Nashville: Word, 1997], 1423).

17. Robert L. Saucy, *The Church in God's Program* (Chicago: Moody, 1972), 65.

18. Bock, "A Biblical Theology of Luke–Acts", 142.

19. See L. Berkhof, *Systematic Theology* (Grand Rapids: Eerdmans, 1953), 572–78 for a Reformed view on the marks of the church.

20. C. H. Dodd, *The Apostolic Preaching and Its Development* (London: Hodder and Stoughton, 1936), 21–23.

21. Robert Mounce, *The Essential Nature of New Testament Preaching* (Grand Rapids: Eerdmans, 1960), 61.

22. Roland H. Bainton, *Here I Stand: A Life of Martin Luther* (New York: Abingdon-Cokesbury, 1950). Bainton traces the emerging doctrine of the church in Luther's life. He states that Luther never went beyond the cardinal tenets of the apostle Paul's theology, but only heightened, intensified, and clarified them.

CHAPTER 2
THE CHURCH IN HISTORY:
THE SPREAD OF GLOBAL WILDFIRE

1. Henry Bettenson, ed., *Documents of the Christian Church* (London: Oxford University Press, 1963), vi.
2. F. F. Bruce, *The Spreading Flame* (London: Paternoster Press, 1958).
3. I am indebted to the work of Christopher Rowland, *Christian Origins: From Messianic Movement to Christian Religion* (Minneapolis: Augsburg, 1985). Rowland presented a contextual interpretation of the rise of the church that few other authors have done.
4. Hans Conzelmann, *History of Primitive Christianity*, trans. John E. Steely (Nashville: Abingdon, 1973), 86.
5. W. R. Inge, *Things Old and New* (1933), quoted in Bruce, *The Spreading Flame*, 161.
6. Walker, *A History of the Christian Church*, 31.
7. For an authoritative review of the apostolic fathers and their writings, see Robert M. Grant, ed., *The Apostolic Fathers* (New York: Nelson, 1964), vol. 1.
8. Bruce L. Shelley, *Church History in Plain Language* (Waco, Tex.: Word, 1982), 92.
9. Kenneth Scott Latourette, *A History of Christianity* (New York: Harper, 1953), 221–35.
10. Ignatius, quoted in *A History of Christianity*, 130.
11. Ibid.
12. F. F. Bruce, *The Dawn of Christianity* (London: Paternoster, 1950), 88.
13. Latourette, *A History of Christianity*, 483.
14. G. H. W. Parker, *The Morning Star: Wycliffe and the Dawn of the Reformation* (Grand Rapids: Eerdmans, 1965), 99–100.

15. Latourette, *A History of Christianity*, 639.
16. For Hus's theology of the church see *The Church*, trans. David S. Schaff (Westport, Conn.: Greenwood, 1974).
17. Steven Ozment, *The Age of Reform 1250–1550: An Intellectual and Religious History of Late Medieval and Reformation Europe* (New Haven, Conn.: Yale University Press, 1980), 180.
18. Roland Bainton, *The Reformation of the Sixteenth Century* (Boston: Beacon, 1952), 41. In Bainton's earlier work, *Here I Stand: A Life of Martin Luther* (New York: Abingdon, 1950), he noted that Luther never intended that the Theses would be distributed among the people; he simply wanted to invite scholarly debate.
19. Bainton, *Here I Stand*, 78.
20. John Calvin, quoted in Ozment, *The Age of Reform, 1250–1550*, 355.
21. Ibid., 366.
22. Howard Mumford Jones, *O Strange New World: American Culture, The Formative Years* (New York: Viking, 1952), 193.
23. Quoted in David Lovejoy, *Religious Enthusiasm in the New World* (Cambridge, Mass.: Harvard University Press, 1985), 9.
24. John Wesley, quoted in James Richard Joy, *John Wesley's Awakening* (New York: Methodist Book Concern, 1937), 64.
25. Robert E. Webber, *Common Roots* (Grand Rapids: Zondervan, 1978), 29.
26. An exception is Mark A. Noll, David W. Bebbington, and George A. Rawlyk, eds., *Evangelicalism: Comparative Studies of Popular Protestantism in North America, the British Isles and Beyond 1700–1900*, (New York: Oxford University Press, 1994). See also David Wells, *No Place for Truth* (Grand Rapids: Eerdmans, 1993); Stanley J. Grenz, *Revisioning Theology* (Downers Grove, Ill.: InterVarsity, 1993); Donald Bloesch, *The Future of Evangelical Christianity* (Garden City, N. Y.: Doubleday, 1983); and Mark A. Noll, *Between Faith and Criticism: Evangelicals Scholarship and the Bible in America* (Grand Rapids: Baker, 1991).

CHAPTER 3
THE CHURCH AND THE HEADSHIP OF CHRIST

1. Otto Weber, *Foundations of Dogmatics*, trans. Darrell Guder (Grand Rapids: Eerdmans, 1983), 2:511.
2. Jean Daniélou, *The Origins of Latin Christianity*, trans. David Smith and John Austin Baker (London: Garton, Longman, and Todd, 1977), 3:430.
3. Donald G. Bloesch, *A Theology of Word and Spirit* (Downers Grove, Ill: InterVarsity, 1992), 272. See pages 267–72 for his complete argument. See also John R. W. Stott, *Christ the Controversialist* (Downers Grove, Ill.: InterVarsity, 1974).
4. Thomas à Kempis, *The Imitation of Christ*, 12.
5. Hans Küng, *The Church*, 94.
6. Ibid., 94.
7. Geoffrey W. Bromiley, *Christian Ministry* (Grand Rapids: Eerdmans, 1959), 19.
8. Luther's seven rights of the universal priesthood of all believers are summarized in Paul Althaus, *The Theology of Martin Luther*, trans. Robert C. Schultz (Philadelphia: Fortress, 1966), 313–18.
9. For a fuller investigation of the views of the Anabaptists, see George Huntston Williams, *The Radical Reformation* (Philadelphia: Westminster, 1962); William R. Estep, *The Anabaptist Story*, 3d ed. (Grand Rapids, Eerdmans, 1996); and C. Arnold Snyder, *Anabaptist History and Theology: An Introduction* (Kitchen, Ont.: Pandora, 1995)
10. Thomas à Kempis, *The Imitation of Christ*, 1–2.
11. Dietrich Bonhoeffer, *Life Together*, trans. John W. Doberstein (San Francisco: Harper, 1954), 17.

CHAPTER 4
THE CHURCH AND THE BIBLE

1. Frank E. Gaebelein, "Perspective on American Christianity," *Christianity Today*, 23 April 1965, 785.

2. G. C. Berkhouwer, "Hearing and Doing the Word," *Christianity Today*, 28 October 1966, 128.
3. Ulrich Zwingli, quoted in W. P. Stephens, *The Theology of Huldrych Zwingli* (Oxford: Clarendon, 1986), 51. Zwingli developed the doctrine of scriptural authority in an early work, *The Clarity and Certainty of the Word of God*, Library of Christian Classics, vol. 24 (Philadelphia: Westminster), 90–91.
4. Emile Cailliet, *Journey into Light* (Grand Rapids: Zondervan, 1968), 11, 18 (italics his).
5. On the differences between revelation, inspiration, and illumination, see Roy B. Zuck, *Spirit-Filled Teaching: The Power of the Holy Spirit in Your Ministry*, Swindoll Leadership Library (Nashville: Word, 1998), chapter 4.
6. See Bernard Ramm, *The Witness of the Spirit* (Grand Rapids: Eerdmans, 1959), 11–27. Ramm traces the historical roots of this false charge and gives an overview of the development of the doctrine of divine illumination of the truth of the Bible.
7. Oscar Cullmann, *Christ and Time* (Philadelphia: Westminster, 1964), 172–73.
8. Donald G. Bloesch, *Crumbling Foundations: Death and Rebirth in an Age of Upheaval* (Grand Rapids: Zondervan, 1984), 87–88.
9. Philip Schaff, *The Creeds of Christendom* (New York: Harper, 1877), 2:11–12.
10. Ibid., 3:499.
11. Ibid., 3:219 (translated from the German).
12. Ibid., 3:419.
13. William L. Lumpton, ed., *Baptist Confessions of Faith* (Valley Forge, Pa.: Judson, 1959), 165.
14. Ibid., 365.
15. Schaff, *The Creeds of Christendom*, 3:703.
16. Ibid., 2:83.
17. F. S. A. Hort, quoted in Richard N. Longenecker, *Biblical Exegesis in the Apostolic Period* (Grand Rapids: Eerdmans, 1975), 217–18.
18. Stanly Hauerwas and William H. Willimon, *Resident Aliens: Life in the Christian Colony* (Nashville: Abingdon, 1989), 24–25.

19. Peter L. Berger, *A Far Glory: The Quest of Faith in an Age of Credulity* (New York: Free, 1992), 10–11.

CHAPTER 5
THE CHURCH AND HOLY SPIRIT POWER

1. Sargeant Shriver, "Acceptance Speech," *Vital Speeches* 38 (15 August, 1972), 646.
2. Pasquala Villari, *Life and Times of Girolamo Savonarola*, trans. Linda Villari (London: T. Fischer Unwin, 1899), 639–40.
3. Jim Elliot, quoted in Elisabeth Elliot, *Through Gates of Splendor* (New York: Harper, 1957), 18.
4. Os Guinness, *The American Hour* (New York: Free, 1994), 65–66.
5. William Barclay, *The Promise of the Spirit* (Philadelphia: Westminster, 1960), 35.
6. Schaff, *The Creeds of Christendom,* 3:325. .
7. See Grudem, *Systematic Theology*, 1049–88. Grudem includes one of the most thorough and useful treatises on the subject of spiritual gifts in the literature of the subject. He cautions the reader against fragmentation in the body of Christ over categorizations of gifts.
8. René Pache, *The Person and Work of the Holy Spirit*, trans. J. D. Emerson (Chicago: Moody, 1954), 6.
9. For a full discussion of the doctrine of sanctification see Henry W. Holloman, *The Forgotten Blessing*, Swindoll Leadership Library, (Nashville: Word, 1998).
10. See Peter Wagner, *The Third Wave of the Holy Spirit* (Ann Arbor, Mich: Vine, 1988).
11. See James Leo Garrett, Jr., ed., *The Concept of the Believers' Church* (Scottdale, Pa: Herald, 1969). I am indebted to the various contributors to this volume for seed ideas and historic data on the rise of the believers' church idea and ideal.
12. John Calvin, "The Necessity of Reforming the Church," in *Calvin: Theological Treatises*, trans. J. K. S. Reid (Philadelphia: Westminster, 1954), 188.

CHAPTER 6
THE CHURCH AND COMMITMENT

1. Sheila Larson, quoted in Robert Bellah et al., *Habits of the Heart* (New York: Harper, 1985), 221.

2. Karl Rahner, "Church," in *Encyclopedia of Theology*, ed., Karl Rahner (New York: Crossroad, 1982), 205–27. Besides describing traditional Catholic theology, Rahner also summarizes Protestant beliefs about the church as well.

3. *Luther's Works*, 26:66–67.

4. "Reply of the Churches in Membership with the Baptist Union to the 'Appeal to All Christian People,'" issued by the Lambeth Conference of 1920, adopted by the Assembly of the Baptist Union at Leeds on Tuesday, 4 May 1926 (Henry Cook, *What Baptists Believe* [London: Kingsgate, 1947], 245–46).

5. Saucy, *The Church in God's Program*, 195.

6. Cook, *What Baptists Believe*, 246.

7. For a full discussion of arguments for and against infant baptism and a discussion of the "age of accountability," see Roy B. Zuck, *Precious in His Sight: Childhood and Children in the Bible* (Grand Rapids: Baker, 1996), 226–41.

8. See Thomas N. Tentler, *Sin and Confession on the Eve of the Reformation* (Princeton, N. J.: Princeton University Press, 1977) for a full discussion of the rise of sacramental confession and Protestant reaction.

9. Ibid., 107.

10. John Stott discusses three forms of legitimate confession: private confession to God, private confession to an offended individual, and public confession to the church. Oral confession to a third party is deplored. "It is God who forgives through Christ; it is the Church which proclaims His forgiveness through its ministers" (*Confess Your Sins* [Waco, Tex: Word, 1964], 63).

11. Ibid., 85–86.

12. For an extensive discussion of church discipline—when, where, and how it should be done—see J. Carl Laney, *A Guide to Church Discipline* (Minneapolis: Bethany, 1985).

13. H. Wayne House and Thomas O. Ice give a helpful critique of the shortcomings of theonomy in *Dominion Theology: Blessing or Curse?* (Portland, Oreg.: Multnomah, 1988). Also see Robert P. Lightner, "A Despensational Response to Theonomy," *Bibliotheca Sacra* 143 (July–September 1986): 228–45.

14. Martin Luther, quoted in Althaus, *The Theology of Luther*, 111.

CHAPTER 7
THE CHURCH AND ITS MINISTRY AND ORGANIZATION

1. See Grudem, *Systematic Theology*, 904–45, for a thorough discussion of the scriptural basis for governance. He states that individual believers should be "willing to live and minister within any of several different Protestant systems of church government in which they may find themselves from time to time" (904).

2. F. J. Forrester, "Church Government," in *International Standard Bible Encyclopedia*, 1 (1979), 697.

3. Berkhof, *Systematic Theology*, 590.

4. "Congregationalism," in *The Oxford Dictionary of the Christian Church*, ed. F. L. Cross (Oxford: Oxford University Press, 1997), 399.

5. On the meaning of "husband of one wife," see Grudem, *Systematic Theology*, 916–17, and Robert L. Saucy, "The Husband of One Wife," *Bibliotheca Sacra* 131 (July–September 1974): 229–40.

6. For a helpful discussion of each of these qualifications see Mark L. Bailey, "A Theology of Paul's Pastoral Epistles," in *A Biblical Theology of the New Testament*, 360–64.

7. Ibid., 364–65.

8. Karl Barth, "Church and Culture," in *Theology and Church: Shorter Writings 1920–1928*, trans. Louise Pettebone Smith (New York: Harper, 1962), 334.

9. Martin Luther, quoted in Althaus, *The Theology of Luther*, 314.

10. Bromiley, *Christian Ministry*, 24.

11. Ibid., 25.

12. Thomas à Kempis, *The Imitation of Christ*, 114–15.

13. Ibid., 117–18.

14. See Paul A. Cedar, *A Life of Prayer: Cultivating the Inner Life of the Christian Leader,* Swindoll Leadership Library (Nashville: Word, 1998).

15. Richard Halverson, introduction in Richard Baxter, *The Reformed Pastor* (reprint, Portland, Oreg.: Multnomah, 1982), xvii.

16. See Marjorie Warkentin, *Ordination: A Biblical Historical View* (Grand Rapids: Eerdmans, 1982). She documents the practice of ordination from the Anabaptist believers' church and Baptist traditions.

CHAPTER 8
THE CHURCH AND WORSHIP

1. Samuel Butler, quoted in Warren W. Wiersbe, *Real Worship* (Nashville: Oliver-Nelson, 1986), 20.

2. Martin Luther, quoted in Althaus, *The Theology of Martin Luther,* 131.

3. Edmund P. Clowney, *The Church* (Downers Grove, Ill.: InterVarsity, 1995), 117.

4. William D. Maxwell, *An Outline of Christian Worship: Its Developments and Forms* (London: Oxford University Press, 1936), 4–5. The author blends history with biblical insight.

5. Charles Haddon Spurgeon, *Lectures to My Students* (1875; reprint, Grand Rapids: Zondervan, 1980), 54.

6. See Cedar, *A Life of Prayer.*

7. This earliest preserved hymn is titled "Bridle of Colts Untamed," which was composed in the second century. Other early hymns appeared before the Council of Nicaea (325).

8. Nikolaus Ludwig von Zinzendorf, quoted in S. Paul Schilling, *The Faith We Sing* (Philadelphia: Westminster, 1983), 25.

9. Willy Rordorf, *Sunday: The History of the Day of Rest and Worship in the Earliest Centuries of the Christian Church* (Philadelphia: Westminster, 1968), 296.

10. For a critique of contemporary worship forms see Robert Wenz, *Room for God? A Worship Challenge for a Church-Growth and Mar-*

keting Era (Grand Rapids: Baker, 1994). For a balanced view of renewal in worship, see Ralph P. Martin, *The Worship of God: Some Theological, Pastoral and Practical Reflections* (Grand Rapids: Eerdmans, 1982).

CHAPTER 9
THE CHURCH AND THE GOSPEL

1. Ewald M. Plass, comp., *What Luther Says: A Practical In-home Anthology for the Active Christian* (St. Louis: Concordia, 1972), 560.
2. Origen, *Homily on Luke.* For insight into the turbulent years of the postapostolic church see F. F. Bruce, *Jesus and Christian Origins Outside the New Testament* (Grand Rapids: Eerdmans, 1974); and Robert M. Grant, *After the New Testament* (Philadelphia: Fortress, 1967).
3. See Walter Rauschenbusch, *Theology for a Social Gospel* (New York: Abingdon, 1945). Gospel work to him was establishing a community of righteousness among humankind, the "energy of God realizing itself in human life" (141).
4. Kenneth Copeland, *The Laws of Prosperity* (Fort Worth: By the author, 1974); and Robert Tilton, *God's Laws of Success* (Dallas: Word of Faith, 1983).
5. Rodney Clapp, "Why the Devil Takes Visa," *Christianity Today,* 7 October 1996, 19–33.
6. Martin Marty, quoted in *Newsweek,* 9 August 1993, 48.
7. John R. W. Stott, *Christian Mission in the Modern World* (Downers Grove, Ill.: InterVarsity, 1975), 57. Stott was one of the framers of the Lausanne Covenant in 1974.
8. James I. Packer, "The Gospel: Its Content and Communication," in *Down to Earth: Studies in Christianity and Culture,* ed. Robert T. Coote and John R. W. Stott (Grand Rapids: Eerdmans, 1980), 97.
9. "The Cambridge Declaration," 35. This statement appeared as "Thesis Two: *Solus Christus,*" prepared by the Alliance of Confessing Evangelicals, 20 April 1996.
10. See Donald McGavran, *Understanding Church Growth* (Grand Rap-

ids: Eerdmans, 1970); C. Peter Wagner, *Your Church Can Grow* (Ventura, Calif.: Regal, 1976); and Elmer Towns, *Evangelism and Church Growth* (Ventura, Calif.: Regal, 1995).

11. Martin Luther, quoted in Althaus, *The Theology of Martin Luther*, 318.

12. John Bunyan, *Pilgrim's Progress* (Westwood, N. J.: Christian Library, 1984), 3–4.

13. J. B. Phillips, *The Young Church in Action* (New York: Macmillan, 1955), vii.

14. J. B. Phillips, *Letters to Young Churches* (New York: Macmillan, 1947), xiv.

15. Gnosticism holds a wide range of belief, including an impersonal God, special "knowledge" to the enlightened, and denial of a need for personal redemption. Nestorianism posited two distinct persons in the incarnate Christ, one divine and the other human. Manichaeanism was a radical offshoot of second-century Gnosticism, promoting a myth of salvation as essentially a release from satanic captivity, with deliverance of the soul dependent on celestial phenomena and ritualistic asceticism.

CHAPTER 10
THE CHURCH AND THE WORLD

1. Ellul, *The Subversion of Christianity*, 191.

2. I. Howard Marshall, "Culture and the New Testament," in *Down to Earth: Studies in Christianity and Culture*, 31.

3. *Saint Augustine's Prayer Book: A Book of Devotion for Members of the Episcopal Church*, ed. Loren Gavitt and Archie Drake (New York: Holy Cross, 1947).

4. Thomas Altizer and William Hamilton, *Radical Theology and the Death of God* (Indianapolis: Bobbs and Merrill, 1966), 125.

5. Ellul, *The Subversion of Christianity*, 18.

6. Quoted in Stott, *The Contemporary Christian*, 94.

7. Plass, comp., *What Luther Says: An Anthology*, 966.

8. This quotation from chapter 5 of the *Epistle to Diognetus* appears in

Roots of Faith: An Anthology of Early Christian Spirituality, Robert Van de Weyer, ed. (Grand Rapids: Eerdmans, 1997), 83. For the original Greek text see J. B. Lightfoot, *The Apostolic Fathers,* ed. J. R. Harmer (London: Macmillan, 1898), 490–500.

CHAPTER 11
THE CHURCH AND SUFFERING

1. Bruce, *The Spreading Flame,* 161 (italics his).
2. For a useful exegetical discussion of this verse see Peter T. O'Brien, *Colossians, Philemon,* Word Biblical Commentary (Waco, Tex.: Word, 1982), 44:75–81.
3. This insight comes from the exegesis of the Greek word *paschō* in *New International Dictionary of New Testament Theology,* 3:724.
4. Polycarp, quoted in *Documents of the Christian Church,* 15.
5. For a full discussion of suffering and martyrdom in the New Testament, especially Jesus as a martyr, see William Horbury and Brian McNeil, eds., *Suffering and Martyrdom in the New Testament* (Cambridge: Cambridge University Press, 1981). The chapter by Brian Beck, "'Imitatio Christi' and the Lucan Passion Narrative" presents the case for the martyrdom theory of Jesus' suffering and death.
6. John Foxe, *Foxe's Christian Martyrs of the World* (Westwood, N. J.: Barbour, 1985), 12. This reprint of the classic sixteenth-century work is under the title *The Christian Library.* Along with the Bible, Foxe's *Book of Martyrs,* as it came to be called, was one of the most readily available books of the sixteenth century.
7. Plass, comp., *What Luther Says: An Anthology,* 1036.
8. This estimation comes from materials presented to the American churches in preparation for the November 11, 1997 Day of Prayer for the persecuted church. Persecution is difficult to quantify and even martyrdom may be subject to interpretation by various researchers.
9. Bettenson, *Documents of the Christian Church,* 12.
10. Eusebius referred to martyrs at Lyon, France, as early as A.D. 177. See F. W. Danker, "Martyr," in *International Standard Bible Encyclopedia,* 3 (1986), 267.

11. See Thieleman J. van Braght, *Martyrs Mirror*, 10th ed. (Scottdale, Pa.: Herald), first published in Dutch in 1660.

12. These insights are gained from conversations with Christian leaders in former Soviet-bloc nations. At the time of the publication of this book, nearly a decade has passed since the removal of the Berlin Wall and the fall of communism in Eastern Europe.

13. F. W. Krummacher, *The Suffering Savior* (1854; reprint, Chicago: Moody, 1947), 440.

CHAPTER 12
THE CHURCH AND ITS HOPE

1. Ernst Hoffmann, "Hope," in *New International Dictionary of New Testament Theology*, 2:243.

2. Bertrand Russell, *Why I Am Not a Christian* (New York: Simon and Schuster, 1957), 115.

3. Milton, *The Works of Milton*. A modern version of these two quotations may be found in *The Portable Milton*, ed. Douglas Bush (New York: Viking, 1949), 234, 548.

4. Charles Wesley, *Victorious Faith* (n. p., 1850), 265.

5. David A. Hubbard, *What We Evangelicals Believe* (Pasadena, Calif.: Fuller Theological Seminary, 1979), 168..

6. In his exposition of Isaiah 8:17 Luther included brief remarks about the hope of the church. See *Luther's Works*, 16:93.

7. John F. Walvoord, "The Hope of the World," in *The Word for This Century*, ed. Merrill C. Tenney (New York: Oxford University Press, 1960), 177.

8. Lewis Sperry Chafer, *Systematic Theology* (Dallas: Dallas Seminary Press, 1948; reprint, 8 vols. in 4, Grand Rapids: Kregel, 1993), 4:261.

9. See Romans 13:11–14; 1 Corinthians 15:58; 2 Corinthians 7:1; Philippians 4:5; 1 Thessalonians 5:23; 2 Thessalonians 2:16–17; 1 Timothy 6:14–16; Titus 2:11–13; 2 Peter 3:11–12; 1 John 5:21; Jude 21.

10. Helmut Thielicke, *The Evangelical Faith* (Edinburgh: Clark, 1982), 465.

11. Saucy, *The Church in God's Program*, 84.

12. See "King," in *New International Dictionary of New Testament Theology*, 2:372–90.

13. The "glory song" was sung often at Bible conferences sponsored by the Mount Hermon Association in Mount Hermon, California, the oldest conference center in the West. Its namesake, the Mount Hermon of Northfield, Massachusetts, was begun by D. L. Moody. The hymn, "O That Will Be Glory for Me," by Charles Gabriel, is copyrighted by the Rodheaver Company.

14. See Ryrie's explanation of the future Millennium (*Basic Theology*, 508–11).

15. See Craig A. Blaising and Darrell L. Bock, eds., *Dispensationalism, Israel and the Church* (Grand Rapids: Zondervan, 1992); and John S. Feinberg, ed., *Continuity and Discontinuity: Perspectives on the Relation between the Old and New Testaments* (Westchester, Ill.: Crossway, 1988).

16. Bruce A. Demarest and Gordon R. Lewis, *Integrative Theology* (Grand Rapids: Zondervan, 1994), 3:307–63.

17. Charles Ryrie, *Dispensationalism Today* (Chicago: Moody, 1965), 131.

18. Robert L. Saucy, quoted in Lewis and Demarest, *Integrative Theology*, 3:356.

19. See Berkhof, *Systematic Theology*, 565.

20. The original hymn had eight stanzas. Worship leaders might wish to compare this Roman Catholic version with other texts as they appear in recent hymnals of the church.

21. Tacitus, quoted in F. F. Bruce, *New Testament History* (London: Oliphants, 1971), 380.

22. For a concise description of this doctrine see David K. Lowery, "A Theology of Paul's Missionary Letters," in *A Biblical Theology of the New Testament*, 294–95. See also Walvoord, *The Rapture Question*, rev. ed. (Grand Rapids: Zondervan, 1979).

23. For a helpful discussion of the Bible's teachings on many end-time events, see John F. Walvoord, *End Times: An Explanation of World Events in Bible Prophecy*, Swindoll Leadership Library (Nashville: Word, 1998).

CHAPTER 13
THE CHURCH AND RENEWAL

1. P. T. Forsyth, *Positive Preaching and the Modern Mind* (London: Independent, 1907), 11.
2. Lesslie Newbigen, *Honest Religion for Secular Man* (Philadelphia: Westminster, 1966), 76.
3. D. M. Lloyd-Jones, *What Is an Evangelical?* (London: Banner of Truth, 1993).
4. John R. W. Stott, *Evangelical Essentials* (Downers Grove, Ill.: InterVarsity, 1988), 85.
5. Nathan Hatch and Michael Hamilton, "Will Success Spoil Evangelicalism?" *Current Thoughts and Trends* (November 1992): 2.
6. Christopher Lasch, *The Culture of Narcissism: American Life in an Age of Diminishing Expectations* (New York: Norton, 1979), 7.
7. David W. Bebbington, *Evangelicalism in Modern Britain* (London: Unwin Hyman, 1989), 2.
8. See Vernon C. Grounds, "The Nature of Evangelicalism," *Eternity,* (February 1956): 12–13, 42–43. Grounds, himself a theologian educated in modern psychological thought, is convinced that theological thought is foundational in all fields of scholarly investigation.
9. This charge is made by James Hunter in *American Evangelicalism: Conservative Religion and the Quandary of Modernity* (New Brunswick, N. J.: Rutgers University Press, 1993). See also David F. Wells, *No Place for Truth: Or Whatever Happened to Evangelical Theology?* (Grand Rapids: Eerdmans, 1993).
10. Charles Colson, *The Body* (Dallas: Word, 1992). The entire book is a call for renewal.
11. "Culture Wars: What the World Needs Now," *Leadership* 14 (spring 1993): 20–28.
12. Leonard Sweet, "Target the Trends," *Leadership* 14 (spring 1993): 21.
13. James Montgomery Boice, "Exposition not Entertainment," *Leadership* 14 (spring 1993):27.
14. Cyprian of Carthage, "De catholicae ecclesiae unitate," in *Documents of the Christian Church,* 101.

15. Michael Novak, "Awakening from Nihilism: The Templeton Prize Address," *First Things* 45 (August/September 1994): 18 (italics his).

16. Mark A. Noll, *The Scandal of the Evangelical Mind* (Grand Rapids: Eerdmans, 1994), 4.

17. Douglas Groothuis, "Arguing with Success," *Christian Research Journal* 18 (spring 1996): 55.

18. Vernon C. Grounds, "The Truth about Truth," *Journal of the Evangelical Theological Society* 38 (June 1995): 219.

19. For the full "Statement of Intent," issued by the Hoddesdon Conference, see Ronald Sider, ed., *Evangelicals and Development: Toward a Theology of Social Change* (Philadelphia: Westminster, 1981), 15–16.

20. Larry Brown, "Ring around the Collar: American Comedy and Clergy," *Christian Scholars Review* 22 (June 1993): 411.

21. James E. White, *A Brief History of Christian Worship* (Nashville: Abingdon, 1993), 13.

22. A. W. Tozer, *The Knowledge of the Holy* (San Francisco: Harper, 1961), 1.

23. Lewis Sperry Chafer, *He That Is Spiritual* (Findlay, Ohio: Dunham, 1918; reprint, Grand Rapids: Zondervan, 1967), preface.

24. Dallas Willard, *The Spirit of the Disciplines* (San Francisco: Harper, 1988), 10.

25. Donald G. Bloesch, *The Future of Evangelical Christianity: A Call for Unity amid Diversity* (Garden City, N.Y.: Doubleday, 1983), 84.

26. Francis A. Schaeffer, *The Church at the End of the 20th Century* (Downers Grove, Ill.: InterVarsity, 1970), 152.

Bibliography

Bainton, Roland. *The Reformation of the Sixteenth Century.* Boston: Beacon Press, 1952.

Bloesch, Donald G. *A Theology of Word and Spirit.* Downers Grove, Ill.: InterVarsity Press, 1992.

Bromiley, Geoffrey W. *Christian Ministry.* Grand Rapids: Wm. B. Eerdmans Publishing Co., 1959.

Bruce, F. F. *The Spreading Flame.* London: Paternoster Press, 1958.

Clowney, Edmund P. *The Church.* Downers Grove, Ill.: InterVarsity Press, 1995.

Colson, Charles. *The Body.* Dallas: Word Publishing, 1992.

Coote, Robert T., and John R. W. Stott, eds. *Down to Earth: Studies in Christianity and Culture.* Grand Rapids: Wm. B. Eerdmans Publishing Co., 1980.

Demarest, Bruce A., and Gordon R. Lewis. *Integrative Theology.* 3 vols. Grand Rapids: Zondervan Publishing House, 1987.

Ellul, Jacques. *The Subversion of Christianity.* Grand Rapids: Wm. B. Eerdmans Publishing Co., 1988.

Garrett, James Leo., ed. *The Concept of the Believers' Church.* Scottdale, Pa.: Herald Press, 1969.

Green, Michael. *Evangelism in the Early Church.* Grand Rapids: Wm. B. Eerdmans Publishing Co., 1970.

Grudem, Wayne. *Systematic Theology.* Grand Rapids: Zondervan Publishing House, 1994.

Hesselgrave, David. *Communicating Christ Cross-Culturally.* Grand Rapids: Zondervan Publishing House, 1991.

Hus, Jan. *The Church.* Translated by David S. Schaff. Westport, Conn.: Greenwood Press, 1974.

Kuiper, R. B. *The Glorious Body of Christ.* Grand Rapids: Wm. B. Eerdmans Publishing Co., 1966.

Küng, Hans. *The Church.* New York: Sheed and Ward, 1967.

Latourette, Kenneth Scott. *A History of Christianity.* New York: Harper and Brothers, 1953.

Lloyd-Jones, D. M. *What Is an Evangelical?* London: Banner of Truth, 1993.

MacArthur, John, Jr. *The Church: The Body of Christ.* Grand Rapids: Zondervan Publishing House, 1973.

McGrath, Alister. *Christian Theology.* Oxford: Blackwell, 1994.

Martin, Ralph. *The Family and the Fellowship: New Testament Images of the Church.* Grand Rapids: Wm. B. Eerdmans Publishing Co., 1979.

————. *The Worship of God: Some Theological, Pastoral and Practical Reflections.* Grand Rapids: Wm. B. Eerdmans Publishing Co., 1982.

————. *Worship in the Early Church.* Westwood, N.J.: Fleming H. Revell Co., 1964.

Minear, Paul S. *Images of the Church in the New Testament.* Philadelphia: Westminster Press, 1960.

Morris, Leon. *New Testament Theology.* Grand Rapids: Zondervan Publishing House, 1986.

Oden, Thomas C. *Life in the Spirit.* San Francisco: HarperSan Francisco, 1992.

Packer, J. I. *A Quest for Godliness.* Wheaton, Ill.: Crossway Books, 1990.

Radmacher, Earl D. *The Nature of the Church.* Hayesville, N.C.: Schoettle Publishing Co., 1996.

Ryrie, Charles. *Basic Theology.* Wheaton, Ill.: Victor Books, 1986.

Saucy, Robert L. *The Church in God's Program.* Chicago: Moody Press, 1972.

Schaeffer, Francis A. *The Church at the End of the 20th Century.* Downers Grove, Ill.: InterVarsity Press, 1970.

Schaff, Philip. *Creeds of Christendom.* New York: Harper and Brothers, 1877.

Smith, David L. *All God's People: A Theology of the Church.* Wheaton, Ill.: Victor Books, 1996.

Stott, John R. W. *Guard the Gospel.* Downers Grove, Ill.: InterVarsity Press, 1996.

————. *The Contemporary Christian.* Downers Grove, Ill.: InterVarsity Press, 1992.

Walker, Williston. *A History of the Christian Church.* New York: Charles Scribner's Sons, 1959.

Wiles, Maurice, and Mark Santer, eds. *Documents in Early Christian Thought.* Cambridge: Cambridge University Press, 1975.

Zuck, Roy B., ed. *A Biblical Theology of the New Testament.* Chicago: Moody Press, 1994.

Scripture Index

Genesis
1:28   256
3:18   202
4:10   5
15:18–21   244
38:24   223
50:20   217

Exodus
16:29   170
19:1–8   244
20:8   170
30:35   204
31:15   170

Leviticus
11:44, 45   109
19:2   109
20:7   109
20:14   223
23:3   170

Deuteronomy
9:10   3
21:22–23   223
23:3   3
25:2–3   223

Joshua
7:25–28   223

Judges
8:23   240

9:45   204

2 Kings
2:19–22   204

1 Chronicles
29:11   240

2 Chronicles
6:3   3

Ezra
10:8, 12   3

Nehemiah
8:2, 17   3

Job
14:14   234

Psalms
2   240
16:8   154
23:1–6   14
27:1   205
34:12–16   207
34:14   209
44:3   205
45   240
47:8–9   240
51:1–6   160
68:18   103
80:1   14

103:19   240
104:4   96
110   45
110:1   57
119:16   89
119:105   89, 206
136   165
145:13   240
149:9   246

Proverbs
12:1   217
13:1   217

Isaiah
5:14   226
6:1   154, 264
6:5   57, 240
40:11   14
42:6   244
43:2   223
53   217
53:4–6   178
56:7   162

Jeremiah
5:14   96
20:9   96
23:29   95
31:10   14
31:31–40   244

293

Ezekiel
34:11–22   14
36:24–58   244

Daniel
7:13–14   240
9:24–27   248

Hosea
6:6   150

Micah
2:5   3

Zechariah
10:3, 8   14

Malachi
3:1   17
4:5–6   17

Matthew
3:17   28
4:10   155
4:17   239, 241
4:18   17
5:9   209
5:11–12   215
5:12   218
5:13   204, 205
5:14   205
5:14–16   206
5:18   245
6:9–13   163
6:10   128, 203, 241
6:24   148
6:33   239
7:1   125
7:13   184
7:13–14   184
8:1–4   181
9:27–34   181
10:11–13   91
10:32, 33   86

10:39   148
11:4–5   175
11:27, 28   181
12:7   150
12:32   245
13   240
13:33   206
14:1–2   16
15:8–9   155
15:12–14   78
15:15   17
16:11   206
16:14   16, 17
16:15   17
16:16   16, 17, 78
16:18   xvi, xix, 3, 5, 16, 17, 18, 19, 53, 78, 241
16:26   201
18:1–5   64
18:15–17   67
18:15–18   127
18:17   3
18:18   22, 66
18:20   20
19:27   17
20:20–28   64, 246
20:22   218, 219
20:25–28   65
20:26   126
20:28   181
21:13   162
22:1–14   122
22:21   128
22:24   57
24:24   91
24:35   77
25:35–40   219
26:26   121
26:26–28   120
26:30   165
26:39   149
26:53   181
26:64   57

27:22–25   243
27:29, 37, 42   58
28:18   180
28:19   22, 117
28:19–20   117, 180, 256

Mark
1:1   174
1:5   117
1:15   239
1:24   109
3:7–8   28
3:13–19   147
3:14–19   137
7:7, 8   117
8:29   16
9:33–37   64
9:49   204
10:15   243
10:29–30   179
10:30   245
10:35–45   64
13:9   219
13:13   215
14:22–26   120
14:24, 25   122
15:9   57
16:15   180, 181
16:16   135

Luke
1:35   109
3:21   163
4:18–19   150
5:31–32   180
6:12   163
6:14   17
6:36   150, 209
9:18   163
9:20   16
9:23   69, 147, 219
9:41–48   64
11:2–4   163
12:13–21   162

12:21	162	15:1–4	19	2:46	157
14:24	122	15:5	69	2:47	134
16:8	202	15:7	77	3:14	109
21:28	245	15:18, 20	215	3:16–20	18
22:17–20	120	15:26	98	4:4	132
22:19	157	16:7, 8	98	4:12	18, 184
22:27–30	219	16:13	75	4:20	221
23:2, 3	57	16:28	69	4:32	113
23:43	135	16:33	199, 215, 248	4:36–37	10, 28, 100
24:27	77	17	163	5	10
24:32	96	17:6	193	5:1–11	10, 22
24:47	180, 181	17:11	257	5:2, 3–4	100
24:49	97	17:13–19	193	5:11	100
		17:18	69, 180, 181	5:14	134
John		17:21, 23	210	5:29	224
1:1–14	182	18:33	239	5:40	223
1:9	205	18:36	xvi, 98, 129, 201	6:1	143
1:12–13	12	18:37	221	6:1–6	151
1:15	205	20:21	181	6:2–4	132
1:17	77	20:22–23	122	6:3	141, 144
1:29	15	21:15–17	142	6:3–5	138
1:42	17, 18	21:15–19	15	6:5	29
2:15, 16, 17	193	21:25	xxii	6:5–6	28
3:3	245			6:7	143
3:23	118	**Acts**		6:8–15	28
4:23	155	1:4	97	7:2–60	28
4:24	153	1:5	20	7:38	4, 100
5:19	245	1:8	28, 180, 182,	7:57–60	222
5:39	94		221, 244	8:1	28, 100
6:38	149	1:22	140	8:10	100
6:68	77	1:26	63	8:12	118, 136, 240
8:12	205	2	20	8:16	118
10:11, 14	15	2:1	140	8:17	151
10:35	93	2:1–4	15	8:19	100
12:36	206	2:4	244	8:22	101
12:44	57	2:12–13	162	8:26–39	29
13:13	17	2:25	154	8:36	118
13:35	209	2:34, 36	57	8:38	136
14:2	13	2:38	118	8:38–39	118
14:6	73, 188	2:38–39	18	9:16	218
14:16	97, 98	2:41	118, 132, 134, 136	9:17	151
14:17	98	2:42	9, 22, 131, 157	9:31	6, 100
14:23	69	2:42–47	132	10	29
14:26	75, 98	2:43–47	9, 22	10:34–43	18

10:44–48	118	22:20	221	12:2	202
10:48	136	22:25	223, 224	12:3	107, 149
11:15	15, 20, 244	23:12, 27–29	20	12:3–8	103
11:19	29	24:10–16	161	12:6	149
11:22	100	27:3	29	12:8	138
11:26	xvii, 20, 29	28:31	240	12:9	201
13–14	29			12:15	125
13:1	100	*Romans*		12:18	209
13:1–3	64	1:2	109	13:1–6	224
13:2	76	1:7	135	13:1–7	129
13:2–3	151	1:9	230	13:7	128
14:19	222	1:14	198	14:7	xxii, 124
14:21	180	1:16	176, 244	14:13, 19	125
14:23	100, 132, 138, 151	1:18–32	201	15:1–3	125
15	137	1:21	167	15:4	250
15:2–4	64	2:16	175	15:13	233, 235, 249
15:5	29	3:4	74	15:15–16	29
15:11	30	3:23	203	15:16	176
15:22	100	3:25	217	15:18	104
15:28	76	4:25	234	15:26	157
15:41	100	5:3	230	15:27–29	162
16:4	64	6:4	118, 135, 234	16:1	4, 144
16:5	100	8:1	203	16:16	4, 157
16:13	162	8:11	234	16:17	127
16:37	223	8:14, 16, 21	12	16:25	175
17:5	20	8:16	75		
17:11	76, 91	8:17	241	*1 Corinthians*	
17:13	20	8:18	215, 218	1:2	4, 23, 63, 134, 258
17:28	12	8:18–27	215	1:10–17	127
18:7, 11	162	8:22	203	1:16	118
19:6	151	8:24	232, 233	1:17	175
19:8–10	162	8:26	63	1:18	148, 183
19:18	66	8:26–27	215	1:18–25	129, 159
19:32, 40	100	8:30	63, 242	1:24	63
20:7	134, 157	9–11	243	1:24–25	193
20:7–12	169	10:1	244	2:1	221
20:17	142	10:2	221	2:13	77
20:22	76	10:9	57, 81, 234	3:1–9	127
20:28	6, 100, 132, 142	10:9–10	17, 161	3:9	12, 59
21:3–4	29	10:14	89	3:9–10	4
21:7	29	10:17	94	3:11	xxii, 17, 54
21:17–18	137	11:25–28	243	3:16	12
21:27–36	20	12	106	3:19	201
22:16	118	12:1	x	4:9	222

4:10–16	218	12:26–27	11	1:10	233
4:13	xvii	12:28	138, 141	1:23	230
4:18–21	127	12:31	107	2:5–11	127
5	134	13	210	2:12	175
5:1–5	22	13:1–3	106	2:14–17	xii
5:1–13	127	13:7	230	2:16	257
5:2	127	13:10	107	2:17	177
5:5	127, 138	13:12	239	3:1–5	216
5:9–13	127	13:13	107, 233	3:2	174
6:1–11	127	14:3–5	104	3:5	150, 257
6:2	245	14:4–5	125	3:6–7	244
6:12–20	127	14:12	104	3:7, 18	242
7:15	209	14:15	168	4:1	176
7:31–33	201	14:16	157	4:3	175, 262
8:1–13	127	14:23–24	134	4:4	176
9:12, 14	176	14:26	104, 114	4:4–6	176
9:16	159	14:33	108	4:7	104, 176
9:19–23	182	14:40	22, 108, 132	4:10	217
10–11	127	15	127, 246	4:14–15	234
10:16	157	15:1–4	157	5:7	149
10:16–17	122	15:1–8	175	5:8	246
10:17	121	15:1–11	1	5:14	180
11:1–16	127	15:2	176	5:18–21	190
11:3	56	15:4	234	5:19	2
11:16	4	15:6	175	5:20	180, 241
11:18–20	134	15:9, 11	6	6:14	201
11:20	3	15:15	221	6:14–17	126
11:22	4	15:17–18	234	6:17	201
11:23	77, 157	15:19	233, 239	7:1	112
11:23–25	120	15:23	248	7:10	123
11:23–26	157	15:24–28	241	8:1–15	125, 162
11:23–30	22	15:25	57	8:3–5	221
11:26	90	15:32	222	9:1–15	10
11:28, 31	161	15:42–44	242	9:10–13	157
12–14	127	16:1	10	9:13	161
12	10, 105, 106	16:1–2	125, 157, 170	10:3	128
12:1	103	16:1–4	162	10:3–4	199
12:3	57, 81, 161	16:2	157	10:4	129
12:4–6, 7	103	16:19	6	11:1–6	91
12:11	107	16:20	157	11:1–15	127
12:13	11, 101, 102, 258	16:22	204	11:2	14, 250
12:14–27	108			11:4	177
12:18, 25	11	*2 Corinthians*		11:24	223
12:26	228	1:1	4, 23	12:12	108

12:20–21	127
13:1–10	127
13:11	125

Galatians

1:1	234
1:6–7	177
1:10	155
1:11–24	75
1:13	6
1:16	29
1:19	137
1:21	29
1:22	4
2:9, 10	10, 79, 137
3:13	223
3:28	192
3:28–29	244
4:4	26
5:1–12	135
5:5	232
5:9	206
6:2	65, 125, 150
6:6	125
6:10	10, 12, 125, 208
6:15	2

Ephesians

1:1	134
1:3	245
1:12	233
1:20	234
1:22	56
1:22–23	11
2:8–9	118, 177
2:10	192
2:12	199, 232
2:13	199
2:14, 18	11
2:19	12
2:20	13, 18, 78, 141
2:20–22	13
2:21	13, 109
2:21–22	102

2:22	13
3:5	109
3:6	244, 245
3:10–11	207
3:21	150
4	106
4:1	266
4:3	209, 257
4:4	233, 257
4:4–6	xii
4:7–8	103
4:7–13	104
4:11	63, 141, 142
4:12	137
4:12–13	141
4:13	266
4:13–16	69
4:15–16	11
4:17	207
4:18	206
4:19	232
4:32	66
5:1	68
5:5	241
5:8, 9	206
5:15	207
5:17, 18	149
5:19	157, 164, 165
5:22	6
5:25	13
5:25–26	251
5:25–33	13
5:27	xii, 4, 251
5:29, 30–31	14
5:32	13, 14
6:10	256
6:12	98
6:15	176

Philippians

1:1	23, 132, 134
1:8	184, 230
1:27	176, 207
1:29	218

2:4	126
2:4–5	65
2:5–11	81, 165
2:6–11	157
2:8	217
2:11	57, 81, 161
2:14–16	208
3:3	100
3:10	115, 217
3:10–11	270
3:20	245, 249
3:20–21	242
3:21	215
4:1	250
4:8	194

Colossians

1:2	134
1:5	233
1:6	177
1:10–12	266
1:15–20	56
1:16–17	79
1:18	53
1:23	16, 233, 237
1:24	6, 216, 217
1:27	232
2:4–23	91
2:6–7	69
2:9–10	68
2:11–12	119
2:12	118, 234
2:19	56
3:1–10	234
3:4	242
3:16	157, 164, 165, 168
4:5	205
4:6	204
4:13	221
4:15	6
4:16	157

1 Thessalonians

1:1	4, 135

1:6	68, 218	3:16	12, 81, 157, 165	2:13	249
1:9	178	4:2–5	177	3:2	208
1:10	178, 248	4:7	112	3:5	177
2:2, 4	178	4:10	17	3:8	192
2:5	230	4:12	207	3:10–11	127
2:8	176	4:13	157		
2:14	68, 178	4:15	151	*Philemon*	
2:19–20	234	4:16	207	2	6
3:13	4	5:17	138, 142		
4:5	175	5:22	151	*Hebrews*	
4:13	232	6:12	157, 161	1:1–2	182
4:15	8	6:13	161, 219, 226	1:3	57, 235, 236
4:17, 18	248	6:15	165	1:7	96
5:9	230, 248	6:17	202	1:13	57
5:10	8	6:20	176, 201	2:10	12, 218
5:11	125			2:13	237
5:15	208	*2 Timothy*		3:14	235, 236
5:17	149	1:6	151	4:2, 6	175
5:22	201	1:8	218	4:12	74
5:27	157	1:9	109	5:8	214, 217
		1:12	218	7:27	121
2 Thessalonians		1:14	72, 176	8:8–13	244
1:1	135	2:11	245	9:15	217
1:8–9	176	2:11–13	165, 245	10:19	5
2:8, 14	29	2:12	241, 245	10:22	167
3:5	230	2:15	91	10:22–25	168
3:6	127, 138	2:17	177	10:23	167, 250
3:14–15	127, 138	2:19	4	10:24	125, 167
		2:20–21	12	10:25	125, 134, 167
1 Timothy		2:22	201, 209	10:36	230
1:1	232	3:1–5	255	10:37	249
1:20	127	3:1–13	91	11	221, 225
2:1	157, 163	3:2–13	216	11:1	233, 235, 236
2:1–2	128, 157	3:16	73	11:7	201
2:3–4	163	4:1	240	11:32–40	229
2:5	114, 164	4:1–2	159	11:34	223
3:1–7	142	4:3	xvi, 160	11:38	xv, 201
3:2, 5	142	4:10	201, 202	12:1	221
3:7	208			12:1–3	54
3:8	144	*Titus*		12:2	53, 217
3:8–13	143, 144	1:5	138, 142	12:14	209
3:11, 12, 13	144	1:6–9	142	12:23–24	5
3:14–15	xvii, 12	1:7	142	12:28	241
3:15	4, 12, 17, 81	2:11–12	202	13:2	125

13:7	68, 141, 142	2:25	15	3:1–2	12
13:15	161	3:1–3	207	3:2	242, 249
13:16	10	3:7	56	3:3	123, 249
13:17	142	3:9	63	4:1–3	21
13:20–21	60	3:10–12	208	4:1–6	260
13:21	149	3:11	209	4:2–3	91
13:24	142	3:15	237	4:10	217
		3:19	175	4:16	125
James		4:1	68	5:19	202
1:2	218	4:6	175		
1:3, 12	230	4:11	104, 106	**Jude**	
1:27	201, 210	4:12–19	214	3	75, 190
2:8, 13	209	4:13	249	8–19	91
2:14, 26	192	4:16	218	24	4
3:18	209	5:2	15, 142		
4:1	200	5:2–3	142	**Revelation**	
5:8	245, 249	5:3	142	1:6	58, 241, 245
5:11	230	5:4	15, 243, 249	1:8	238
5:15	125	5:6	60	1:10	3, 169
5:16	66, 123, 125, 161	5:10	63, 218	2–3	135
5:19–20	125			2:9–10	219
		2 Peter		2:13	221
1 Peter		1:1	134	2:14–15	23
1:1	134	1:4	201	3:14	229
1:3	233	1:6	230	5:10	58, 241, 245
1:6	218	2:1–3, 12–22	91	5:12	165
1:9	58	2:20	201	7:12	246
1:12	175	3:7, 10	247	11:15	241
1:13	249	3:11–14	250	13:8	243
1:15	109	3:14	4, 250	14:6	175, 183
1:21	234			15:3–4	165
1:22	123	**1 John**		17:6	221
1:23	92	1:3	120	19:6–8	14
1:25	175	1:5	205	19:9	14, 122
2:2	92	1:7	160	19:11	243
2:4	13	1:8–10	123	19:16	58
2:5	13, 111, 174	1:9	161	20	243
2:6	13	1:10	66	20:6	241, 245
2:7	56	2:2	217	20:14–15	235
2:9	109, 111	2:6	263	21:4	219, 235
2:9–10	63	2:15	201	21:7, 9	8
2:11	29, 192	2:15–17	201	22:3–5	241, 243
2:12	207, 208	2:16	99	22:17	8, 165
2:21	216	2:17	201	22:18–19	77
2:22	68	2:28	249		

Subject Index

—A—

Act of Supremacy, 88
Acton, John, 77
Altizer, Thomas, 196
Ambrose, 34
America, pluralism in, 48
Amish, 46
Anabaptists, 46, 62, 86, 111, 120–21, 123, 129, 195, 226
    on Luther, 77.
    See also Baptists
Ananias, 22, 100
Anderson, Leith, 251
Anglicanism, 41, 46–47, 52, 63, 88
    and dissent, 46
    bishops, 136–37, 144.
    See also Church of England;
        Episcopalianism
Anthony, 33
Apocryphal gospels, 177–79
Apologetics, 31
    Gospels as, 31
    weakened apologetics, 258–60
Apology (of Justin Martyr), 32
Apostles
    authority of, 79–80
    before church, 3
    duties, 131–32
    proclamation of good news, 1–3
Apostles' Creed, 82, 124, 161
Apostolic fathers, 31–32
Apostolic succession, 62
    lay apostolate, 63.
    See also Popes

Aquila, 6
Arius, 35–36
Asceticism, 31, 33–35
Assemblies of God, 136
Athanasian Creed, 82
Athanasius, 33, 35–36, 82
Augsburg Confession, 83
Augustine, 5, 34, 82, 153, 194–95, 240
Authority
    abuses, 76–77
    centralized, 91
    of Bible, 73–74
    of church, 74–75
Authorized Version, 47
Avignon popes, 38
Azusa Street revival, 110

—B—

Babcock, Maltbie, 203
Bach, Johann Sebastian, 149–50, 166
Bainton, Roland, 23, 42
Bakker, Jim, 53, 179
Baptism, 101–2
    as Christian circumcision, 135
    believers', 101, 116, 119–20
    infant, 119, 135
    of the Holy Spirit, 19–20, 101
    on profession of faith, 135–36
    salvation and, 102, 135–36
    water, 101
Baptist Society for Propagating
    the Gospel, 50
Baptists, 4, 11, 195

and Lord's Supper, 44
Confession of the Baptists, 84–85
in New World, 48
origin, 46
revival, 50.
See also Anabaptists; Baptism
Barclay, William, 102
Baring–Gould, Sabine, 11
Barnabas, 2, 3, 6, 9, 7, 100
 appointing elders, 138
 ordaining elders, 151
Barth, Karl, 145
Baxter, Richard, 49, 150–51, 153, 267
Bebbington, David, 254
Belgic Confession, 84
Believers' baptism. *See* Baptism, believers'
Bellah, Robert, 113
Benedict, 34
Bereans, 76
Berger, Peter L., 93
Berkhof, Louis, 138
Berkouwer, G.C., 72
Bernard of Clairvaux, 165
Bettenson, Henry, 25
Bible
 as authority, 55, 73–77, 80–81
 church and, 71–94, 111
 consequences of neglect, xx
 decline in Bible literacy, 71–72
 right of laity to interpret, 62–63
 translation, 39–40, 72
Bishops, 136–37, 141
Black Plague, 41
Blaurock, Georg, 46
Bloesch, Donald B., 55, 81, 269, 173
Bock, Darrell, 15
Body of Christ, church as, 10–11
Boice, James Montgomery, 256
Bonhoeffer, Dietrich, 69
Book of Common Prayer, 158
Booth, William, 111
Brethren of the Common Life, 67
Brethrenism, 46, 111
Bride of Christ, church as, 13–14

Bromiley, Geoffrey, 59, 146–47
Brown, Larry, 263
Bruce, F.F., 26, 36, 216
Bucer, Martin, 45, 62
Building of God, believers as, 12–13
Bunyan, John, 117, 187–88
Burton, John, 89
Butler, Samuel, 153

—C—

Caesar Augustus, 27
Cailliet, Emile, 74
Caligula, 222
Calvin, John, 45, 54, 82, 87–88, 92, 112,
 114, 115, 120, 123, 129, 138, 145,
 158, 165, 266
 on Bible, 72
 on church, xviii, 5, 16, 18
Calvinism
 in America, 50
 in Scotland, 46
Cambridge Declaration, xix–xx
Canada, 47–48
Canon of Scripture, 31. *See also* Bible
Carey, William, 50
Catherine of Siena, 39
Catholic church, 35. *See also* Roman
Catholicism
Celibacy, 34
Cephas, 18. *See also* Peter
Cessationism, 107–8
Chafer, Lewis Sperry, 239, 265
Chalcedonian Creed, 82
Charismata, 103–9
Charismatics, 108
Charlemagne, 37
Charles V, 112
Chief Shepherd, Jesus Christ as, 15
Chloe, 6
Christ. *See* Jesus Christ
Christian witness
 light metaphor, 205–6
 salt metaphor, 204–5
Christianity. *See* Church

Christlikeness, 67–70
Church
    as community of servants, 64–65
    as community of the forgiven, 65–67
    as communion of saints, 124–26
    as discipling community, 266–69
    as divine institution, xviii, xxii
    as invincible by hell, xvi–xvii, 18–19
    as described in New Testament, 2–16.
    See also Church in New Testament
        times
    Bible and, 71–94, 90–94
    church militant, 7–9
    church triumphant, 238–43, 245–47
    church universal, 4, 5–6
    creeds, 80–89
    eschatology, 236–43
    false church, 92–93
    foundation of church, 16–20, 77–80
    history, value of study, 25–26
    hope of, 231–50
    kingdom of God and, 239–43
    marks of true Church, xxi, 20–23
    meaning of word, 3–4
    ministries listed, 60
    New Testament autonomy, 138–39
    Old Testament imagery, 15–16
    organization, xx–xxi, 131–45
    preaching the Word, 21–22, 89–91
    priesthood of all believers, 61–67
    relation to world, 32–33, 72, 100–
        101, 128–30, 191–211
    rise of central authority, 35–36
    spiritual power of weakness, xvii–xviii
    split between East and West, 36–38
    translocal, 4–5, 6–7
    witness to world, 204–6
    words of Christ, 77–78.
    See also Church growth; Clergy;
    Discipline; Early church; Eastern
    Orthodoxy; Elders; Evangelical
    Christianity; Evangelism; Gospel;
    Holiness; Holy Spirit, church and;
    Jesus Christ; Martyrs; Ministry;

Missionary activity; Persecution;
    Peter; Renewal; Roman Catholicism;
    Worldliness; Worship
Church fathers, doctrine of church,
    xviii–xix
Church governance, 136–45
Church growth, 184
    non–Western growth, 80
Church in New Testament times, 27–31.
    See also Early church
Church leadership. *See* Leadership
Church membership, differing views,
    23. *See also* Membership
Church of England, 84, 88, 117
    in New World, 48.
    See also Anglicanism; Episcopalianism
Church unity, 23, 257–58. *See also* Unity
Clement of Alexandria, 165, 190
Clement of Rome, 31
Clergy
    vs. laity, 61, 63, 146. *See also* Ministry
Clowney, Edmund, 156
Coenen, L., 3
Colson, Charles, 251, 255
Commitment, 113–30
Communion, 120–22
Communion of saints, 5, 124–26
Concerts of prayer, 163
Confession of sin, 66–67, 122–28, 160–62,
    164
    as sacrament, 122–23
Confessors, 32
Congregationalism, 64, 139–40
Conscience, freedom of conscience, 87–89
Conservative Christian Congregational
    Churches, 140
Constantine, 32–33, 170, 225
Constantine VI, 36–37
Constantinople, as seat of Church, 36–37
Consubstantiation, 120–21
Consultation on the Theology of
    Development, 262
Conversion, 198–200
Conzelmann, Hans, 30

Copeland, Kenneth, 179
Cornelius, 29, 136
Cornerstone, Jesus Christ as, 13
Council at Carthage, 36
Council of Chalcedon (451), 36, 55
Council of Constance, (1414–18), 36, 38
Council of Constantinople (381), 35–36,
    55
Council of Ephesus (431), 55
Council of Jerusalem, 29–30, 64, 139
Council of Nicaea (325), 35–36, 55
Council of Nicaea (787), 36–37
Council of Trent (1545–63), 36, 88
Cowper, William, 165
Creeds
    early formulations, 81–82
    historic creeds, 82–86
    importance of, 86–87
Cullmann, Oscar, 78, 198, 234
Cyprian, 32, 257
Cyprian of Carthage, 114
Cyril of Jerusalem, xxii

—D—

Daniel, 203
Day of Pentecost, 4, 26–27
    baptism at, 102
    beginning of Church, 15, 19–20
Deacons, 132–33
    in New Testament, 141, 143–44
    today, 144–45
Decius, 32
Defenses of the faith. See Apologetics
Deism, 48
Desert Fathers, 31
Desmarest, Bruce A., 244
Didache, 163
Diet of Speyer, 112
Diet of Worms, 42, 43
Diocletian, 32, 225
Diognetus, Epistle to, 210–11
Discipline, 22–23, 126–28
    eroded under Constantine, 33
    Gospel pattern, 67

membership and, 134
purpose, 127–28
Doctrine, xvi, xviii–xix, 86–87
Dodd, C.H., 21–22
Doddridge, Philip, 165
Dominicans, 34, 47
Dominion theology, 129
Domitian, 230
Donatist schism, 227
Dwight, Timothy, 240

—E—

Early church, 2
    accommodating to culture, xix
    after Pentecost, 26–27
    apostles' proclamation, 1–3
    as "the Way", xvii, 1
    as the "Nazarenes", xvii
    content of preaching, 21–22
    holiness, 247–48
    in Acts, 9–10
    worship, 31
Eastern Orthodoxy, 33, 36–37, 63, 225
Ebionites, 34
Ecclesia. See Ekklesia
Eck, John, 220
Edict of Milan, 115, 225
Edwards, David J., 253
Edwards, Jonathan, 50
Ekklesia, 3–4
Elders, 132–33
    in early Church, 132
    in New Testament, 141–43
    in Presbyterianism, 137–39
Elliot, Jim, 96, 148
Ellul, Jacques, xix, 173, 193, 197
England. See Anglicanism; Church of
    England; Nonconformism
Enlightenment, 48
Episcopalianism, 118, 136–37.
    See also Anglicanism
Epistles, when written, 31
Erasmus, 42, 44, 90
Eschatology, 236–43

Eucharist, 121
Eusebius, 226
Evangelical Christianity, 210–11
    accommodationism, xv–xvi, xix, 55,
        258–60
    defined, 51
    evangelical revival, 48–50
    Luther's views and, 43
    present day, 50–52
    rise of evangelicalism, 46–48.
        See also Church; Fundamentalism;
        Jesus Christ
Evangelism, 184
    as necessity, 187–88
    culture and, 207–10
Excommunication, 127

—F—
Faber, Frederick W., 79–80
Faith alone principle, 62
Fellowship, church as, 9–10
Fénelon, François, 130
Ferdinand, 41
Five Fundamentals, The, 51
Flock of God, church as, 14–15
Forgiveness, Church as forgiven, 65–67
Forms of Prayers, 158
Forsythe, P.T., 251
Fourth Lateran Council (1215–16), 36,
        37–38
Foxe, John, 219
Franciscans, 34, 47
Franck, Johann, 166
Frederick the Wise, 43
Free churches, 111
Fundamentalism, 51, 196–97
    doctrinal vs. cultural, 200.
        See also Evangelical Christianity
Fundamentals, The, 196

—G—
Gabriel, Charles, 241
Gaebelein, Frank E., 71
Gallicanism, 41

Gates of Hell, church and, 18–19
Gifts, spiritual. See Spiritual gifts
Gnostics, 35
God, as father of household, 11–12
God's building, believers as, 12–13
God's field, believers as, 12–13
God's household, church as, 11–12
God's Kingdom. See Kingdom of God
Gordon, A.J., 111
Gospel
    apocryphal Gospels, 177–79
    as counterculture, 192–204
    Bible as foundation, 174–75
    Christ as center, 175–76
    Great Commission, 180–82
    success gospels, 179–80
    when written, 31
    word origin, 174
Gospel of Thomas, 178
Great Awakening, 48–49
    emotionalism, 158
    social reform, 50
Great Commission, 180–82
Great Schism, 38
Great Tribulation, 248
Grebel, Conrad, 46
Greek Orthodoxy, 37, 136. See also
        Eastern Orthodoxy
Green, Fred Pratt, 169
Gregory of Nyssa, 190
Gregory VII, 39
Groothuis, Douglas, 259
Grounds, Vernon, 260
Guiness, Os, 99
Gutenberg, 42
Guyon, Madame, 130

—H—
Hades, 18–19
Hagner, Donald, 17
Halverson, Richard, 151
Hamilton, Michael, 253
Handel, G. F., 58, 246
Hatch, Nathan, 253

Hauerwas, Stanley, 93
Heidelberg Catechism, 103
Hell, Church prevailing against, 18–19
Hellenistic influence in Church, 29
Helvetic Confession, 84
Henry, Carl, 91
Henry VIII, King, 41, 46
Heresy, 35–36
Hermas, 31
Herod, 27
Herod Agrippa, 222
Herod Antipas, 27
Hildegard of Bingen, 165
Hippolytus of Egypt, 158
Hoffmann, Ernst, 232
Holiness, 23, 109–12, 247–50
Holy priesthood, 111
Holy Roman Empire, 37
Holy Spirit
    as Christ's gift, 98–101
Holy Spirit, church and, xxi
    secular powers, 96–97
    spiritual gifts, 103–9
    zeal and, 95–97
Hort, F.S.A., 89
Household of faith, church as, 11–12
How, William W., 247
Hubbard, David, 236
Hus, John, 38, 39, 40, 86
Hussites, 41
Hutterites, 46, 195
Hymns, 165–66, 168

—I—

Iconoclastic controversy, 36–37
Ignatius, 31, 35
Ignatius of Antioch, 218
Illumination, 75–76
Imitation of Christ, 67–69
Incarnation, 69–70
Individualism in church life, 20–21
Infant baptism. See Baptism, infant
Inge, W. R., 30
Innocent III, 37–38

Irenaeus, 3, 10, 113
Isabella, 41
Islam, 41
Isolationism, church growth and, 261
Israel, church and, 243–47

—J—

James (apostle), 28, 63, 64, 136–37, 225
James I, King, 47
Jerome, 34, 39
Jerusalem Council. See Council of
    Jerusalem
Jesuits, 47
Jesus Christ
    as head of Church, xxi, 53–54
    as martyr, 219
    centrality of Christ, 54–56
    contemporary views of, 16–17
    giving Holy Spirit, 98–101
    his ministry as model, 59–60
    rule of Christ, 56–58,
    second coming, 236–43, 248–50
Joan of Arc, 39
Johannes Eckhart, 39
John (disciple), 63, 225
John the Baptist, 27–28
Joseph, son of Jacob, 203
Josephus, 222
Judas, 63
Julian of Norwich, 39
Justin Martyr, 25, 32, 101, 170

—K—

Keith, George, 92
Kempis, Thomas á, 39, 53, 58, 67–69, 148
Keswick movement, 110
King James Version, 47
Kingdom of God, 58–59, 239–43
Knox, John, 46, 54
Koinonia, 9–10, 124
Krummaker, F.W., 230
Küng, Hans, 2, 58–59, 197
Kyriakos, 3–4

—L—

Laity, vs. clergy, 63
Lamb of God, 15
Larson, Sheila, 113
Lasch, Christopher, 254
Latourette, Kenneth, 34–35, 39
Lausanne Conference on church
     mission, 181–82
Laval, François, 48
Lawrence, Brother, 130
Lay apostolate, 62–63
Leadership, 63–64, 131–52
     distinctions of office, 140–45
Leo III, Pope, 36
Leo IX, Pope, 37
Lewis, Gordon R., 244
Liberal Christianity, 55, 189, 190
Little Flock church, 14
Living stones, believers as, 13
Lloyd–Jones, Martyn, 253, 269
Local church, 6. See also Church
Lollards, 40, 41, 90
London Missionary Society, 50
Lord's Day, 169–70
Lord's Prayer, 163
Lord's Supper, 116, 120–22, 158, 170
     Luther's view, 43
     Zwingli's view, 44
Lord's Table, 90
Luther, Martin, 1, 19, 38, 41, 67–68, 69,
     71, 79, 86, 87–88, 96, 101, 111,
     114, 115, 120, 123, 129, 137, 145,
     150, 155, 158,165, 170, 174, 176,
     187, 202, 220, 239, 257, 266
     and tradition, 76–77
     Augsburg Confession, 83
     break with Rome, 42–44
     influence on Wesley, 49
     on confession, 66–67
     on priesthood of all believers, 61–62
     views listed, 43
Lutheranism, 48, 118, 129, 136

—M—

Magisterium, 75
Manz, Felix, 46, 226
Marcionites, 35
Marshall, I. Howard, 194
Marty, Martin, 179
Martyrs, 32, 219–30
     as intercessors, 225
     execution, 222–23
     meaning of word, 221
Mary, veneration of, 38
Matthias, 63
Maxwell, William, 157
McGavran, Donald, 184
Megachurches, 268
Melanchthon, 83, 86, 236
Melitian schism, 227
Membership, in church, 133–36.
     See also Church; Discipline
Mennonites, 46, 195
Merrill, W.P., 97
Methodism, 46, 49–50, 110, 118, 136
Meyer, F.B., 70
Michelangelo, xii
Milton, John, 231, 234–35
Ministry, 145–52
     key concepts, 146
     ministers as executives, 15
     ordination, 151–52
     priesthood of all believers, 145–46
     requirements, 147–51
Missionary activity
     adapting to culture, 182–84
     biblical theology, 182–83
     global strategy, 185–87
     Great Commission, 180–82
     in New Testament, 29–30
     loss of urgency, 260–62
     secular methods, 37
     social justice, 261–62
Modernism, 196
Monasticism, 33–35, 194
     missionary effort, 34–35

Moody, D.L., 111
Moravian Brethren, 49, 195
Mosaic Covenant, 244
Moses, 203
Mote, Edward, 236
Mounce, Robert, 22
Mumford, Howard, 47
Münzer, Thomas, 62
Music, 164–66
    abandoned by radical groups, 158
    shallow, 168–69

—N—

National Association of Evangelicals,
    258
Neander, Augustus, xviii
Neoorthodoxy, 55
Nero, 30, 247
New Age ideas, 113, 179, 188–90
New Covenant, 244
New France, 47–48
New Hampshire Confession, 85
New Light, 50
New Testament church. See Church in
    New Testament times
New World, religious ideas, 47
Newbigen, Lesslie, 252
Newton, John, 67, 165
Nicene Creed, 82
Ninety–Five Theses, 42
Noll, Mark, 259
Nominalism, 264–65
Nonconformism, 46–47
Nouwen, Henri, 131
Novak, Michael, 259
Novation, 226–27
Nympha, 6

—O—

Offering, in worship service, 162
Old Testament, imagery of church, 15–16
Ordinances of the church, 22, 116–22
    Scripture and, 90
Ordination, 151–52

Origen, xxii, 178, 190
Orthodoxy. See Eastern Orthodoxy;
    Greek Orthodoxy
Overseers, in New Testament, 141–43
Ozment, Stevens, 41

—P—

Pache, René, 108–9
Pacifism, 195
Packer, J.I., 182
Paedobaptism. See Baptism, infant
Parachurch ministries, 267
Pascal, Blaise, 89, 95
Pastors, in New Testament, 141–43.
    See also Ministry
Paul, 63, 64
    appointing elders, 138
    authority crisis, 74–75
    missionary journeys, 29
    on spiritual power of weakness, xvii
    ordaining elders, 151
Pentecost. See Day of Pentecost
Persecution, 32, 222–27, 245–48
    as normal situation, 69–70
    by church, 220
    Christians reviled as atheists, 225–26
    imprisonment, 223–24
    lapses from faith, 226–27
    potential benefits, 220, 227–30.
    See also Martyrs; Suffering
Peter, 63
    and Gentiles, 29
    as Rock, 17–18, 78–79
    bishop of Rome tradition, 17–18, 30
    Peter's confession, 16–17
Pharisees, 27
Philemon, 6
Philip, 29, 100
Phillips, J.B., 188
Pietism, 46, 48, 195
Pilgrim fathers, 47
Pliny, 170
Pliny the Younger, 213
Polycarp, 31, 218, 226

Popes, 37–38
    as "vicars of Christ," 63
    Great Schism, 38
    Luther's view, 42–44.
    See also Roman Catholicism
Postmodernism, 189, 196
Power, as church's temptation, 100–101
Pragmatism, 255–57
Prayer
    in worship service, 162–64
    Lord's Prayer, 163
    ministry and, 149–50
    types explained, 164
Preaching, 89–91
    as mark of true church, 21–22
Presbyterian Church (USA), 138
Presbyterianism, 118, 137–39
Priesthood of all believers, 61–67, 145–46
    Bible's view, 63
    holy priesthood, 111
    rights of believers, 61–62
Priscilla, 6
Profession of faith, 160–62
Protestant reformation, 40–46
    Calvin, 45
    causes, 40–42
    confession, 66–67
    Luther, 42–44
    radicalism, 46, 62–63
    views of worship, 158, 167
    Zwingli, 44–45
Psalms, 164–65
Puritans, 46–47, 88
    in New World, 47, 48

—Q/R/S—

Quakers, 46, 195
    in New World, 48
Quietism, 129–30, 195
Qumran, 31
Rahner, Karl, 114, 197
Rapture, 4, 248–49
Rauschenbusch, Walter, 178
Reformed churches, 118

Reformers, early reformers, 39–40.
    See also Protestant reformation
Renewal, 251–70
    character vs. competency, 262–63
    management model, 251–52
    need for biblical principles, xvi
    pragmatism, 255–57
    problems in, 262–66
    therapeutic society, 252–55
Revivalism, 158, 165
Robinson, J.A.T., 198
Roman Catholicism, 118, 136
    apostolic succession, 63–64
    authority claims, 75
    Fourth Lateran Council, 37–38
    in New World, 47–48
Rome
    as church authority, 31–32
    early efforts to reform church, 39–40.
    See also Pope; Roman Catholicism
Russell, Bertrand, 232
Ryrie, Charles, 4, 244
Sabbath. *See* Lord's Day
Sacramentalism, 22, 32, 61, 116
Sanhedrin, 27, 28
Sapphira, 22, 100
Sattler, Michael, 83
Saucy, Robert, 118, 244
Saul of Tarsus, 28, 76, 225. *See also* Paul
Savonarola, Girolamo, 96
Saxon Confession, 84
Schaeffer, Francis, 270
Schleithim Confession, 83
Schubert, Franz, 169
Scotland, Church of, 138
    Scottish Confession, 84
Scriptures. *See* Bible
Second coming, 248–50
Sectarianism, 87
Secularism, 128
Separatism, from the world, 31, 46–47,
    200–204. *See also* Worldliness
Severus of Antioch, 31
Shakespeare, 231

Sheler, Jeffrey L., xvi
Shelley, Bruce, 32
Shepherd and Overseer, 15
Shriver, Sargeant, 95
Simon Peter. *See* Peter
Simon the sorcerer, 100–101
Simons, Menno, 86
Sin
    as outdated concept, 123–24
    confession of sin, 122–28
    seriousness of sin, 126–27.
    See also Discipline
Small group ministry, 268
Smyth, John, 47
Social justice, 61–62
Society for the Propagation of the
    Gospel, 50
Soul liberty, 62, 87, 88–89
Spener, Philipp Jakob, 48–49, 195
Spirit baptism. *See* Baptism, of the Holy
    Spirit
Spiritual gifts, 103–9
    cessationism, 107–8
    listed, 106–7
Spiritual life
    ministry and, 149–50
    recovery, 265–66
Spurgeon, Charles Haddon, 105, 159
State
    relations with church, 128–30
    state–enforced religion, 128
    state church under Constantine,
        32–33
Stephen, 28, 221, 225
Stigmata, 224
Stone, Samuel J., 8
Stott, John, 124, 191, 253
Suffering
    as inevitable, 213–17
    biblical meaning, 217–19.
    See also Martyrdom; Persecution
Sunday. *See* Lord's Day
Sutherland, Samuel, 242
Swaggart, Jimmy, 53, 179

Syncretism, 184, 188–90

—T—

Tacitus, 247
Teilhard de Chardin, Pierre, 95
Tertullian, 32, 220
Tetzel, John, 43
Theodosius, 33, 37
Theology, xv–xvi
Therapeutic society, 252–55
Thielicke, Helmut, 239
Thirty–Nine Articles of Faith, 84
Tilton, Robert, 53, 179
Timothy, 63
Titus, 63, 138
Tongues, speaking in, 107
Torrey, R.A., 111
Tozer, A.W., 111, 264
Tradition, as living faith, 85
Trajan, Emperor, xv
Translocal church, 4–5, 6–7
Transubstantiation, 120–21
    adopted by Rome, 38
    denied by Luther, 43
Tribulation, 248
Trueblood, Elton, xix

—U/V/W—

United Church of Christ, 140
Unity, 269–70
Universal church. *See* Church, universal
Universalism, 184, 190, 260
Vespasian, 230
von Bora, Katharina, 44
von Brandenburg, Albrecht, 41
von Zinzendorf, Nikolaus Ludwig, 49,
    168, 195
Wagner, Peter, 110
Waldensians, 83
    Waldensian Declaration of Faith,
        82–83
Walker, Williston, 30
Wallis, S.J., 98
Walvoord, John F., 238

Water baptism. *See* Baptism, water
Watts, Isaac, 165, 236
Webber, Otto, 54
Webber, Robert, 51
Weber, Max, 45
Wesley, Charles, 49, 110–11, 165, 195, 236
Wesley, John, 49–50, 63, 68, 110–11, 165, 195, 262, 268
Wesley, Samuel, 49
Westminster Shorter Catechism, 85
White, James E., 264
Whitefield, George, 49, 110–11
Whitmore, Lucy E.G., 66
Willard, Dallas, 266
Williams, Roger, 48, 88
Willimon, William, 93
Witness. *See* Christian witness
Word, ministry of the, 159–60
Word of God. *See also* Bible; Gospel
World Evangelical Fellowship, 258
Worldliness, 99–100, 199

culture and church, 207–10
Western church, 80
Worship, 153–71, 166–69
as entertainment, 158
Bible and, 157, 159
confession of sin, 160–62
in early church, 31
key elements, 156–66
loss of meaning, 155–56, 263–64
music, 164–66
new catholicity, 159
offering, 162
prayer during service, 162–64
profession of faith, 160–62
style, 156
traditional elements, 153–54, 157–58
Wycliffe, John, 38, 39–40

—X/Y/Z—
Zwingli, Ulrich, 44–45, 74, 120–21, 123, 129, 158